Art Deco

An illustrated guide to the decorative style 1920–40

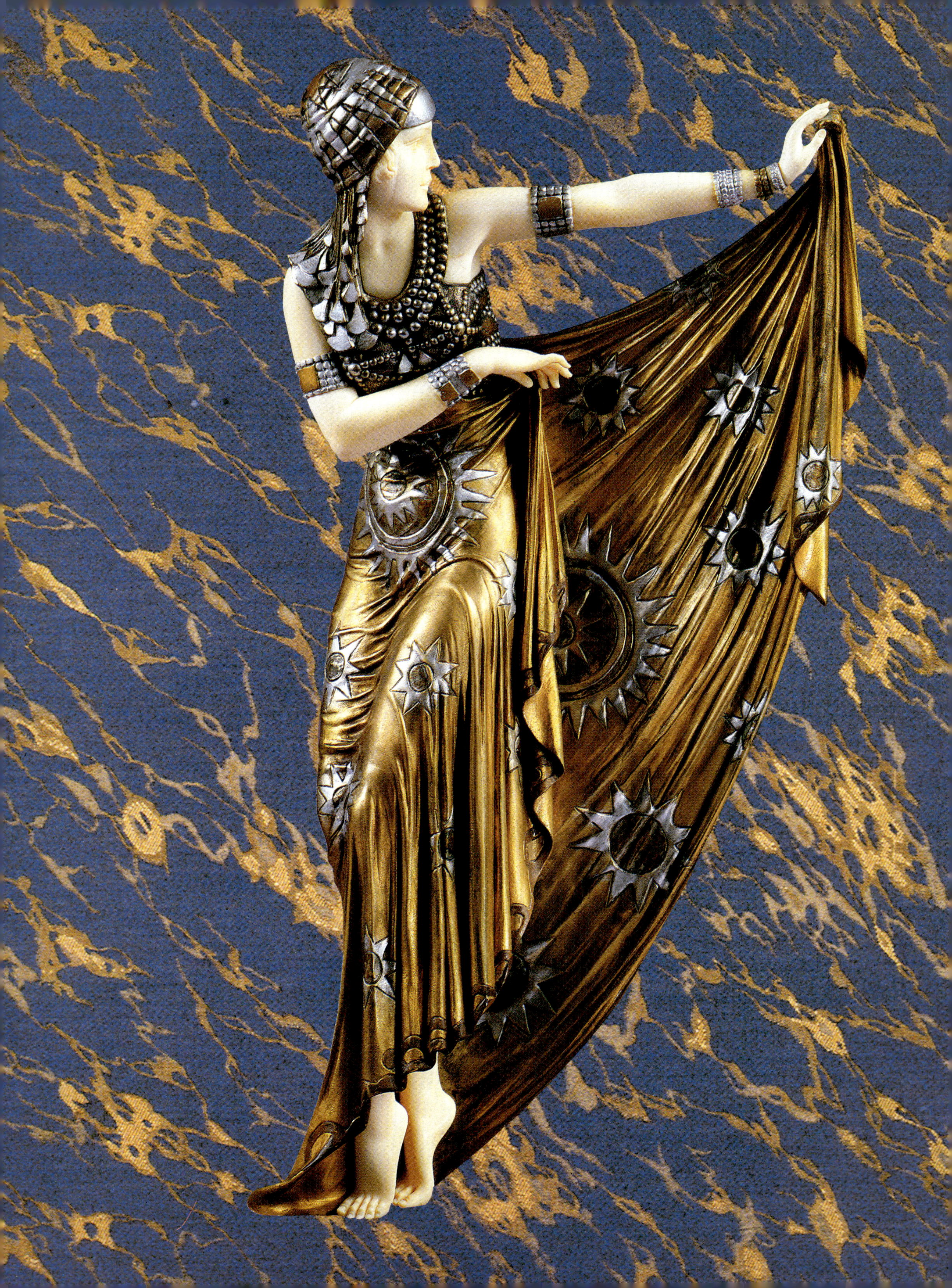

Art Deco

An illustrated guide to the decorative style 1920–40

Arie Van De Lemme

PAST TIMES®

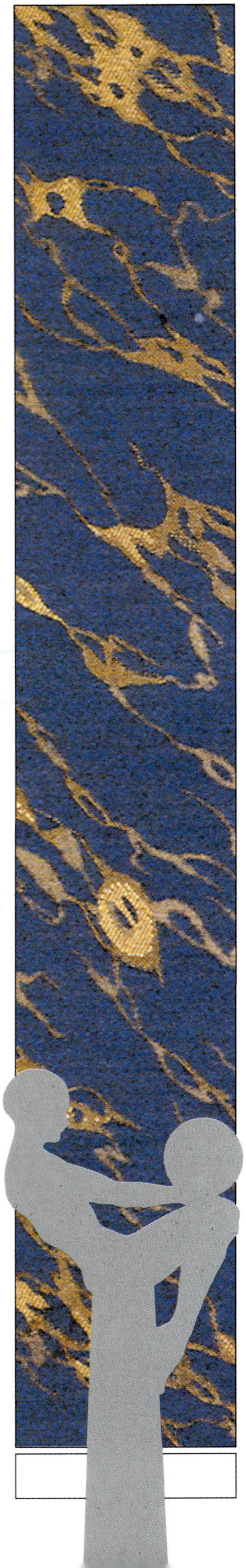

To
Ans and Piet
with gratitude

Special edition for PAST TIMES, Oxford, England

A QUINTET BOOK

1 3 5 7 9 10 8 6 4 2

A CIP catalogue record for this title is available from the British Library

ISBN 1-86155-394-3

This book was designed and produced by
Quintet Publishing Limited
6 Blundell Street
London N7 9BH

Art Director: Peter Bridgewater
Editors: Nicholas Law, Josephine Bacon
Picture Researcher: Anne-Marie Ehrlich
Illustrator: Lorraine Harrison

The editors would like to acknowledge the assistance of Stephen Astley of the Furniture and Interior Design Department, Victoria and Albert Museum, and of Patrick Cook of the Bakelite Museum of London.

Typeset in Great Britain by
Central Southern Typesetters, Eastbourne
Manufactured in Hong Kong by
Regent Publishing Services Limited
Printed in Singapore by
Star Standard Industries (Pte) Ltd.

PAST TIMES®

Photo credits ALLEN EYLES, London: pages 44, 45 (3), 46. ANNELY JUDA FINE ART, London: pages 33, 85 (2). IAN BENNETT, London: page 114. BETTMAN ARCHIVE/BBC HULTON PICTURE LIBRARY: pages 15, 16, 17, 18 (3), 19, 20, 21 (2), 22, 23, 28, 48 (3), 49 (2). BRIDGEMAN ART LIBRARY, London: pages 9, 83, 91, 101, 122. BRITISH FILM ARCHIVE, London: page 110. RICHARD BRYANT/ARCAID, London: page 46. CHRISTIES: pages 2, 7, 8, 12, 35, 41, 42, 55, 56, 57 (2), 58, 59, 60, 61, 62, 64, 67, 68, 73, 74, 75, 76, 77, 79, 80, 81 (2), 84, 85, 86 (2), 87, 88 (2), 89, 90, 91 (2), 93, 105, 109, 111, 117, 119, 120, 121. E.T. ARCHIVE, London: pages 30, 38, 39, 94, 95, 96, 100 (2). GALERIE GEORGE, London: page 9. ANGELO HORNAK, London: pages 68, 70, 71 (2). JOHN JESSE and IRINA LASKI, London: pages 12, 13, 25, 26, 31 (2), 32, 36, 75, 78, 108, 122, 123 (2). LEWIS KAPLAN & ASSOC., London: pages 28, 84, 87, 97, 113, 114, 118, 123. DE LORENZO, New York: page 81. FÉLIX MARCILHAC, Paris: page 106. MUSÉE DES ARTS DÉCORATIFS, Paris: pages 10, 11, 12, 33, 59, 75, 100, 121. MUSÉE DE LA PUBLICITÉ, Paris: pages 24, 110. MUSEUM OF DECORATIVE ART, Copenhagen: page 83. NATIONAL MONUMENTS RECORD, London: pages 43, 50, 52 (2). FOTO RITTER, Vienna: page 115. ROHSSKA KONSTSLÖJDMUSEET, Gothenburg: page 114. SOTHEBY'S, London: pages 26, 69, 83. VICTORIA & ALBERT MUSEUM, London: pages 11, 83, 91, 101, 114. WARNER & SONS LIMITED, London: pages 98 (3), 99 (3)

Marble fabric in blue and gold, created by Warner & Sons' in-house designer Bertrand Whittaker in 1923, has been used as a background pattern on the opening pages to the chapters of this book.

CONTENTS

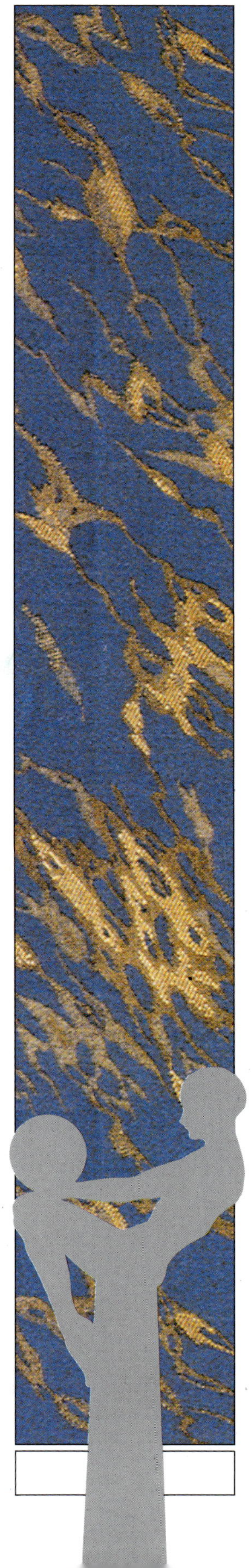

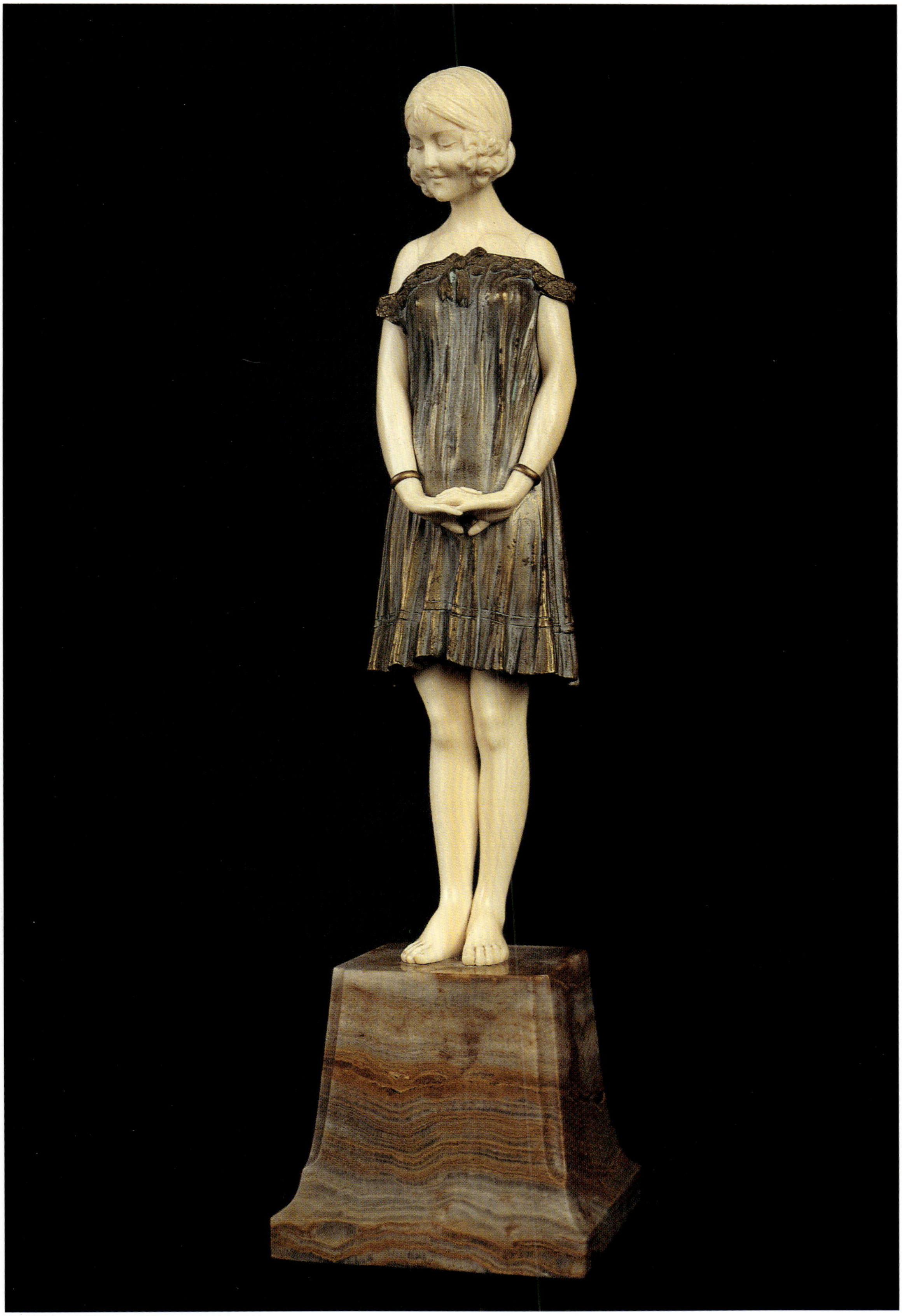

LEFT 'Innocence' by Demetre Chiparus, made from ivory and bronze with a marble base and signed by the artist. A delightfully coy little sculpture, and beautifully worked.

L'EXPOSITION DES ARTS DECORATIFS ET INDUSTRIELS 1925

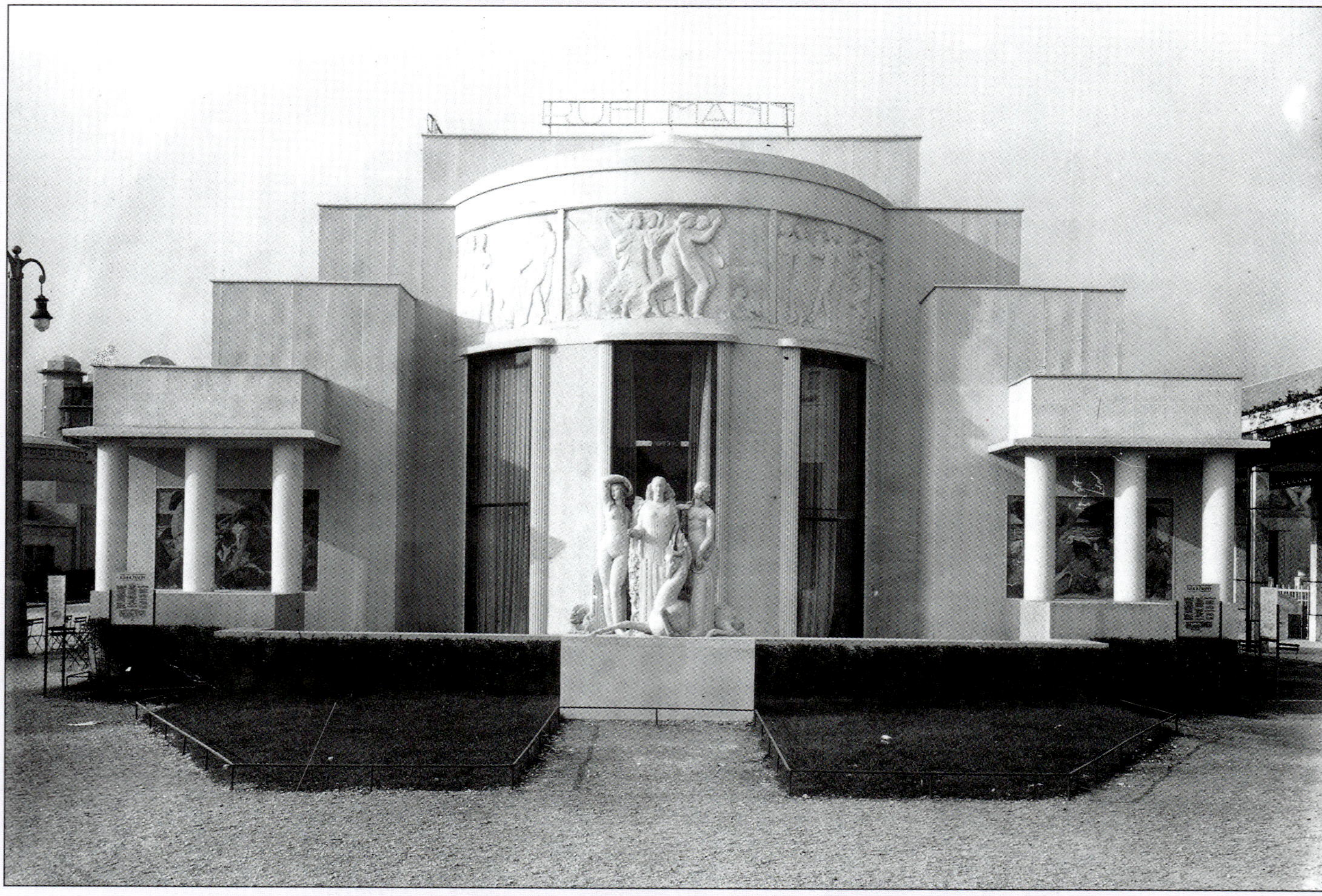

Today, every day of every year there will be a trade fair or international exhibition of some sort or another somewhere in the world. We have become so used to them now we hardly notice them, unless they cater for our particular interest: a motor show, boat show, an art exhibition, or a camping show. Probably the single most famous series of exhibitions we have all heard of is the World's Trade Fair. Throughout the second half of the 19th century, fairs on a massive scale were organized to sponsor and spread the gospel of art and industry; Amsterdam, Milan, Chicago and New York hosted such extravaganzas. The unifying idea behind all these fairs was the sound economic doctrine that lavish advertising and displaying a showcase to the world could promote sales. The success of the Great Exhibition in London in 1851, housed in the Crystal Palace, and with Prince Albert as its enthusiastic Royal patron set the standard for competition abroad.

Paris repeated the formula many times in the late 19th century, culminating in the famous 1900 Exposition which displayed much work in the contemporary Art Nouveau style. It included work by Hector Guimard, the designer of the hundreds of green iron entrance gates to the Paris Métro, and Pierre Chareau. As a result of the Exposition, the Société des Artistes Décorateurs was formed with the objective of repeating the success of the 1900 Exposition as soon as possible. In 1903, the Salon d'Automne was set up. It is best remembered for its huge retrospectives of the work of the painters Paul Cézanne and Gustave Courbet, and the sculptor Auguste Rodin. It also held occasional shows of the decorative and applied arts. Due to interruption by the First World War, and the overwhelming organizational problems, the Société des Arts Décoratifs could not realize its ambitions for over 10 years.

When the entrance gates to the Exposition des Arts Décoratifs et Industriels were finally opened in 1925, it was a sensational *tour de force*. The sheer scope of the Exposition, with almost 150 separate pavilions, cafés, restaurants and theatres, was

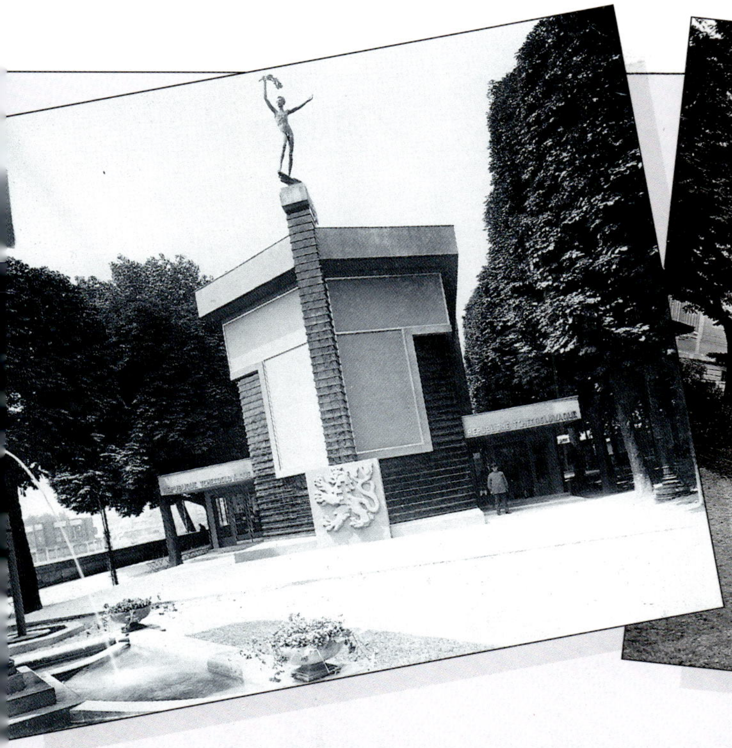

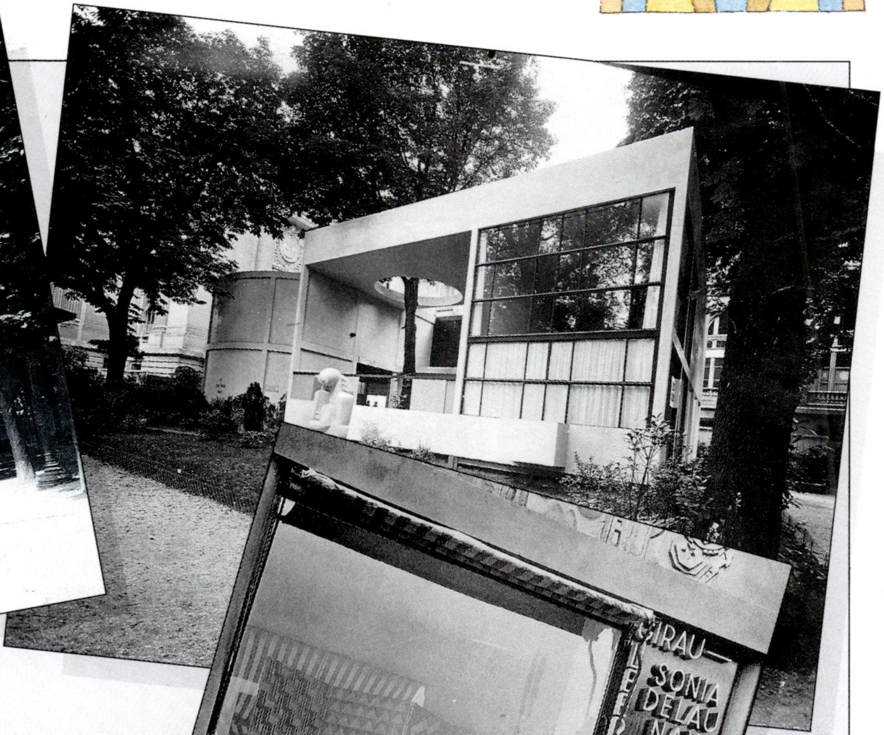

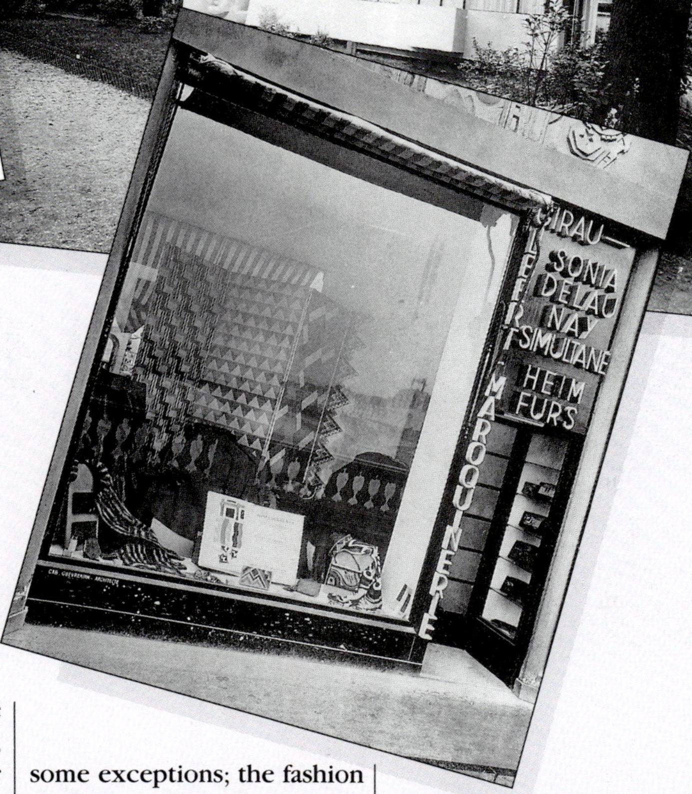

ABOVE The Czechoslovakian pavilion, one of the foreign pavilions on the edge of the Seine at the 1925 Exposition.

OPPOSITE The exterior of Ruhlmann's Hotel d'un Collectionneur by the architect Patout at the 1925 Exposition. The sculpture in the foreground is by Jeanniot and the friezes above by J. Bernard. The overall effect is both modern and classical.

ABOVE RIGHT Le Corbusier's seminal work the Pavillon de L'Esprit Nouveau at the 1925 Exposition. Its modernity sharply contrasts with the fussy fin-de-siècle decoration on the building behind.

RIGHT The Simultanist shop designed for Sonia Delaunay by the architect Gabriel Guevrekian in 1925. As can be seen from the photo, Delaunay applied her designs to almost anything, clothes, furniture, jewellery, and even cars.

as diverse and complex as an Epcot Centre or the Olympic Games. As well as the more serious displays of applied art, the Exposition had fashion shows, shows of photography and the cinema, circuses, fairs, dancing, music, flower displays and hairdressing demonstrations. It was both an opportunity to see the latest in design and a chance for a day out with the family.

Set in the centre of Paris betwen the Place de la Concorde and the Eiffel Tower, the Exposition crossed over the Seine on the modified Alexander III Bridge. The firm of Citroën captured the lion's share of the advertising, illuminating the Eiffel Tower with 200,000 light bulbs, crowned with the Citroën logo. At the other end of the Exposition, the Grand Palais was utilized for its acres of indoor exhibition space. On the Right Bank, along the Cours de la Reine, the organizers placed most of the foreign pavilions, which included those of the USSR, Japan, Great Britain and Belgium, though not the USA. Most of the French pavilions were situated along the Esplanade des Invalides, with some exceptions; the fashion designs of Paul Poiret were exhibited on barges below the Pont Alexandre.

One of the most important aspects of the Exposition was the impact of pavilions of the four major Paris department stores. Each of these stores had realized that quality and price could be supplemented by good design, and each had its own design studios. The recognition that a retail outlet could profit by employing designers provided a boost to the whole industry. Even specialist producers of glass, porcelain and ironwork at the luxury end of the market had to maintain exceptionally high standards in order to compete.

The immediate success of the Exposition could be judged by the number of people who passed through its gates. In the long term, the exhibition highlighted the vitality of French design, and provided the impetus for the dispersal of the Art Deco aesthetic across the globe.

RIGHT Leaded glass skylight, designed by Frank Lloyd Wright for the B. H. Bradley House, Illinois, 1900. The geometric design of the window is convincing proof of Wright's advanced taste, securing him as one of the sources for the Art Deco style.

CENTRE This luxury Bakelite box made by the Paris company Edition E. Furnels, is an example of a more expensive range of plastic objects. The motif stamped into the lid is of a bacchanale, including nude women, a deer and oak trees.

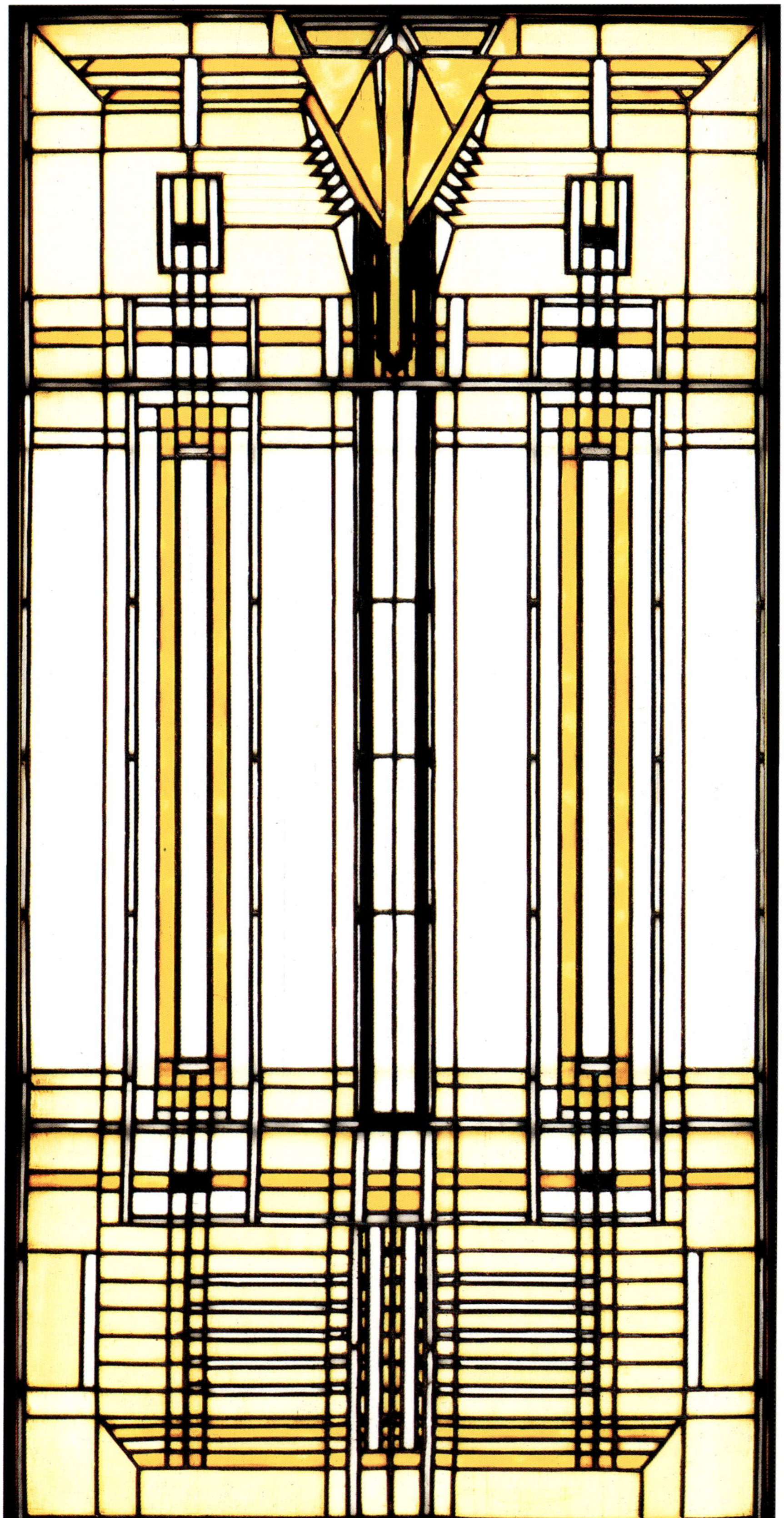

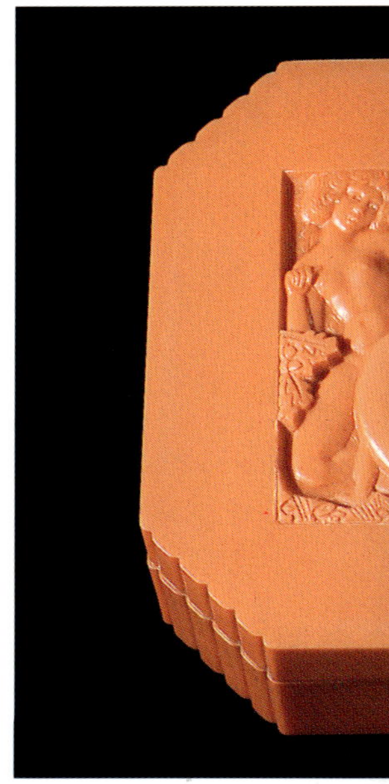

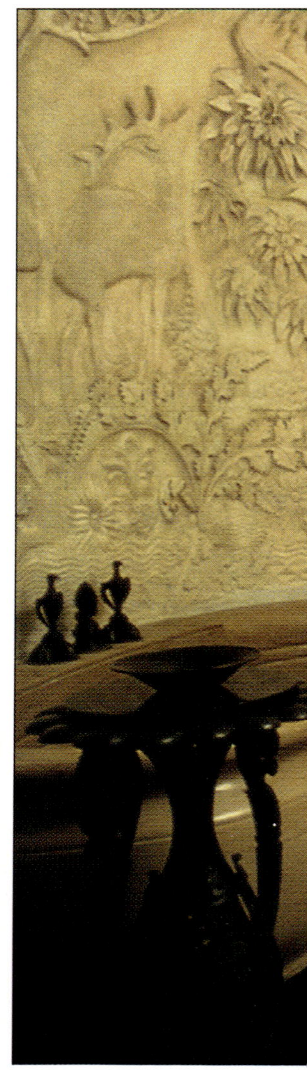

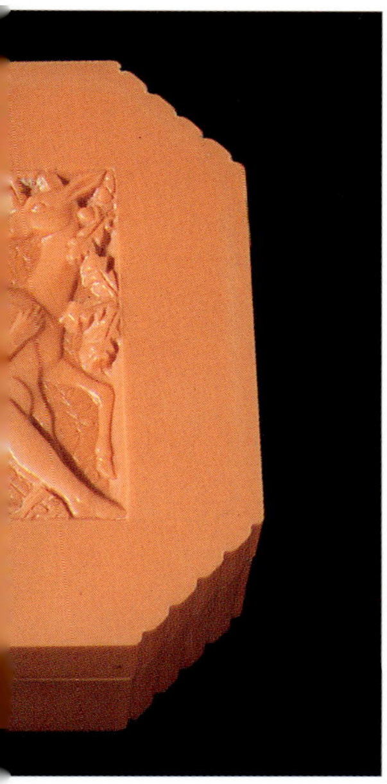

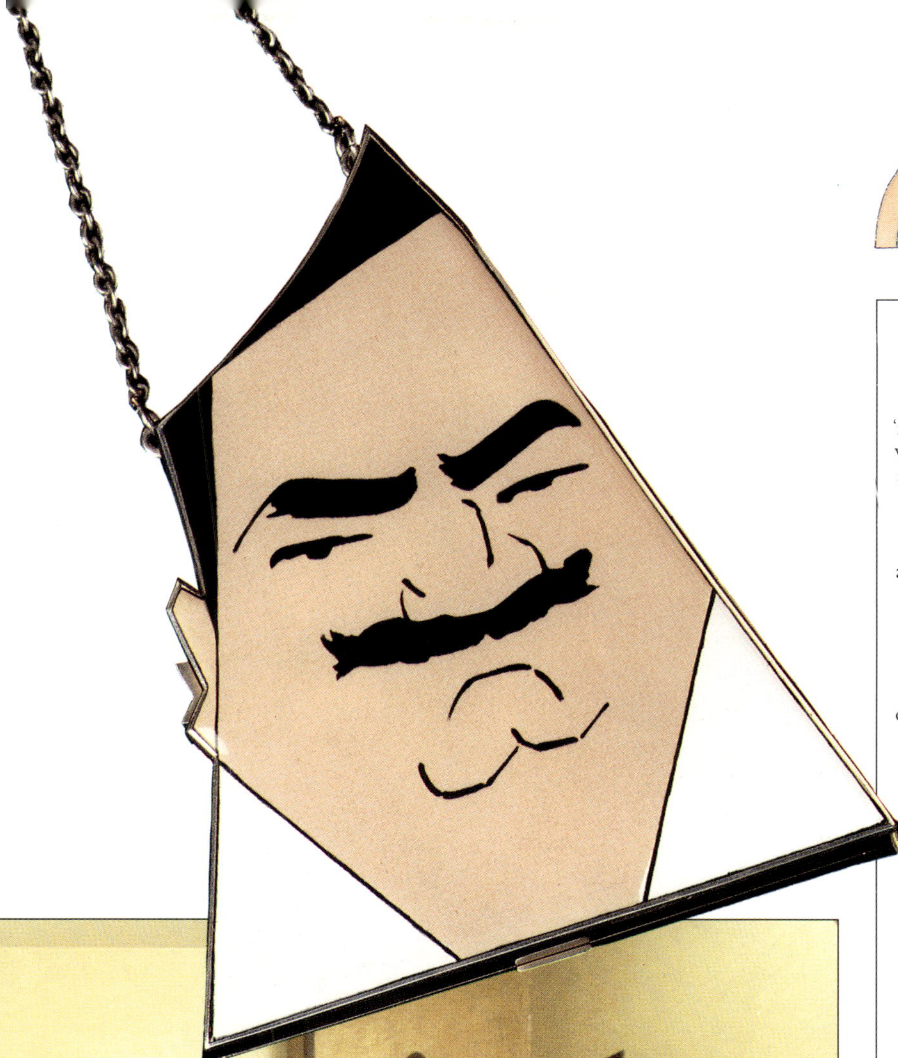

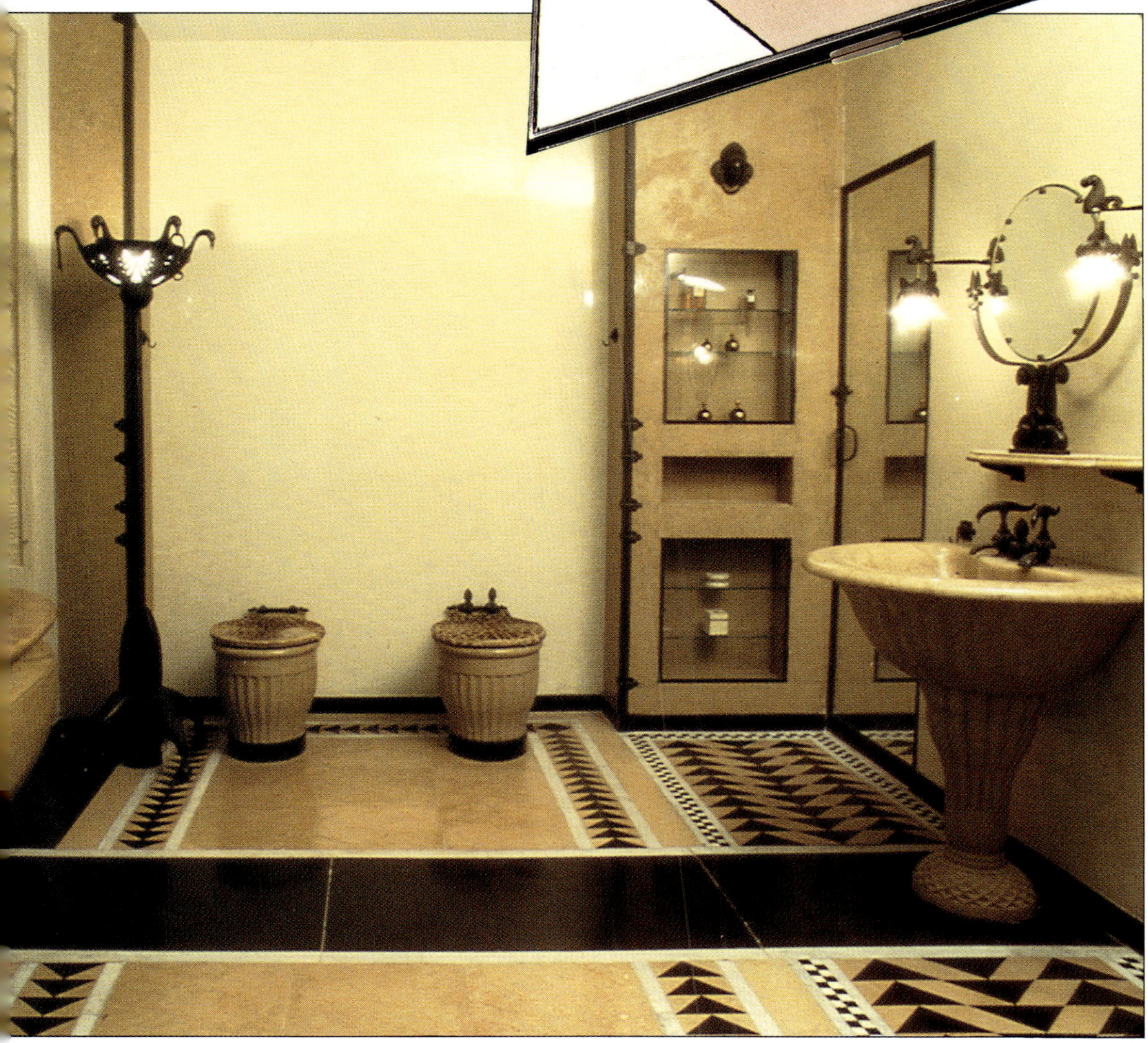

LEFT Enamelled 'minaudière', or compact, with portrait of the opera singer Enrico Caruso, by Lacloche Frères, Paris. This kind of artefact would be used by ladies as a fashion accessory for evening wear. The compact opens out to reveal a clip for bill money, a separate powder and lipstick compartment, along with a mirror, an ivory note pad and propelling pencil.

BELOW This elegant and luxurious bathroom was designed by Rateau for Jeanne Lanvin between 1920–22 and incorporated the use of marble, stucco, wrought iron and patinated bronze.

CHAPTER ONE

THE AGE OF ART DECO

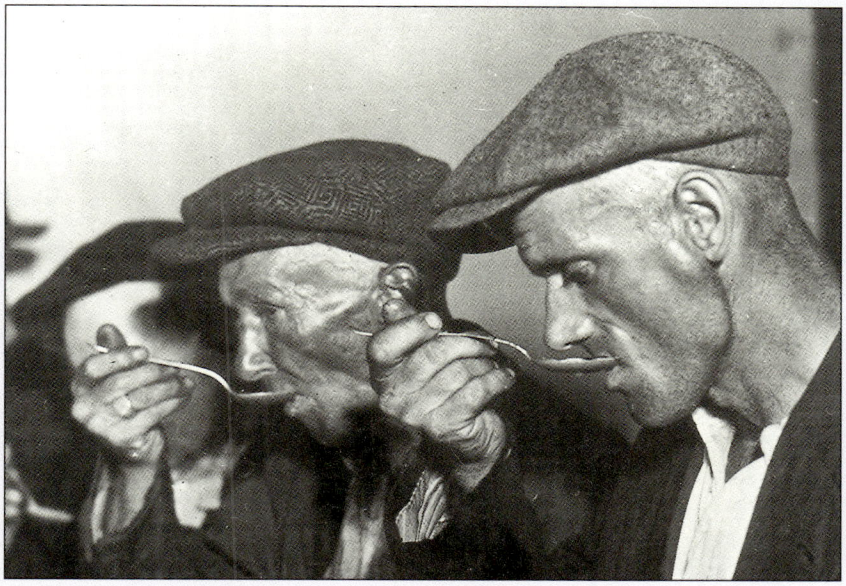

Unemployed men eating their bread and soup at one of the many New York soup kitchens set up during the Depression to prevent mass starvation.

RIGHT Unemployed men eating their bread and soup at one of the many New York soup kitchens set up during the Depression to prevent mass starvation.

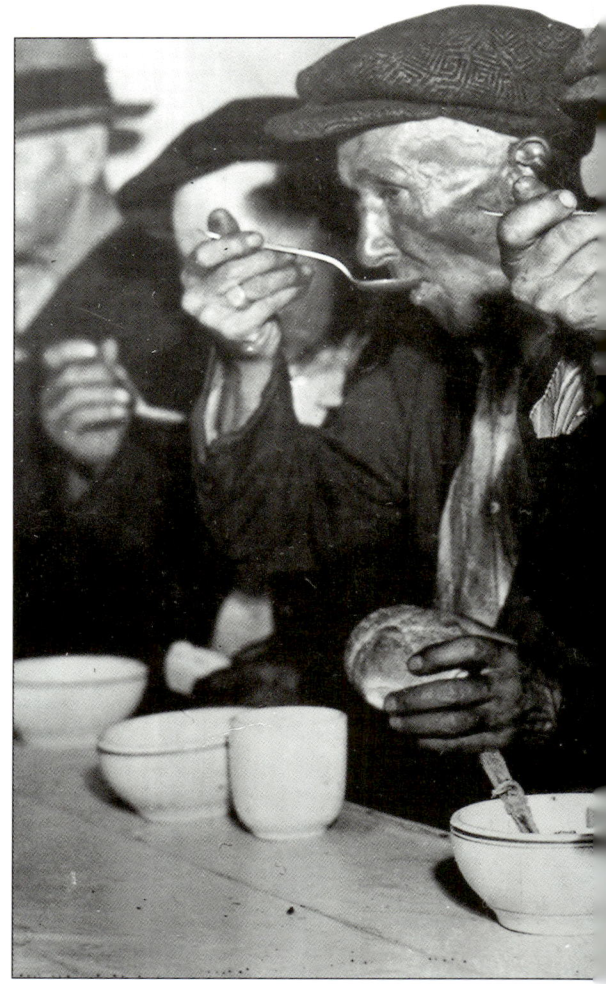

There are many people still alive today for whom the inter-war period is a vague memory of childhood, or a difficult adolescence preparing for a military service that might, or might not, terminate their life. Others will remember the early Hollywood films, dancing, and the courtship of their prospective husbands and wives. All were part of the same world. Sandwiched between the two world wars, the period from 1918 to 1939 had a very distinct, if contradictory, character. It was the age of economic depression throughout the western world yet also the era of feverish, youthful vitality which attempted to ignore what in retrospect seems obvious, the coming war.

In 1918 the Allied forces joined together to form the League of Nations. Following the carnage of the First World War they hoped to ensure that nothing so awful would ever happen again. It all turned out very differently. The 1920s and '30s were, in fact, just a pause. There are as many titles for, and descriptions of, that period as there are historians. It was not only the Age of Jazz, the Age of Swing, the Charleston, the Age of the Flapper, of Hollywood, of Christopher Isherwood's *Goodbye to Berlin*, and of course the Age of Art Deco, but also the Age of the Great Depression, the Wall Street Crash, the Age when money went mad, the Age of Fascism.

It is perhaps a typical quirk of human nature that even in the periods of deepest gloom and depression, the spirit calls on its resources to create and sustain something of beauty. In a small and very practical way the innumerable Art Deco teapots, cups, saucers, plates and cigarette lighters, with their clear colours and simple designs, affordable by almost everyone, provided an innocent boost to flagging spirits. Something else new had also happened with the turn of the century, namely, mass production.

The industrialization of the late 19th century, which in passing had been responsible for destroying many of the age-old arts and crafts that passed from father to son, had also spawned a brand-new marketing system that was, on the whole, efficient, which could produce in quantity for an attractive price. In the United States, the Sears Roebuck mail order catalogue was a hugely successful example of how consumer goods were now easily available to the most distant prairie-dweller or backwoodsman. What this meant in actual terms was that even for the average person, it was now possible to be up-to-date and "modern". An object seen at the 1925 Exposition des Arts Décoratifs et Industriels could be copied, probably with a few alterations, and ready for mass production within the year. To be in style was no longer the domain of just the wealthy European. The flavour of France could be savoured in Eastbourne, England, Munich, Bavaria or Memphis, Tennessee. The Age of Speed had telescoped diverse experiences one into another. Unusual objects from the far-flung corners of the world could be enjoyed at home. Although all of this could have promoted the spread of a greater and deeper understanding between the nations and races, the reality was different. If it was the Age of the Motor Car and the elegant transatlantic liner; it was also the Age of Empire.

The British Empire 'on which the sun never set', the Belgian, French, and more dangerously the Italian and German empires, had controlling positions that ensured the supply of cheap labour

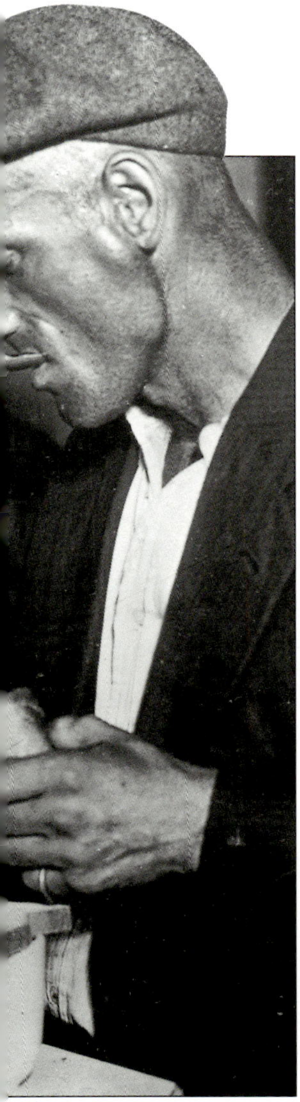

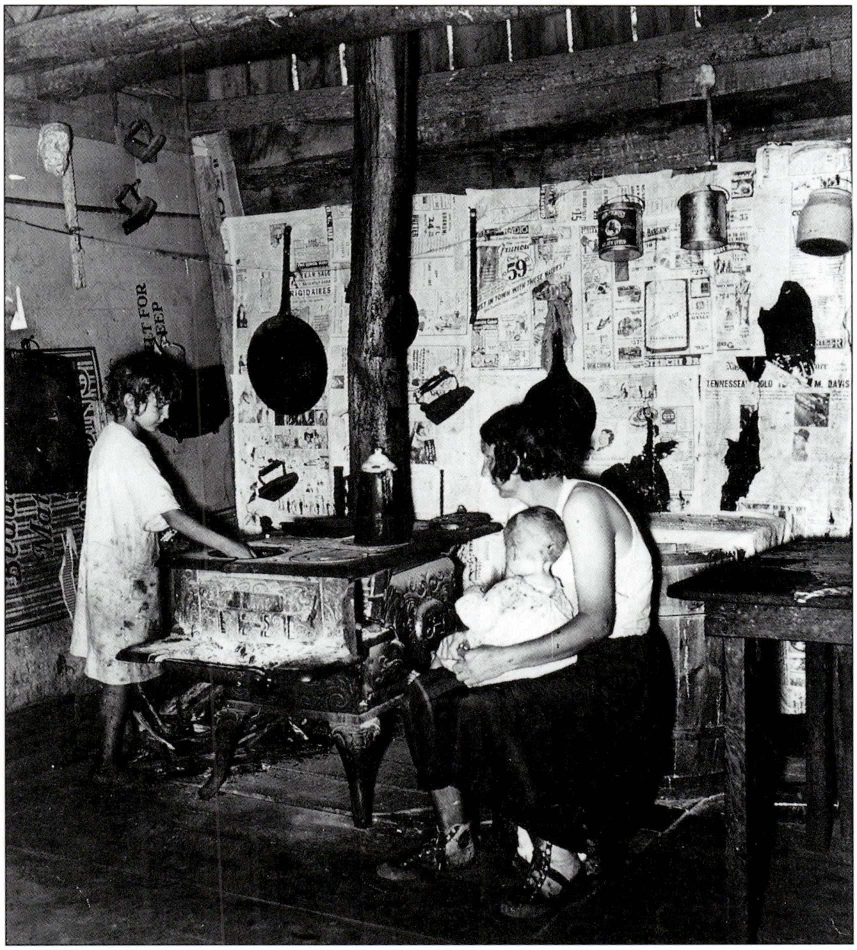

CHAPTER 1

LEFT The immediate effects of the Wall Street Crash were felt throughout the stockmarkets and business communities of the world. By the early 1930s the effects were felt by almost every community, even the most far flung. Those communities that relied on a single industry or agriculture often took a great deal longer to recover. This is a pathetically sad image of the poverty of a single family in Tennessee, United States.

and materials. If nations were powerful, so were their leaders. The 1920s and '30s were the last decades during which private palaces, country houses and yachts could be staffed and used as if their owners had an absolute and divine right to the comfort and pleasure that went with those assets. In the early 1920s, with the First World War far behind them, it must have seemed to the wealthy that nothing would ever change. It was a time to amass riches and enjoy them.

After Art Nouveau, with its intricate, heavily-worked floral patterns and intertwining vines, and Empire and Consulate furniture, the coming of Art Deco and the pure, no-nonsense simplicity of everyday objects must have filled their users with a sense of relief and clean, uncluttered well-being. If Art Deco design was bold, bright and innocent, the reality of the age was far more sinister, far less comfortable and secure.

W H Auden, who had emigrated to America in the early 30s to escape from the Nazi threat, wrote a poem called *September 1, 1939*, a title as unromantic as its subject matter. From that vantage point he wrote hauntingly and hopelessly:

I sit in one of the dives
On Fifty-Second Street
Uncertain and afraid
As the clever hopes expire
Of a low dishonest decade:
Waves of anger and fear
Circulate over the bright
And darkened lands of the earth,
Obsessing our private lives;
The unmentionable odour of death
Offends the September night.

The indication that all was not well with the world, after the high expectations of the League of Nations' founders, occurred as early as 1926. Inflation raged in Germany until finally the currency became utterly worthless. Wealthy shipowners and businessmen went broke overnight. Stories abound; the elderly couple who

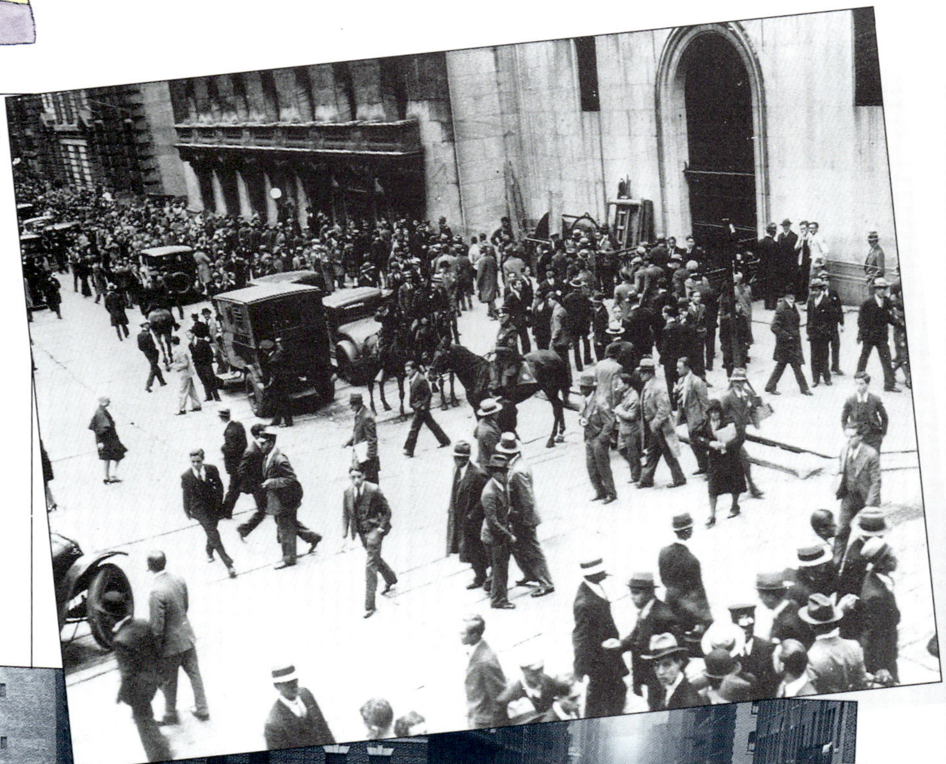

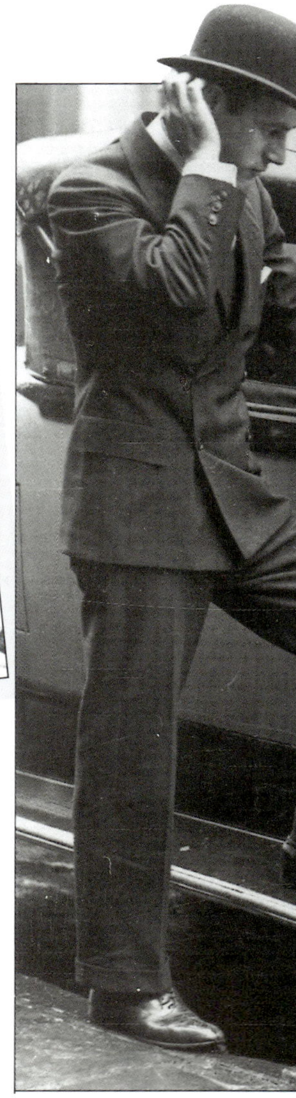

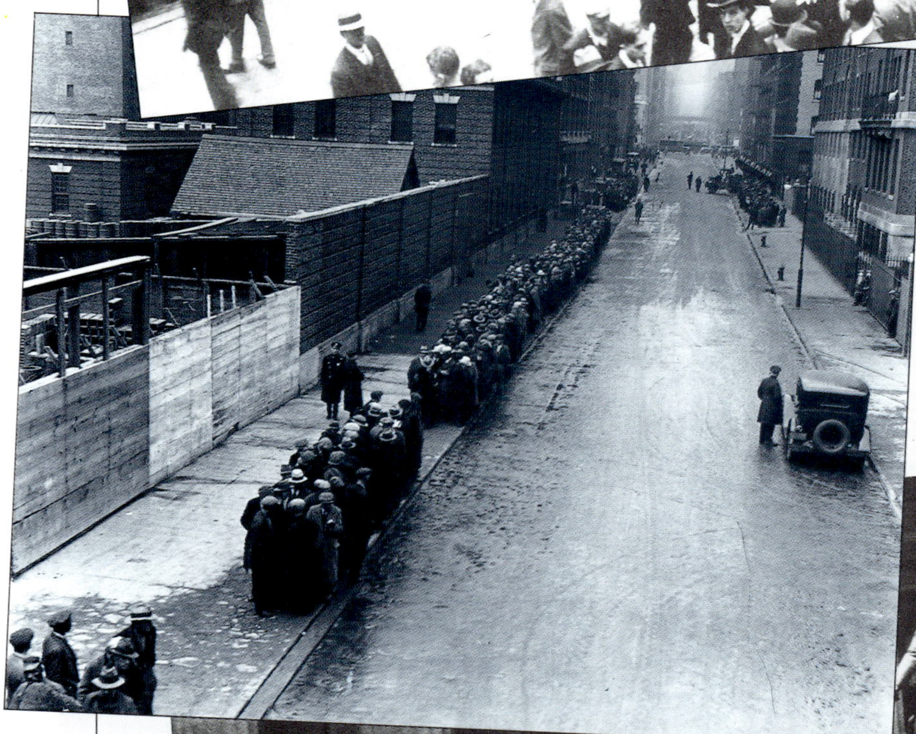

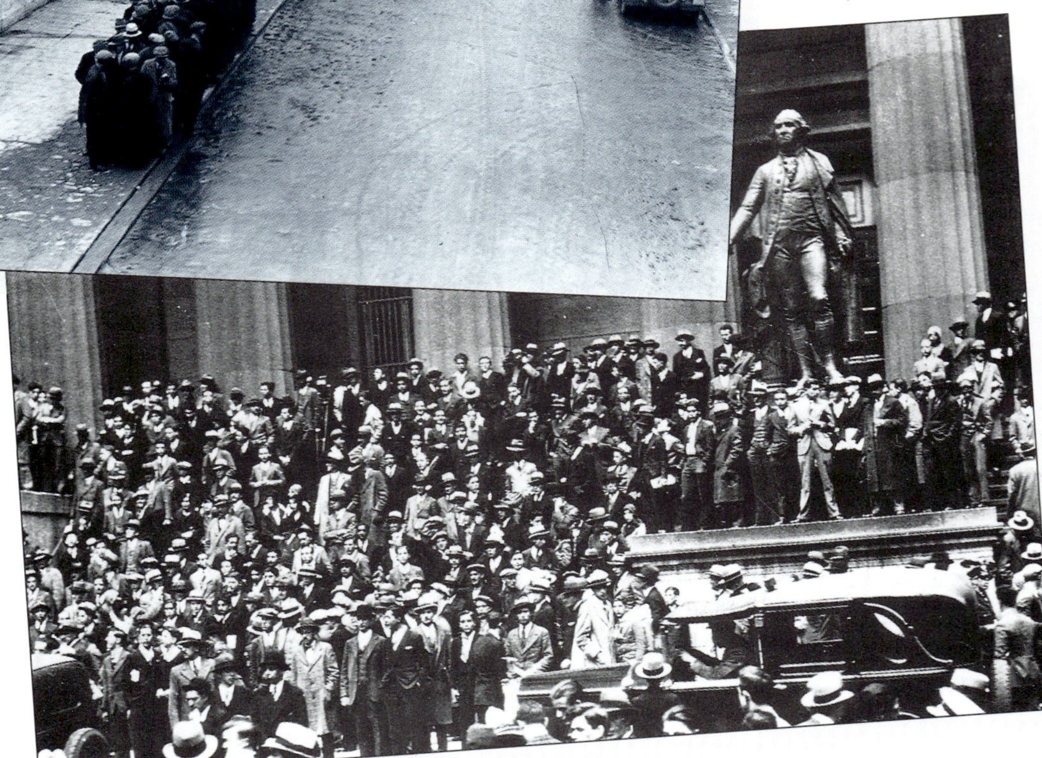

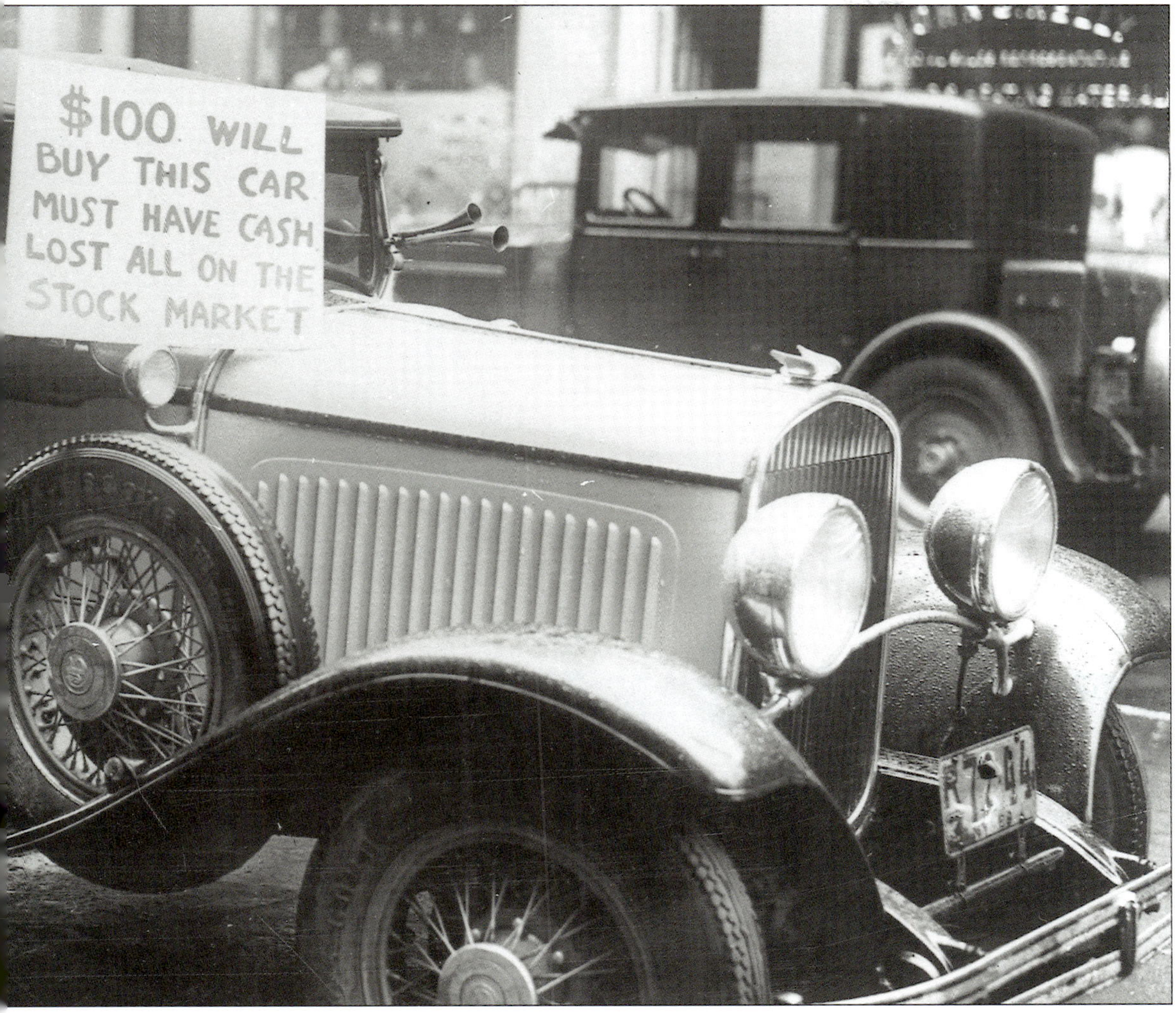

FAR LEFT On the worst day of trading, 24 October, 1929, mounted police are called in to keep law and order outside the New York Stock Exchange building on Wall Street.

LEFT One of the many losers on the stock market seeks to sell his car at a knockdown price.

CENTRE Following the Wall Street Crash, welfare services were stretched to their limits in order to prevent destitution and starvation. These men are waiting for the opening day of a new lodging house.

BELOW Crowds of anxious businessmen wait for news outside the sub-treasury building across from the New York Stock Exchange on the day of the worst collapse in stock market history, that signalled the beginning of the Great Depression.

cashed their life savings and found they could buy only a few strawberries, and the man who took a wheelbarrow full of money to buy a loaf of bread and, leaving it unattended for a few seconds, came back to find a pile of money and no wheelbarrow, are but two examples. The immediate effect of this was limited almost entirely to Germany, but it would take only another ten years for the repercussions to affect the rest of Europe and eventually the whole world.

The Wall Street Crash in October 1929 was of far greater importance. The stock market had been driven up to unprecedented levels, first by professional investors and then by anyone who could release enough cash to speculate on the buoyant market. The fickleness of the stock market is notorious, a sudden loss of confidence can radically alter the state of the market. That was exactly what happened. A sudden run on shares encouraged a further spiralling down, until paper fortunes were not worth the ink they were written in. Companies and banks were dragged down into the morass of bankruptcy, and the shock waves went right through the world economy. Fitful recoveries lasted only a few months as unemployment stayed at record levels in most of the western world. It took well into the mid '30s for the economy to recover, but by that time other, more serious problems, those of Fascism and Nazism, became more pressing.

To describe the 1920s and '30s as a sorry episode in history is perhaps making light of the enormity of the misery and desperation that most experienced. What is surprising is that Art Deco managed to survive and become the style of the age, when its designers and practitioners had such little support. It was partly due to the farsightedness of the French government's patronage.

RIGHT Revealing yet teasing photo of Josephine Baker in 1926 at the Folies Bergères, wearing the barest amount of Art Deco jewellery.

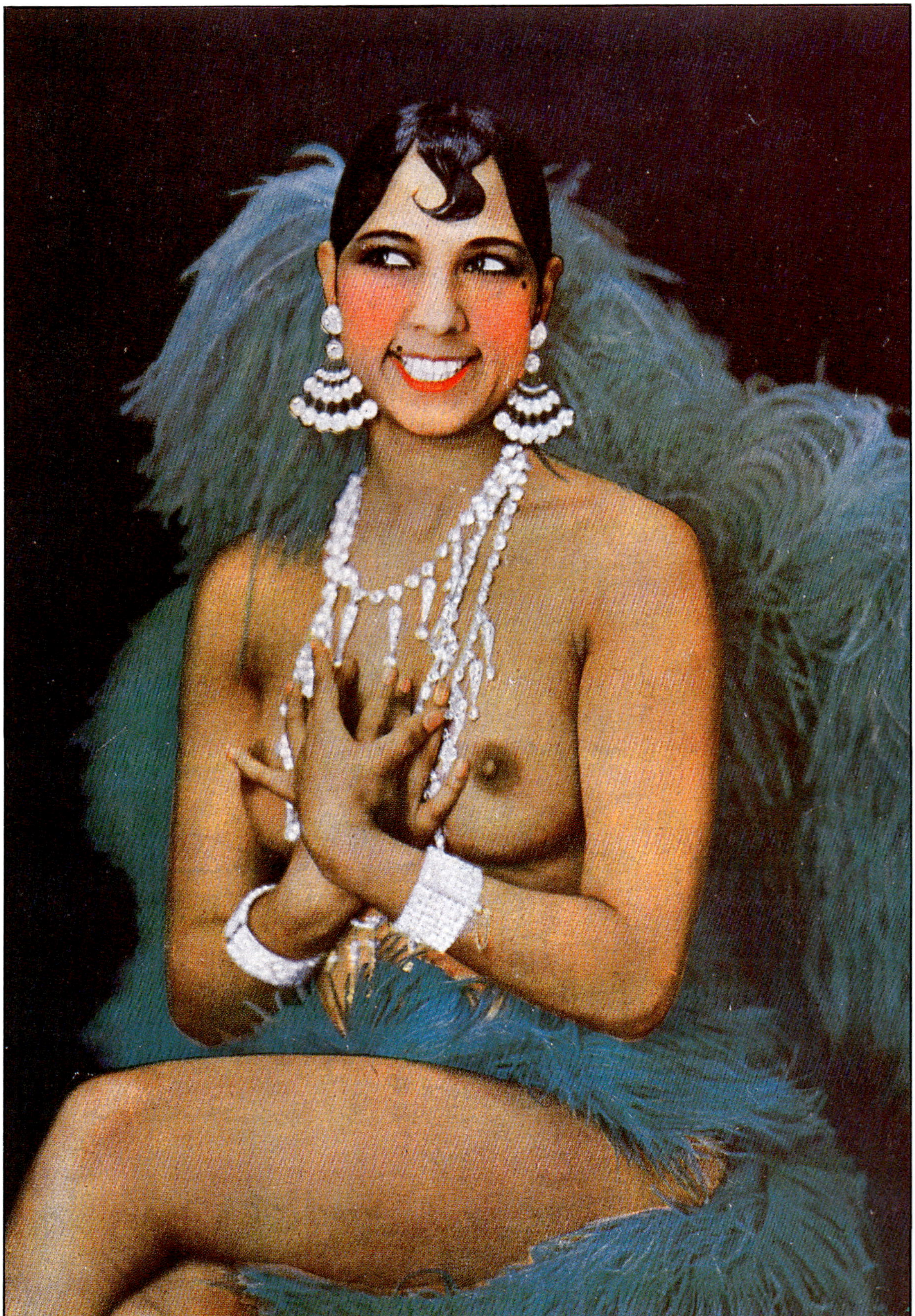

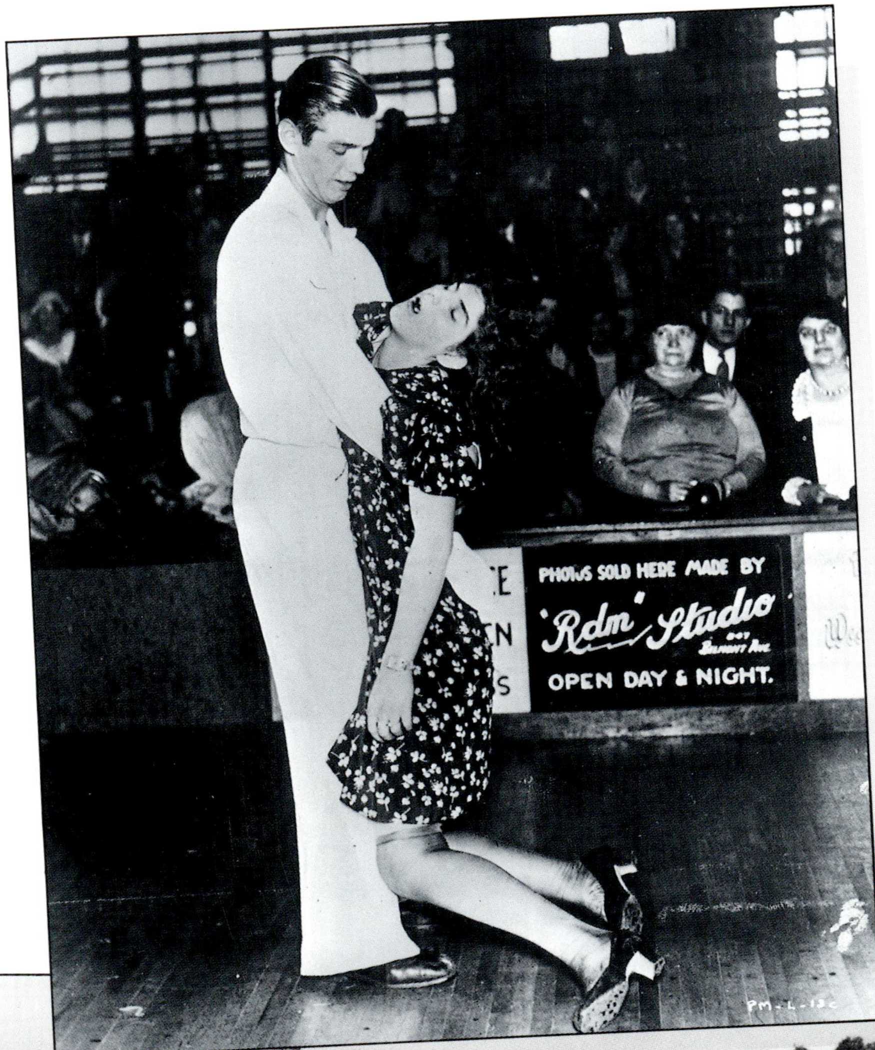

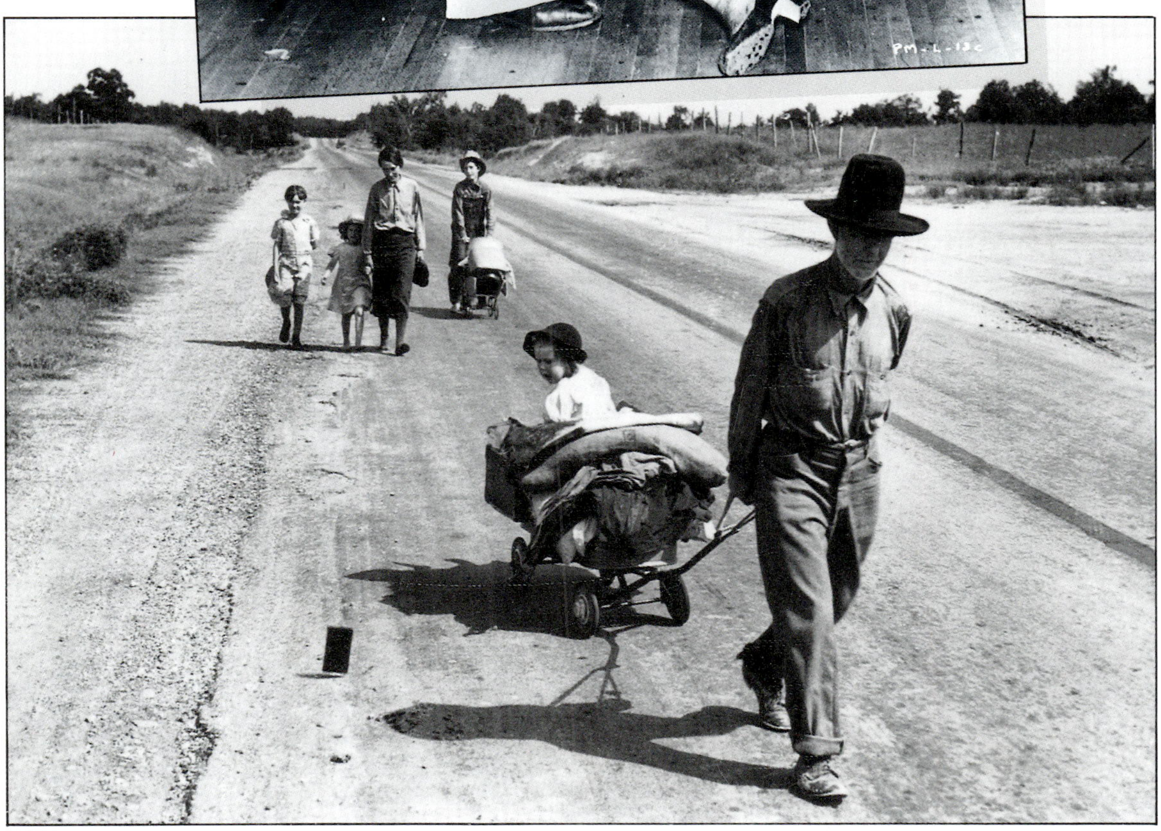

LEFT During the Depression, young couples would literally dance until they dropped in dance marathons that offered prize money to the winning couple. As this touching photo shows, it was a cruel burlesque of all that we associate with dancing: romance, energy and excitement. No picture could contrast more strongly with the hundreds of Hollywood publicity shots of the well-groomed hero looking deep into the heroine's swooning, lovesick eyes.

BELOW With all their worldly belongings, an Oklahoma family trudge westward to California along the Pittsburgh County Highway, in a tragic 1930s parody of the 19th century Wild West pioneers, with seemingly less hope.

RIGHT Couple dancing the Charleston, just one of the new dance crazes of the 1930s.

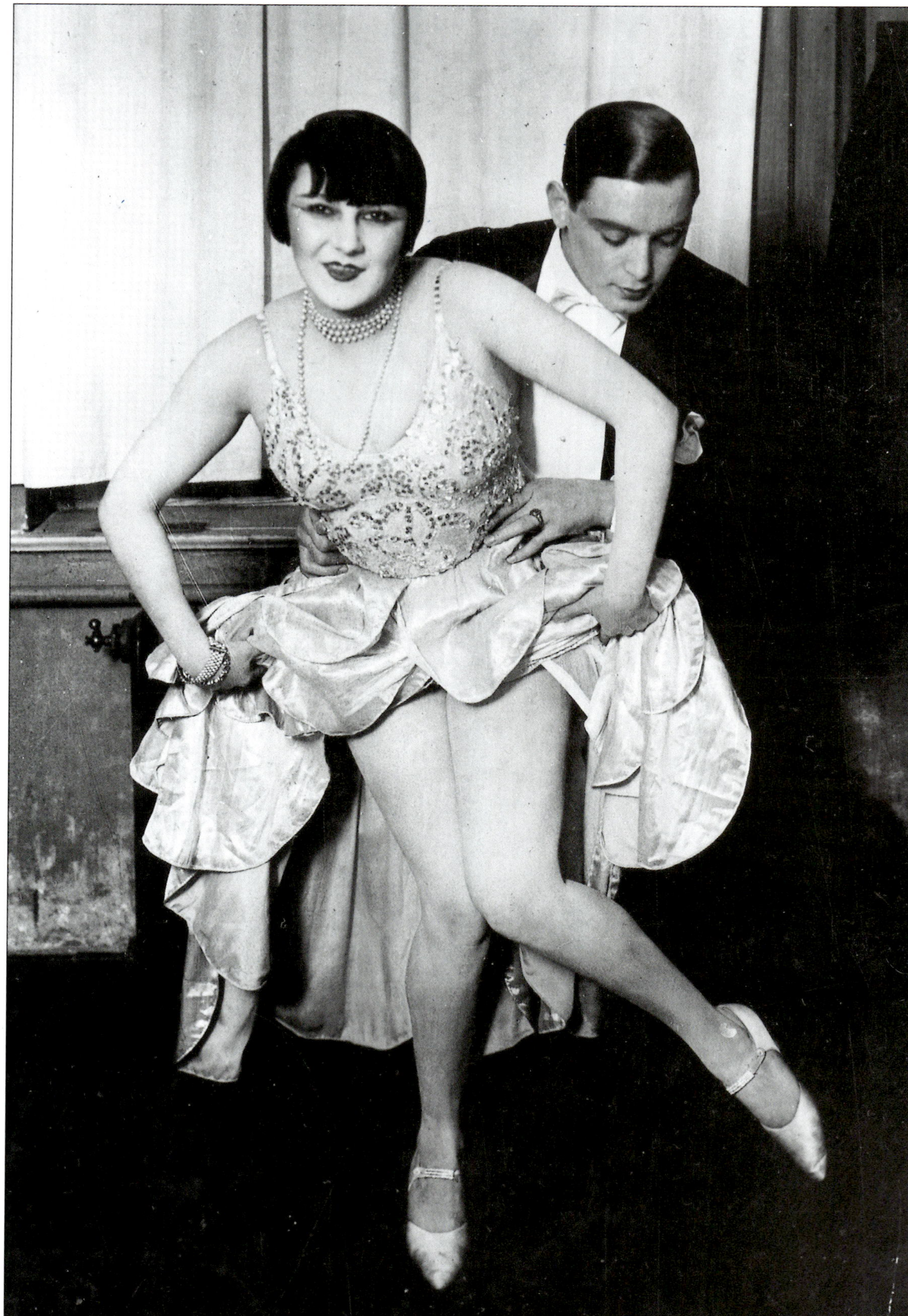

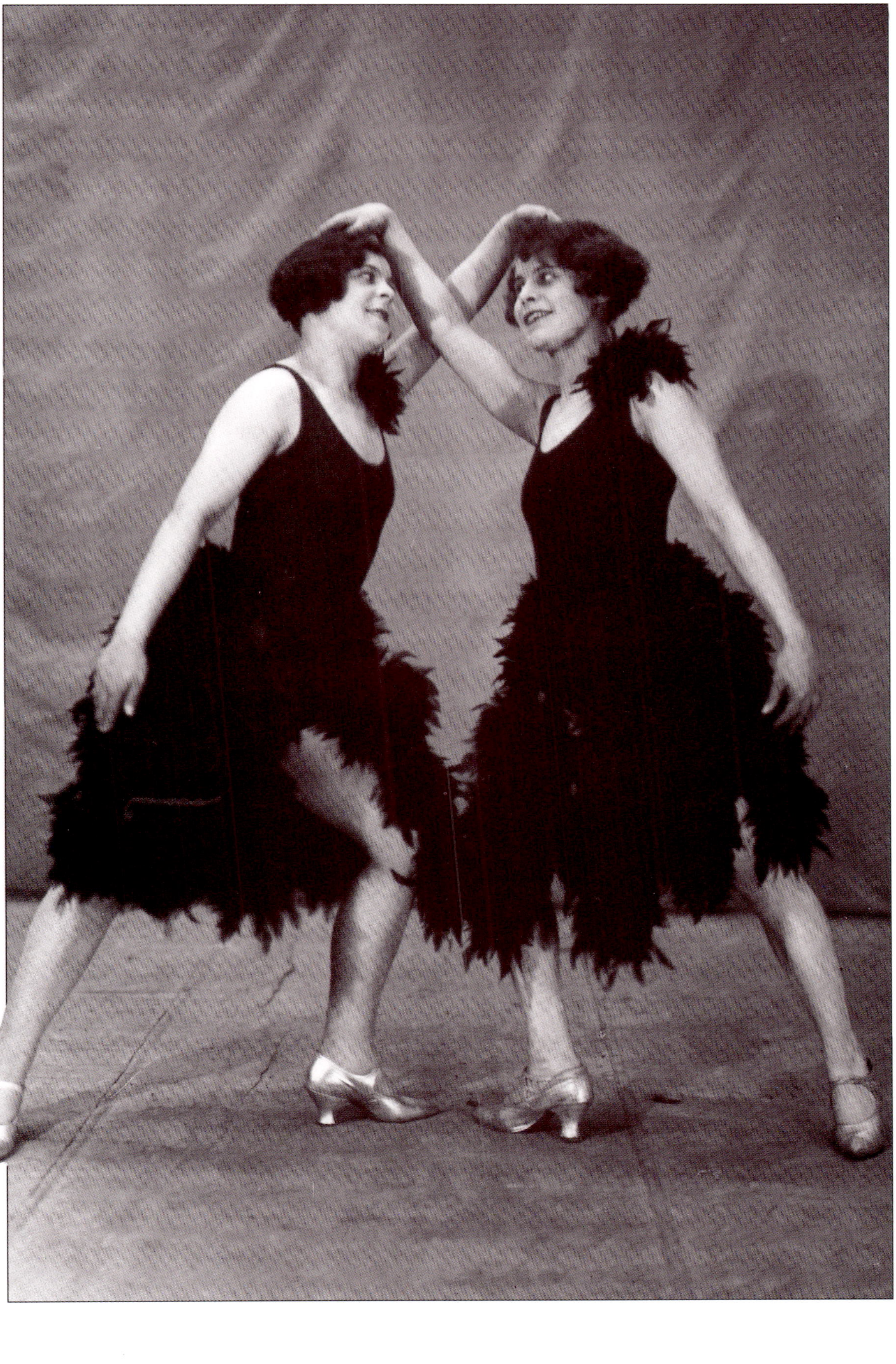

CHAPTER 1

LEFT The Charleston dance and Jazz music were two of America's most important contributions to the spirit of the Art Deco age. This humorous photo has more serious undercurrents. Oblivious to the outside world, it was as if the Charleston dancers were dancing on top of a volcano, blissfully unaware.

CHAPTER TWO

ART DECO STYLE

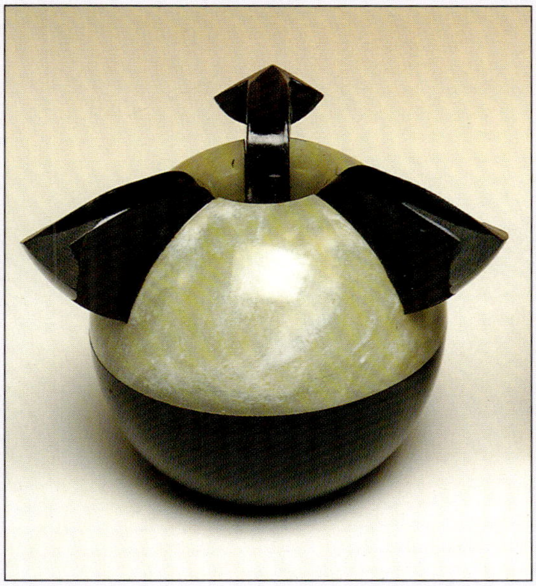

The tennis ball ashtray is an
ingenious creation for the Dunlop rubber Company.

RIGHT Examples of British Art Deco porcelain design from the 1930s by Henry Nixon and W. S. Coleman for the Royal Doulton works.

BELOW RIGHT Two fine examples of promotional advertising objects made of new synthetic materials in a simple Art Deco style. The Bakelite hot drink mug promotes the Bournvita brand for Cadbury's of England, and comes across with 'jolly night cap' lid. The tennis ball ashtray is an ingenious creation for the Dunlop rubber Company. The spherical body is made from urea formaldehyde, while the actual cigarette holders are made from a sister material, phenol formaldehyde.

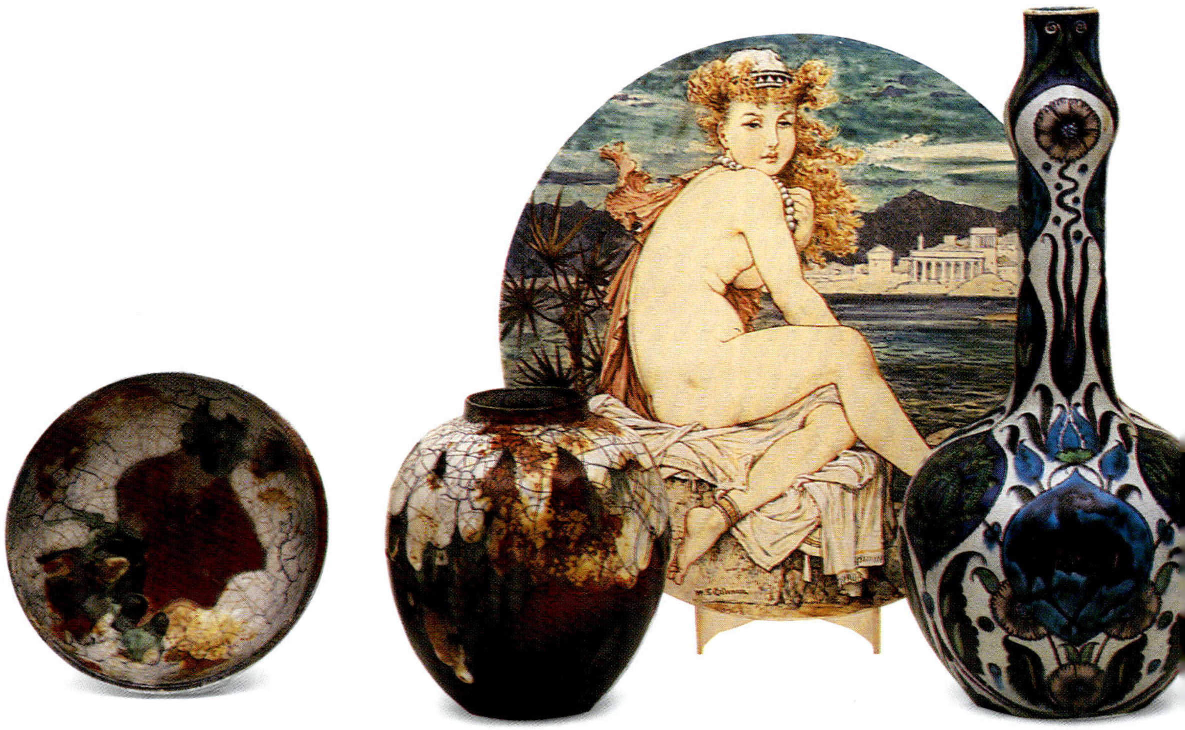

As with all works of art, it is difficult to pinpoint exactly where the ideas, or inspiration for a style come from.

But why was Art Deco so special, and different? There are many reasons. Art Deco was the first truly 20th-century style, moreover, it was international. Arriving when it did, and such timing is seldom by accident, it was a style that could be adapted to every single man-made object, regardless of application or budget. It also arrived at a time when new forms of communication ensured its rapid spread. Finally, and most important, it was the last total style. Like Baroque, Classical or Regency, Art Deco could ornament a house, a yacht, or a knife. Nothing has coloured and illuminated our life so extensively since.

That Art Deco was *the* style in the period between the wars is without question, but why this particular style? Fashions tend to be cyclical; why not neo-Baroque, for instance? Why did people go for the new when they could have revamped the old? That is where the secret lies. Art Deco did exactly that – it re-presented the old but spiced it up with new ingredients. Part of today's interest in Art Deco is pure nostalgia – the Charleston and the early movies – but at the time, the perspective was entirely different.

The spirit of Art Deco was the spirit of the modern. Even though it adapted older styles for its own use, it was still the style of the new. An Art Deco piece can be enjoyed for its form, the craftsmanship involved in the making and, because any object has its place in history, also because it is an indicator of times past. In the 1980s, only our grandmothers and grandfathers can still recall the surprise and excitement of owning their first motor car (automobile), their first trip in an aeroplane, their first radio, telephone and, later, television. Spoilt and jaded by the current overabundance of new technology, it is easy to forget that there is always a first time. Every advance to them must have had the impact of the first man on the moon. Art Deco was the style of the age that wouldn't stay

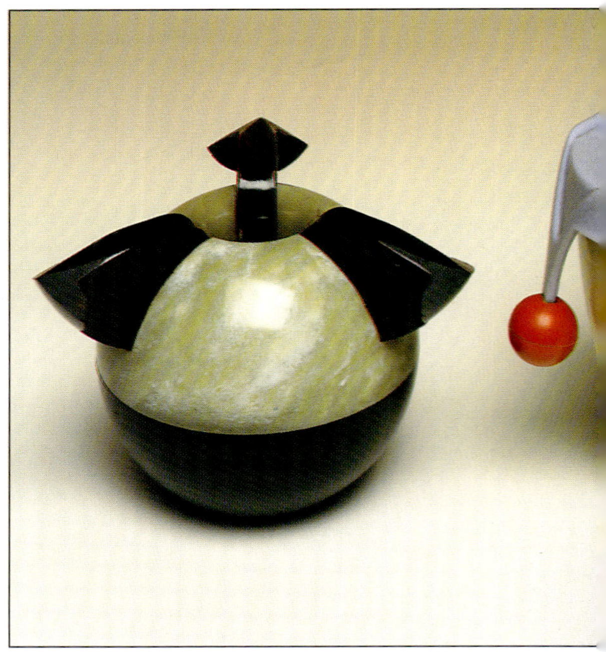

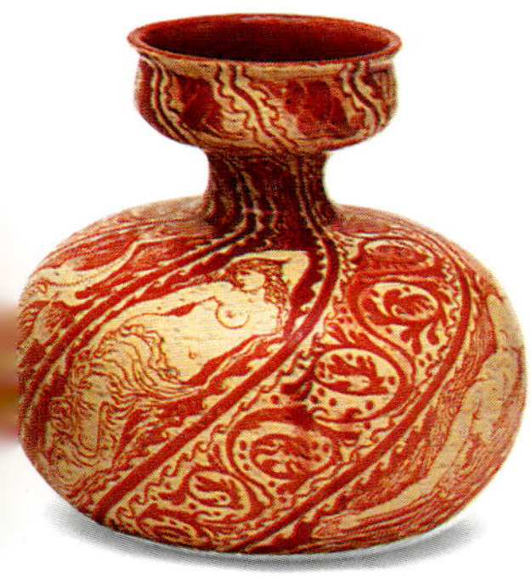

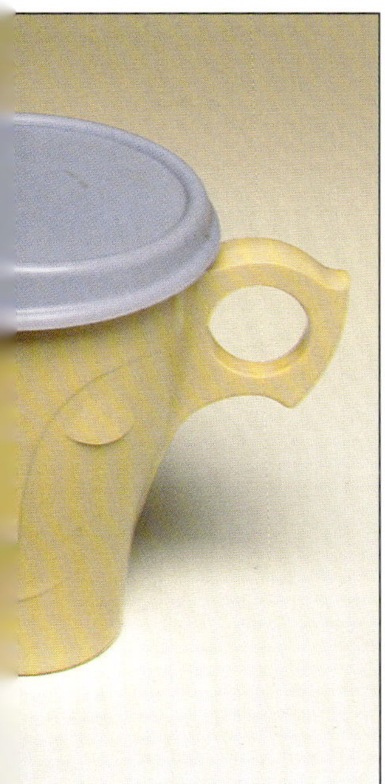

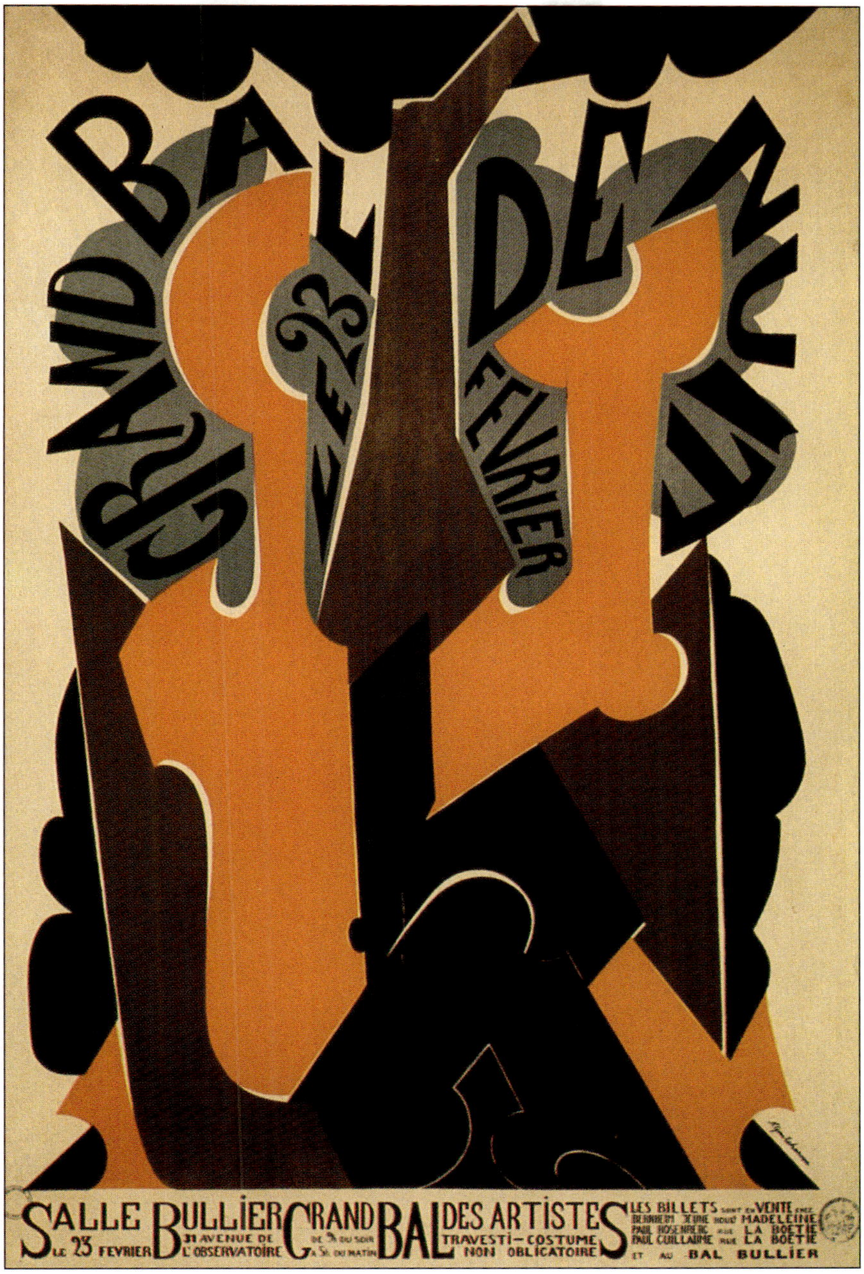

LEFT Poster advertising the Grand Bal de Nuit, designed by the Russian artist Natalia Gontcharova, who also designed stage sets for Diaghilev's Ballets Russes.

still and looked to that age for its content, its meaning, and often its subject matter.

However, Art Deco may have been the modern style, but it emerged from as many different directions as it had applications. Art Deco was given its greatest cohesion in the Paris Exposition of 1925, but it was also the Paris of Pablo Picasso, Georges Braque, Fernand Léger, and Robert and Sonia Delaunay. Such Art Deco pieces as a decorated cigarette lighter by Gérard Sandoz, a silver tea service by Jean Puiforcat, and a plate by the Royal Doulton works, could not have come from any time earlier than 1910. Art Deco is essentially a style applied to applied art, though most of its sources are in the fine arts, architecture, sculpture and painting.

Paris was the stage on which almost all the battles of modern art were fought. The rapidity with which style has since followed on style has made it almost impossible to discern any lasting direction today. From Impressionism through post-Impressionism, Symbolism, Cubism, Futurism, Orphism, Constructivism, Purism, Surrealism, Vorticism, one "ism" has replaced the

TWO TYPES OF CUNARD

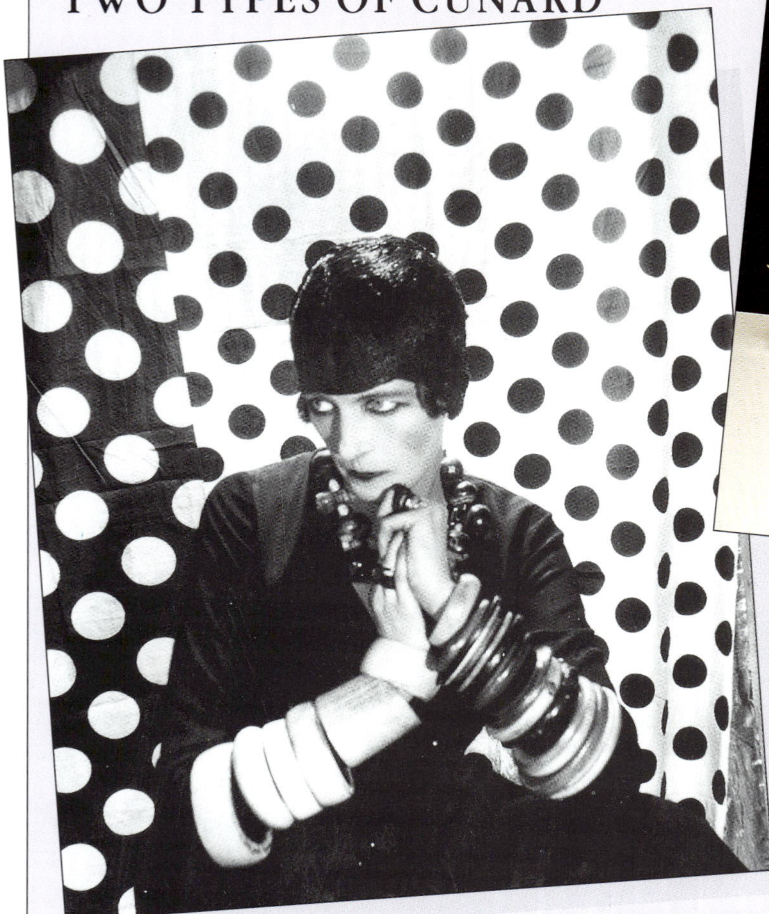

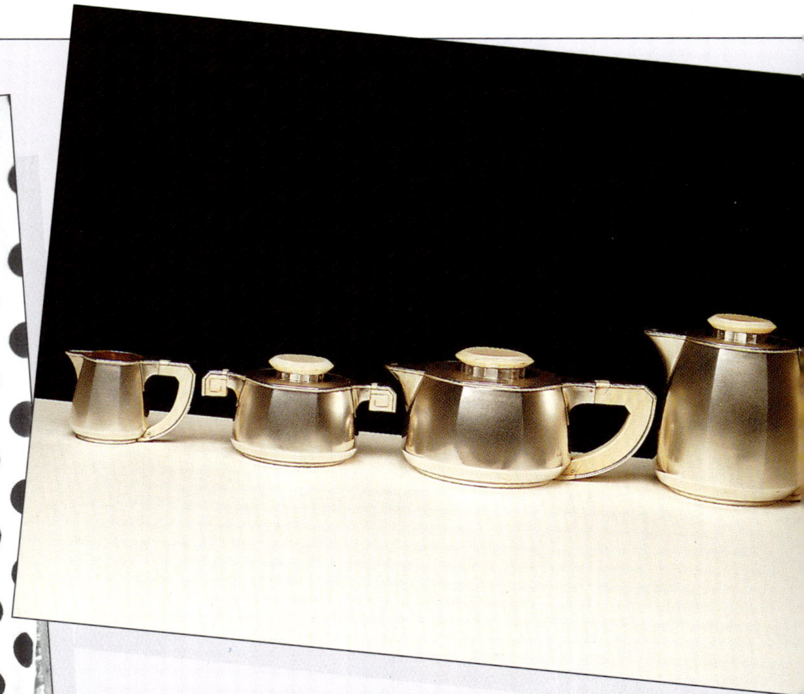

ABOVE A beautifully sympathetic juxtaposition of silver and ivory in this tea service by the master craftsman Jean Puiforcat. The spouts and handles are reminiscent of the ocean liners of that age.

RIGHT Two of the Cunard's most famous liners in a poster from the 1950's.

LEFT Portrait of the illustrious Nancy Cunard by the society photographer Cecil Beaton. Lively, well-connected, and beautiful, this photo shows why Nancy had so many supporters and admirers.

In 1840 Samuel Cunard, based in Halifax, Nova Scotia, established the Cunard Line, a trans-Atlantic passenger service. By the first decade of the 20th century the Cunard liners became so sophisticated they could properly be called "floating palaces". Massive ballrooms, casinos, swimming pools, and restaurants that served the best cuisine were only some of the facilities that passengers could expect. In 1907 the *Mauretania* was launched, and along with her sister ship the *Aquitania*, became standard bearer of the Cunard Line. They were important, not just because they provided the quickest transport between America and Europe at the time, but also because their design played a decisive role in the development of modern architecture, and the Art Deco style.

At the 1925 Exposition des Arts Décoratifs et Industriels there had been one pavilion which seemed completely out of keeping with all the rest. The now famous architect Le Corbusier, arguably the greatest of this century, suggested a pavilion which would be used as a forum in which to discuss his latest ideas. The organisers attempted to dissuade him from entering, but finally had to allow him a space, stuck in a corner behind the Grand Palais. The result was the Pavillon de L'Esprit Nouveau. It was a curiosity, a statement which argued forcefully against the decorative arts that the whole Exposition hoped to promote. Rectangular, and cube-like, with large, plain windows, it was the very latest in modernist architecture. It was as Le Corbusier himself had written in his book *Towards a New Architecture* two years previously, "a machine for living in." Le Corbusier had split *Towards a New Architecture* into sections, of which the major part concentrated on the possibility of looking towards aeroplanes, motor cars, and liners as possible sources of inspiration for the new architecture. The *Aquitania* displayed numerous possible applications for domestic architecture. Le Corbusier's message was that the artist should control the machine and apply it to all aspects of modern life. Liners were supremely functional; the *Mauretania* held the Blue Riband, the transatlantic prize for the fastest crossing, for 22 years, averaging over 27 knots at its fastest. They were also elegant in their simplicity; long colonnaded walkways, metal staircases, and an approach to new materials that had not been thought of pre-

next, with disarming regularity. What many of these "isms" had in common, which would be of great importance to Art Deco, was that they shared a tendency towards abstraction, a move away from obvious subject matter towards a concern for the basic elements of picture-making or sculpting, so that form, colour, line and volume became important in themselves. The artist's feelings and sensibility could be read, it was hoped, through the manipulation of those infinitely flexible variables. Architecture had the additional need to be functional, to keep out the rain, keep in the warmth, and provide a living space. Ornament is not absolutely necessary on a building, nor on everyday objects. Teapots are for pouring tea and keeping it warm, a plate is for eating off.

As for the decorative arts in the Art Deco style, they ranged from the purely functional, through simple and clear decoration, to pure ornament. That is why it is impossible to talk of one Art Deco: there were as many directions, hybrids and strains as there were practitioners. The easiest way to understand and unravel the puzzle is to see where Art Deco came from and what sources it may have used.

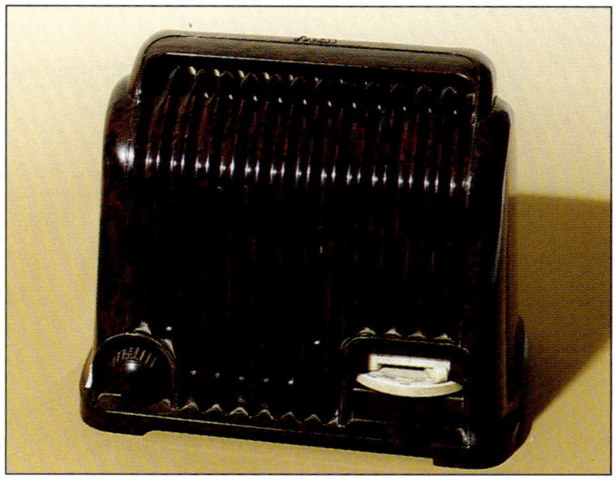

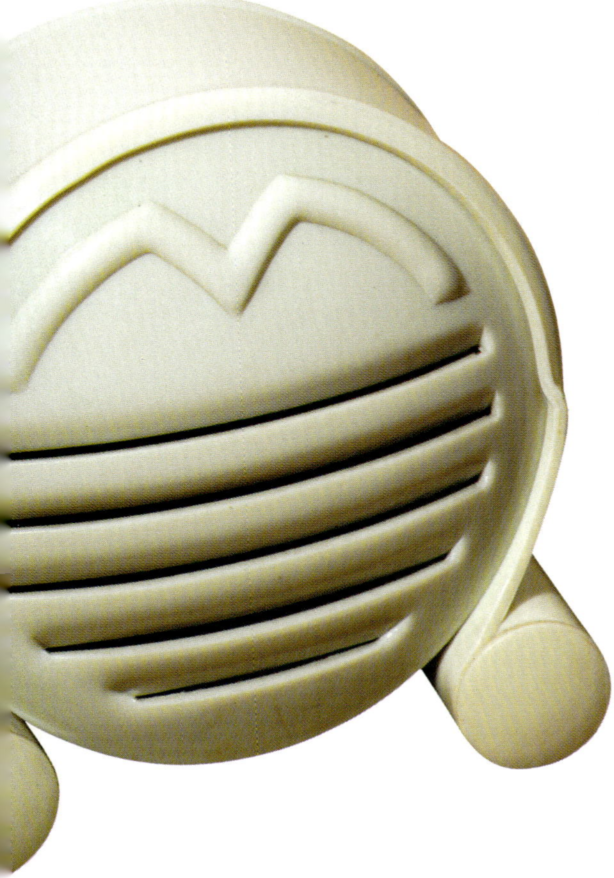

CHAPTER 2

LEFT Bakelite radio set of the 1930s inscribed receiver type 439 is an example of Art Deco applied to the latest technology. How many of these must have been thrown out with the rubbish when technology improved, and styles altered.

BELOW LEFT The M-speaker is typically Art Deco in design. The letter M is distinctly of the period, as are the sound box grilles and the pseudo-classical scrolls at the base. Made in Bakelite by Wavox in Britain, it must have been one of the least expensive speakers on the market.

When Picasso and Braque set off together in 1907–8 on the journey through their radical discoveries that would lead to Cubism, "roped like mountaineers", they turned art, as it had then been understood, on its head. The shock waves pulsed across Europe into Russia, and across to North America in less than five years. The Italian artists Severini, Boccioni, and Marinetti quickly united under their Futurist banner; in Holland the architects, designers and painters Gerrit Rietveld, Bart van der Leck and Piet Mondrian formed de Stijl, and Constructivism was conceived in the U.S.S.R. In England there was Vorticism, in Germany the Bauhaus was formed a few years later, and back in Paris Orphism appeared. Out of Picasso, Abstraction had been born. The process of art had become a search, an experiment. Modernism came into being, the avant-garde invented. It had become viable, and ultimately necessary to test out all the infinite options, to play intellectual games, and extend and expand the boundaries of art. To be ahead of one's time, or at least up there with it, pushing forward, was to be a modernist. Like-minded designers could apply these principles to the decorative arts and arrive at something wholly novel. In a lesser way they could apply the colour schemes of a Mondrian painting, a Goncharova, El Lissitzky, a Wyndham Lewis, or, simpler still, Malevich's painting *White square on a white background*, and arrive at simplicity itself. In the transition from fine art to applied art, the most simple motif had passed from being shocking, avant-garde and bewildering, to being accepted and merely decorative.

Art Nouveau was of central importance to the

RIGHT Cologne bottle, inscribed 'HIS' for the Northwoods company, Chicago, Illinois. The stylized cubist head is in cream-coloured Bakelite; the maroon bottle is made of glass. This hexagonal box with a motif of two birds is an exceptionally fine example of marbleised Bakelite employing various colours.

OPPOSITE ABOVE Simple yet eccentric side-table of 1923 by Pierre Legrain clearly showing African inspiration and displaying Legrain's love of the primitive.

OPPOSITE BELOW 1979–81 reconstruction by Martyn Chalk of a relief produced in 1914 by the Russian avant-garde artist Vladimir Tatlin. Using materials as diverse as sand, plaster, wood, glass, iron and bitumen, Tatlin spearheaded the Russian avant-garde movement that would later produce fine examples of porcelain.

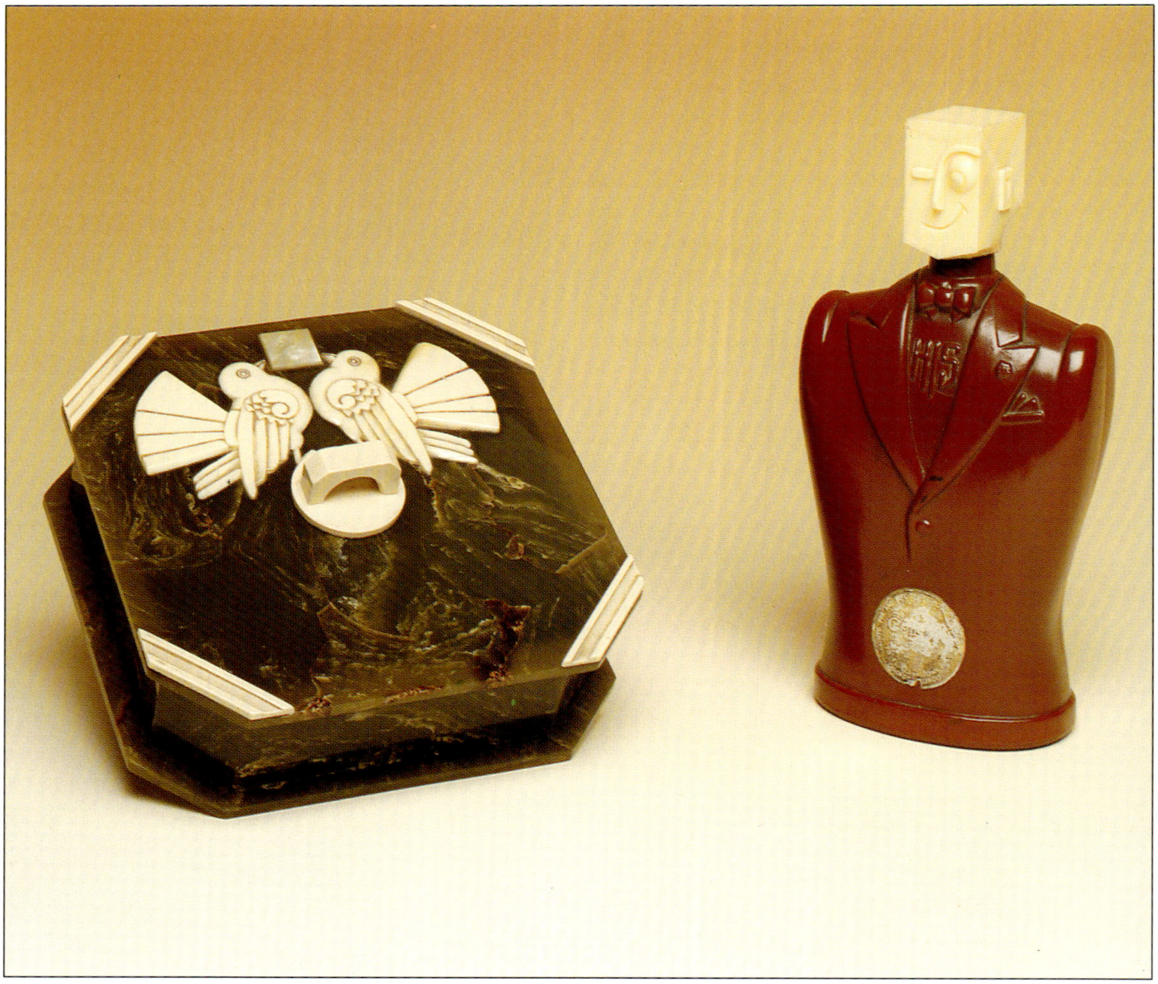

rise of Art Deco, if only as a style to react against. Equally, the work of Hoffman, Olbrich, Peche, and Moser, who founded the Wiener Werkstätte at the beginning of the century, were early practitioners of a style which, when refined, looked like very early Art Deco. Another influence, which probably became the most important of all, was a response to primitive art. Painters such as van Gogh and Whistler had earlier looked at Japanese prints for inspiration. Later Derain and Picasso looked at African art, and later still Matisse looked at the decorative potential of Morocco. What had happened throughout the late 19th century was a reappraisal of primitive art. Museums throughout Europe had rearranged their collections of primitive art, dusted them down, opened up the old showcases jumbled and heaped up with old artefacts, and redisplayed them as works of art. Anything that was not European was recognized at last as having some artistic worth. Indeed, Europe looked away from the products of a diseased society that had chosen to massacre its youth across the battlefields of the Somme, to an art that was primitive, untouched and natural. This was particularly relevant to Art Deco, because by the time the style began to develop, a tendency towards the primitive was not just an option, it was obligatory.

Nobody looking back at Paris in the first quarter of this century could ignore the impact of the Ballets Russes on the arts. Driven by its passionate Svengali and impressario Serge Diaghilev, its stage designs and costumes mixed the oriental with the westernized, the avant garde with the primitive. Leon Bakst, its most famous designer, produced costumes whose lavishness and orientalism came as a complete shock to the Parisian public. Diaghilev's production of *Scheherezade* was a riot of deep, rich colour which inspired the heavier decorative side of Art Deco and interior design. Even more

ART DECO WIT

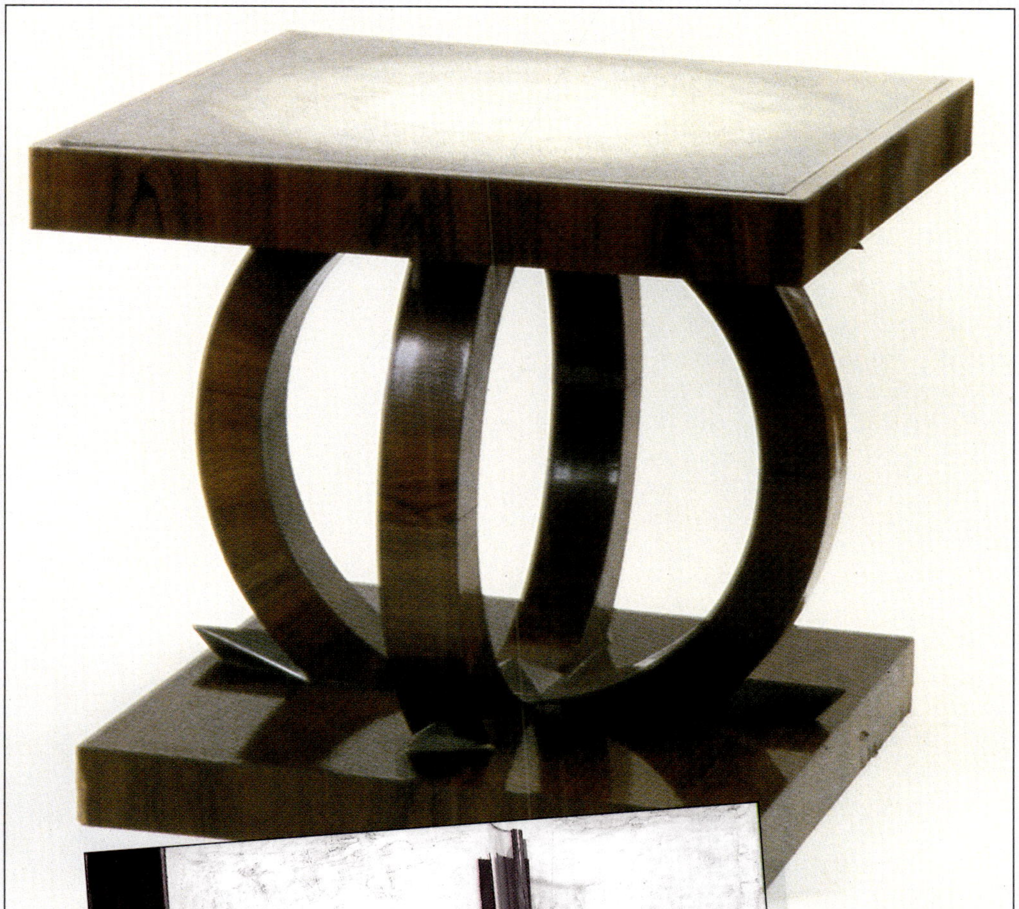

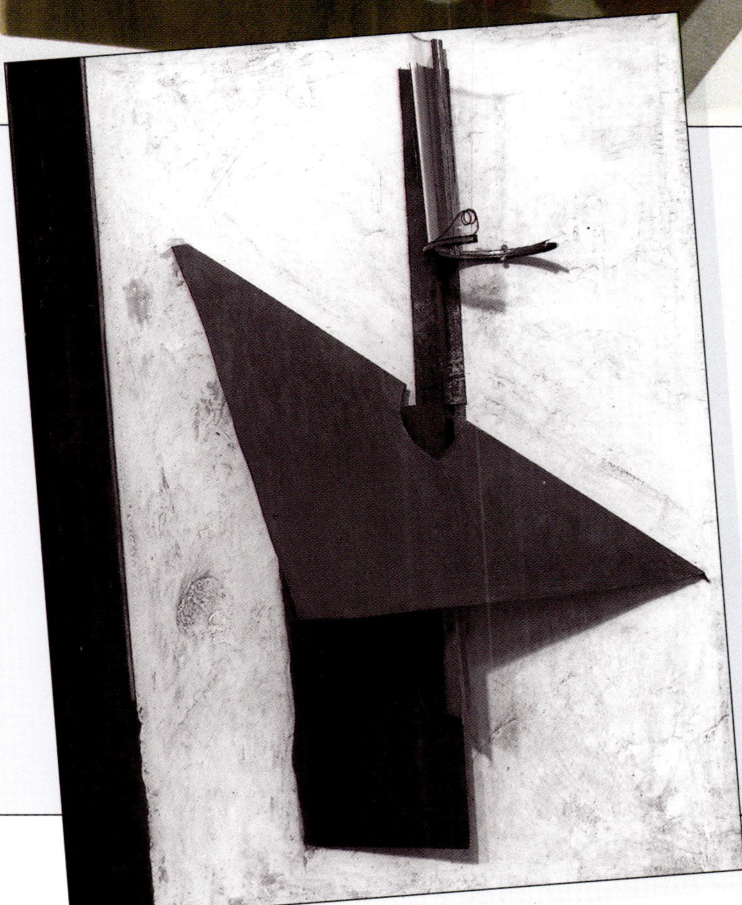

Designers have a habit of taking themselves too seriously. Most styles can be elegant, impressive and imposing, but no fun at all. The Parthenon, the Eiffel Tower and Versailles amaze rather than amuse. One of Art Deco's most endearing qualities, therefore, is its playfulness, its sense of the ridiculous, its knack of taking something out of a context which we all recognize and putting it into another. Often it is downright silly. Art Deco has been responsible for the most tasteless of kitsch. If the dog with the nodding head wasn't invented then, it should have been.

That teapot by Puiforcat looks like an ocean liner but for the perversion of scale involved, so that massive areas become small domestic details – imagine crossing the Atlantic in it. The tables and chairs by Pierre Legrain with their strong African flavour could be just as easily worn as bracelets or strung on a necklace as sat on.

Art Deco producéd teapots disguised as cars, bears and elephants, and table lamps of a landing female parachutist. Some of the most common objects of all, and still among the easiest examples of Art Deco to collect, are the hundreds and thousands of plaster heads. Based on the tradition of portrait busts, these are pure comedy. The simpering dancer, or the haughty, fashion-conscious woman, the golfer, and the pipe smoker, are all distilled into caricatures – cartoons of themselves.

ambitious in the Art Deco style were the thousands of gouache drawings for set designs of Erté. The sinuous, sweeping curves of dresses and curtains fell across a rigidly simple, but still evocative backdrop. Elegantly arched windows looked in on interiors bedecked with leopard skin rugs and abstract rectilinear furniture, enlivened by dancers in oriental costume. That was part of Diaghilev's legacy to Art Deco. If that was not enough, he also incorporated the latest in contemporary dance, design and music. In 1917 the ballet *Parade* employed the talents of Picasso as stage designer, Erik Satie as composer, and Jean Cocteau as the scenario writer. In later years Diaghilev would also involve Russians like Naum Gabo, Antoine Pevsner, and Larionov, whose constructivist sets would display an outrageous purity of form that continued to fuel the starker and more minimal extremes of Art Deco.

If oriental art had been made fashionable by the Ballets Russes, Mexican, Egyptian, North American Indian and South American art was of equal importance. The Egyptian influence, and also that of Africa, are obvious in the chairs of Pierre Legrain. Heavy, solid pieces of furniture they are crude and built to last, much like the early radio sets and triangular clocks for the mantelpiece that instantly recall Egyptian pyramids or Aztec temples. What Art Deco learnt, and taught the public, was bold design. If colours were to be bright, they should knock you over, if lines were to be clear, they should be as stark and severe as the steps up a temple. The obvious could be chic.

The final, and one of the most obvious, influences on Art Deco was there to see at every street corner, in every house, factory and shop, on the sea and in the air. The 20th century was the machine age. Art Deco was modern because it used aspects of machine design as inspiration, the wings of an aeroplane, the bow of a yacht, the porthole of the cabin window of the new ocean liners, the cogs and wheels of a sewing machine or a motor car engine. It was even more modern because it accelerated the adoption of new materials such as plastic, bakelite and chrome.

The mixing of all these influences made Art Deco the style it is. In the hands of genius, the objects transcended their sources. In the hands of competent designers, or plagiarists, they might become drab or garish, but they were, nevertheless, truly Art Deco.

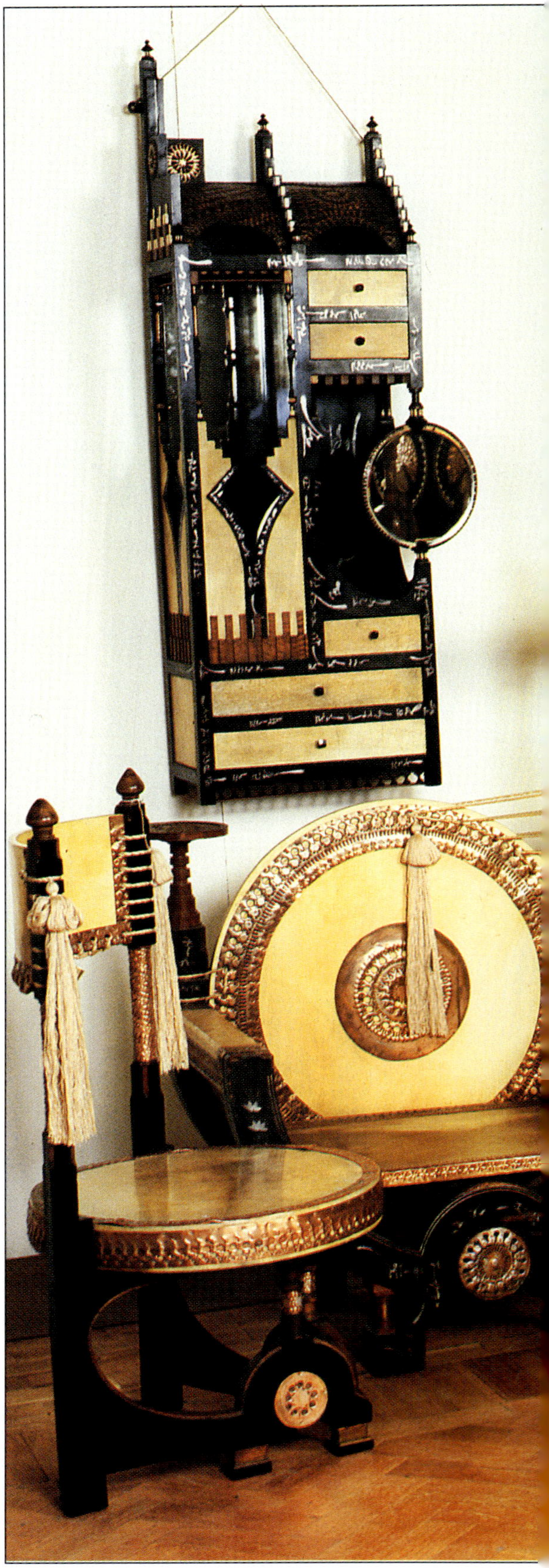

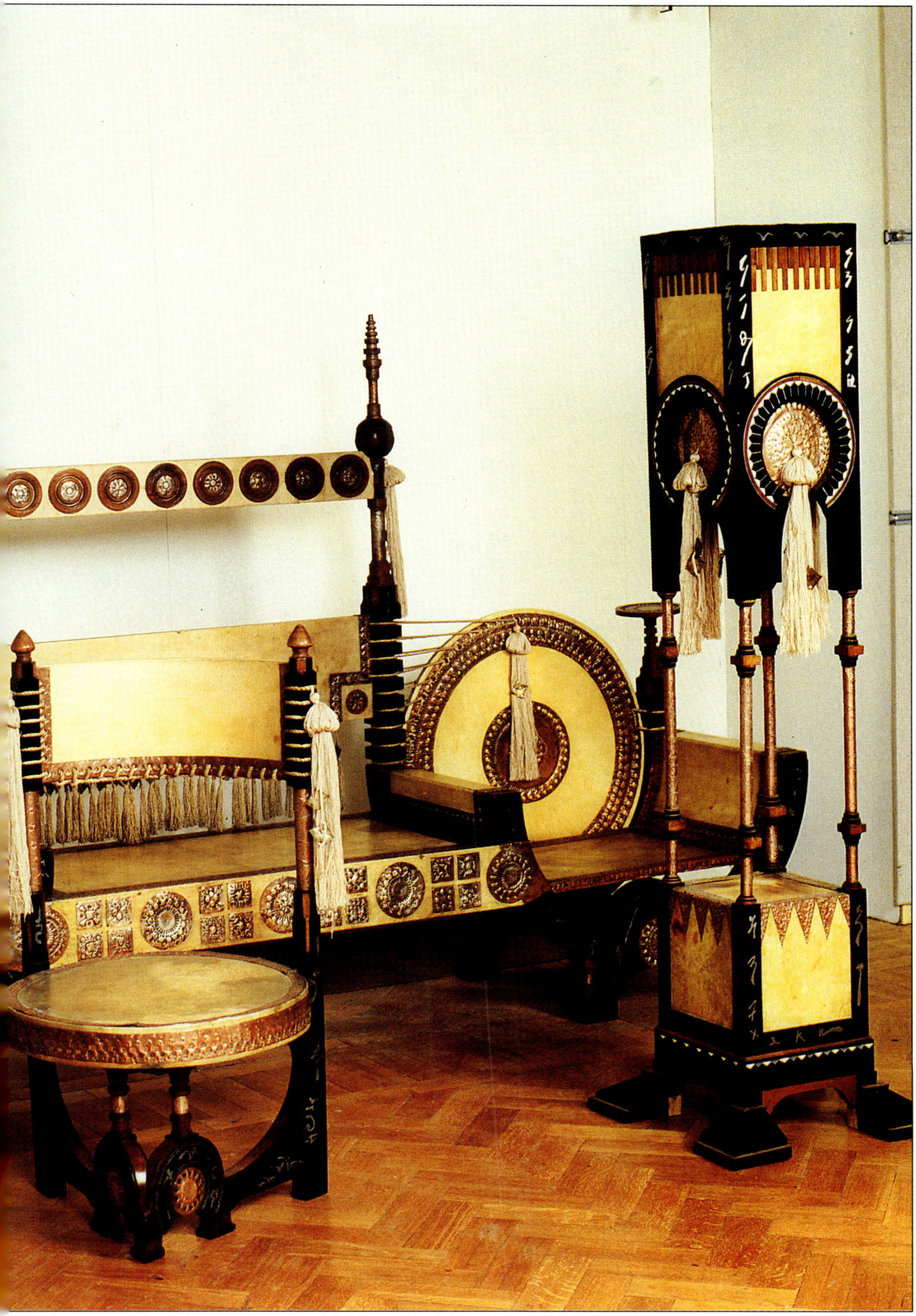

C H A P T E R 2

LEFT Drawing room suite by Carlo Bugatti. As eccentric in its middle eastern and oriental flavour as any piece by Armand J. Rateau, Bugatti furniture runs totally counter to the modernist strain in Art Deco furniture.

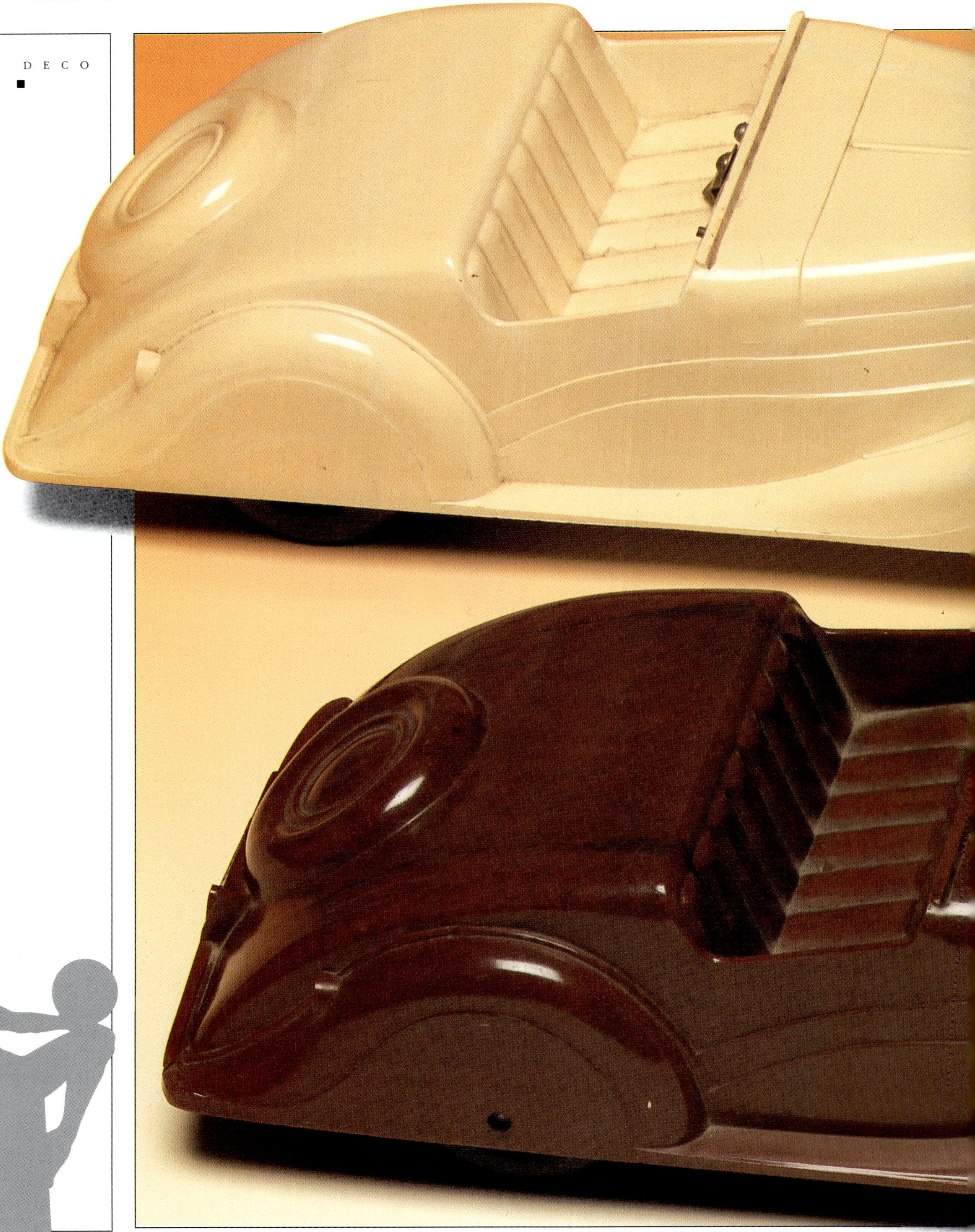

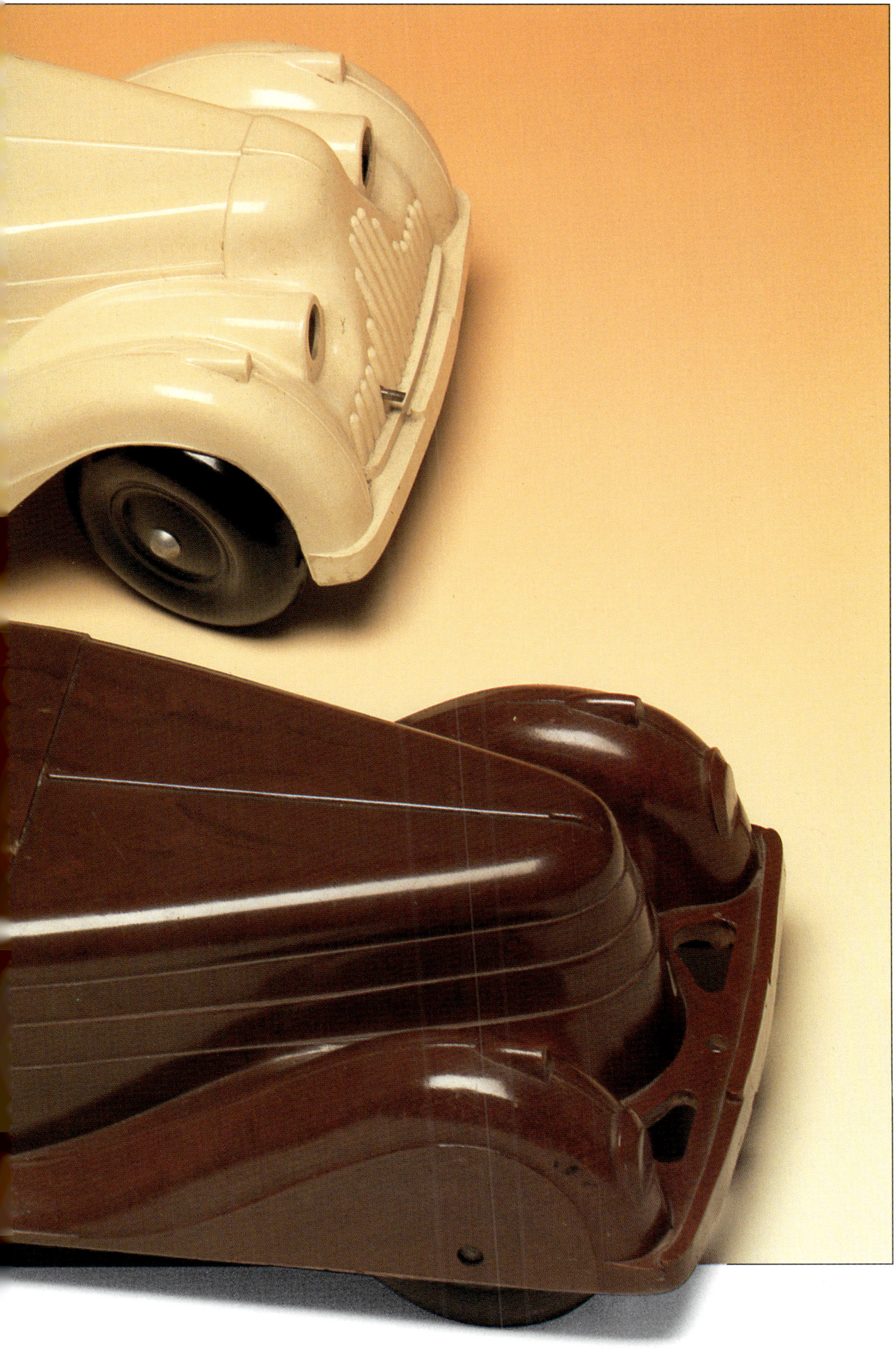

LEFT Two mechanical toy cars in Bakelite, fully operational and hardy enough for the most demanding child.

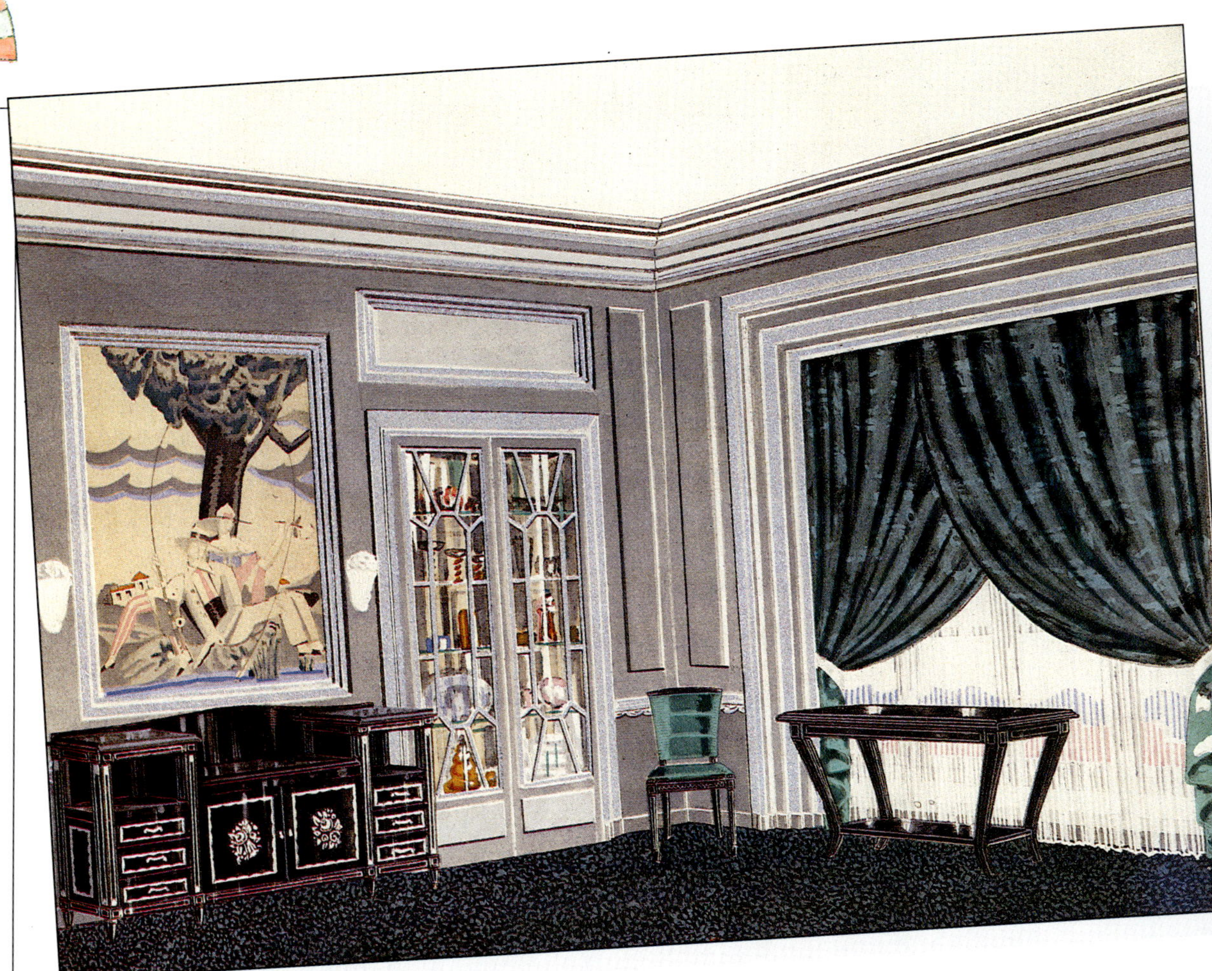

RIGHT Interior design for dining room by André Groult, c. 1920. The furniture has a traditional look but the drapery and wall decorations favour the austere look of the twenties.

THE REDISCOVERY OF THE LOST ART DECO · GERMANY AND RUSSIA

Art Deco has become so closely associated with France and to a lesser degree, Britain and America, that people tend to forget, or ignore, the fact that the decorative arts were alive and well in Weimar Germany and post-revolutionary Russia. Perhaps uninformed opinion of what Russia must have been like immediately after the revolution fostered the assumption that the "luxury" nature of the decorative arts made it impossible for Art Deco to exist there at all. Such an assumption was quite wrong, denying Art Deco one of its most important attributes, that of flexibility. The principles of Art Deco could be applied as successfully to mass-produced clothing or cheap pottery as to the most expensive and opulent piece of Cartier jewellery or piece of inlaid furniture by Ruhlmann. It was a style fit for kings, while at the very same time it was being absorbed and used by the people.

Weimar Germany may have suffered economically under the harsh conditions laid down under the Treaty of Versailles, which resulted in the financial collapse of 1926, and in the Great Depression a few years later, but there was always a demand for the most basic commodities such as a plate, a cushion, a teatowel, or a milk jug. In fact by 1930, the German porcelain and ceramic industry, far from being run down, was the largest in Europe. Companies like Villeroy and Boch, based in Dresden, flourished by meeting the realities of the situation head on. Good, cheap design did not have to be a luxury. Until 1933, at least, it would be true to say that if the supremacy of France as the centre of the art world was under any threat, it was from Germany. From that year on, following Hitler's rise to power, the leading lights of German culture emigrated to America, mostly via London. Figures like Walter Gropius,

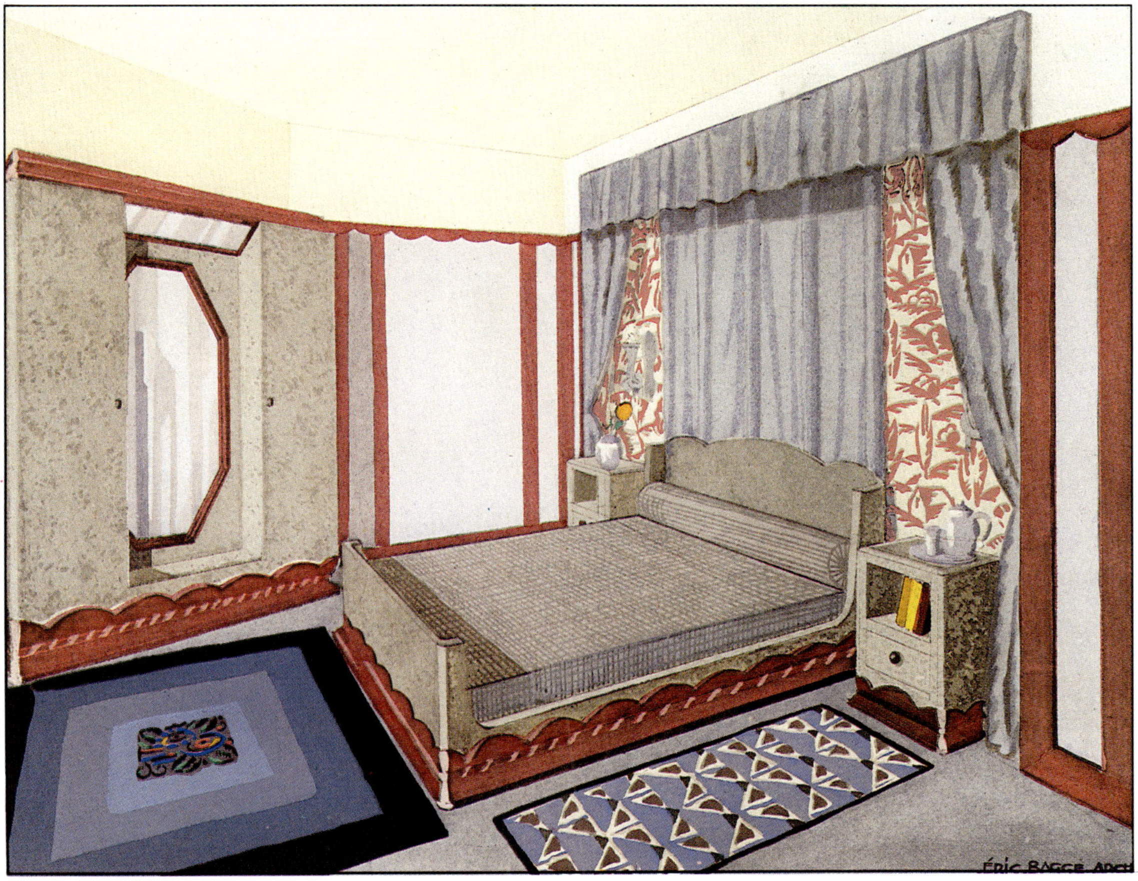

LEFT Interior design for a bedroom by Eric Bagge, c. 1930. Note the starkness of the walls, the absence of pictures, and strong, plain outlines of furniture and fabrics.

Mies van der Rohe, Marcel Breuer, Kurt Schwitters, and George Grosz, were as vital to contemporary German culture as Le Corbusier was to the French. The Bauhaus was the laboratory of the avant-garde. The design of a chair could be broken down into its most basic components, a plywood plank for a seat with bent chrome legs for support. What could be cheaper yet more novel?

The situation in Russia was even more interesting and experimental. Following the revolution, there were two immediate problems to be resolved: initially, how to revive and restore industries that had been disrupted during the revolution, and secondly the role of the artist in the new society. The artist could no longer just serve and respond to the whims of an élite, he had to climb down from his ivory tower and work in harmony – or conflict – with the people. The constant examination of these questions in such conditions promoted exciting new developments and resulted in many fresh approaches.

For many spectators, the Soviet pavilion at the 1925 Exposition must have seemed shockingly innovative.

Designers like Nikolai Suetin and Ilya Chesnik applied their Suprematist designs to dinner services. Highly abstract and directly derived from contemporary painting, these had a clarity and straightforwardness that was marketable – and close to Art Deco. Even when obvious symbols of the revolution were employed, like the hammer and sickle, the worker or the farm hand, they could be incorporated into the most advanced textile or ceramic designs. Even artists of the stature of Rodchenko or Tatlin, whose reputations as avant-garde leaders were without question, turned their hand to dress design. If artists were to be artists at all, their art had to be applied. In Europe the situation was different, and that was one reason why the decorative arts were always thought of as secondary in importance to fine art.

CHAPTER THREE

THE GREAT COMMISSIONS

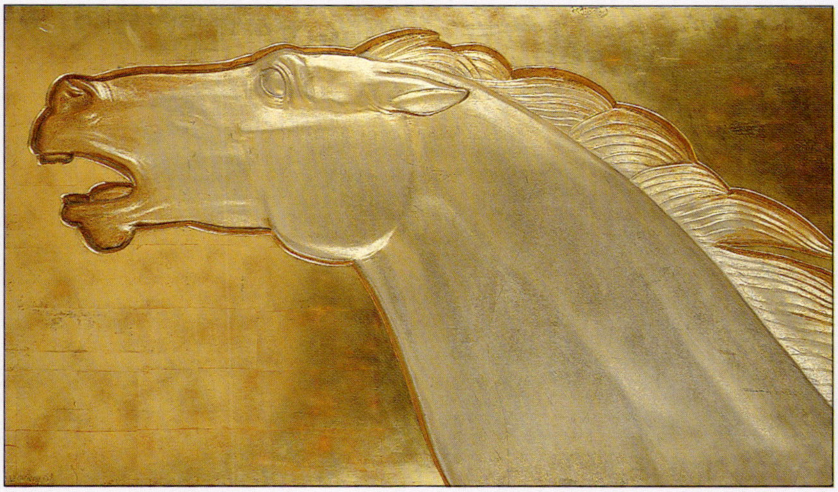

ABOVE Gold-lacquered panel depicting the head of a stallion with streaming mane by Jean Dunand. The design and application link it closely to the designs for the Normandie.

RIGHT Ten of the surviving mural panels designed by Jean Dupas and executed by Champigneulle in 1932–4 for the liner Normandie. These were part of a series on the theme of the history of navigation.

BELOW RIGHT The grand salon of the Ile de France. The decoration of the main public rooms aboard the liner were by Jeanniot, Bouchard and Saupique. A foretaste of the grandeur to come with the Normandie.

OPPOSITE RIGHT An exotic painted panel in the Normandie Salon.

OPPOSITE BELOW RIGHT West elevation of the New Victoria cinema (movie theater), London, England. A grand imposing Art Deco façade

Art Deco was very much a case of reinterpreting old ideas in a new way. Since the middle of the 19th century, there had been great concern about the alienating effect of the industrial revolution. Although welcomed by many, it posed the very immediate problem of how to retain the medieval sense of pride in craftsmanship. Many forward-thinking people were genuinely worried that industrialization would culminate in a situation in which workers would be totally divorced from the creative process, and would ultimately become the tools of the machinery that had been meant to serve them. The concern was genuine. The reality became worse. In a city such as Manchester where the average life expectancy of factory workers had been reduced to thirteen years by the early 1860s, there was a real need to curb the more extreme aspects of the industrial process. It was not very surprising that Britain, the country that had industrialized first, was also the first country to attempt to re-establish an equilibrium between the individual and his workplace.

Following the teachings of Thomas Carlyle, Pugin and Ruskin, William Morris attempted to find some answers. Morris was the founder of the Arts and Crafts Movement; and his follower C R Ashbee attempted to reintroduce a sense of humanity to the workplace. In the face of accelerating industrialization it was a brave attempt to make time stand still.

The most important legacy of the Arts and Crafts movement for Art Deco was the concept of collaboration between craftsmen. The heroic example of the Renaissance Man who could turn his hand to anything had been replaced by specialization in particular trades and crafts. At the turn of the century, there were two men who singlehandedly proved themselves exceptions to the rule. The American, Frank Lloyd Wright, and Josef Hoffman, an Austrian, were geniuses, giants in the history of architecture and design. Both proved to be invaluable examples of and forerunners of the Art Deco style. Frank Lloyd Wright's massive project for the Midway Gardens in Chicago, contemporary with the zenith of the Art Deco style, and his 1912 designs for the Avery Coonley Playhouse in Chicago, Illinois, are well ahead of their time. Hoffmann's Palais Stoclet in Belgium shows a similar attention to detail while still maintaining a sense of the whole. Their work was extraordinary, visionary

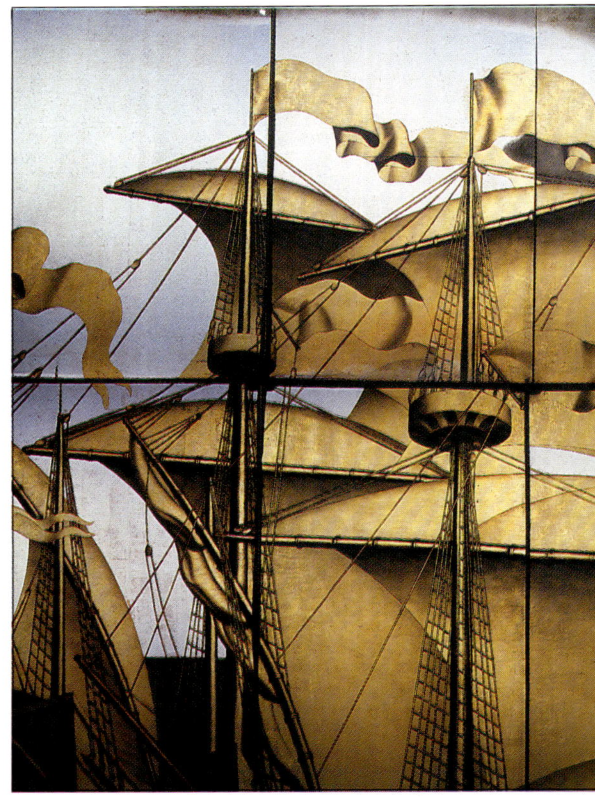

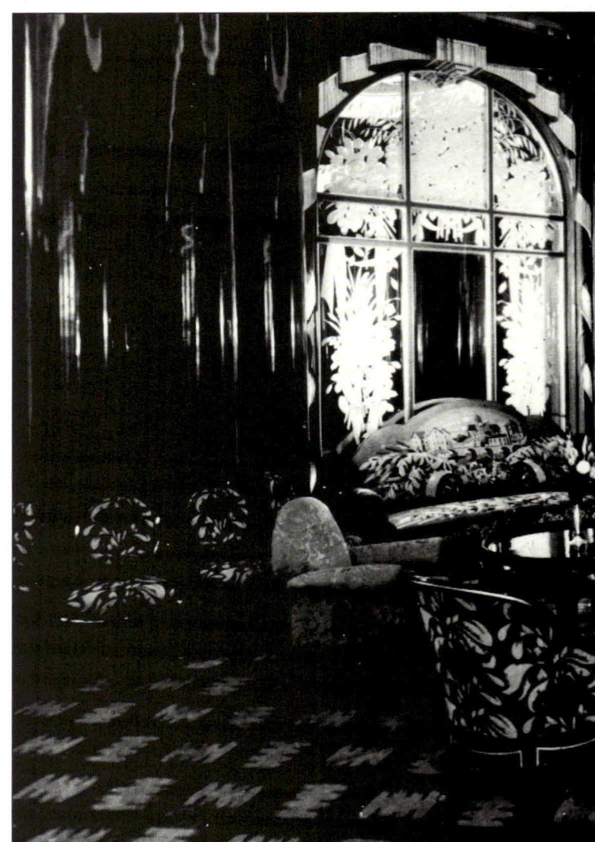

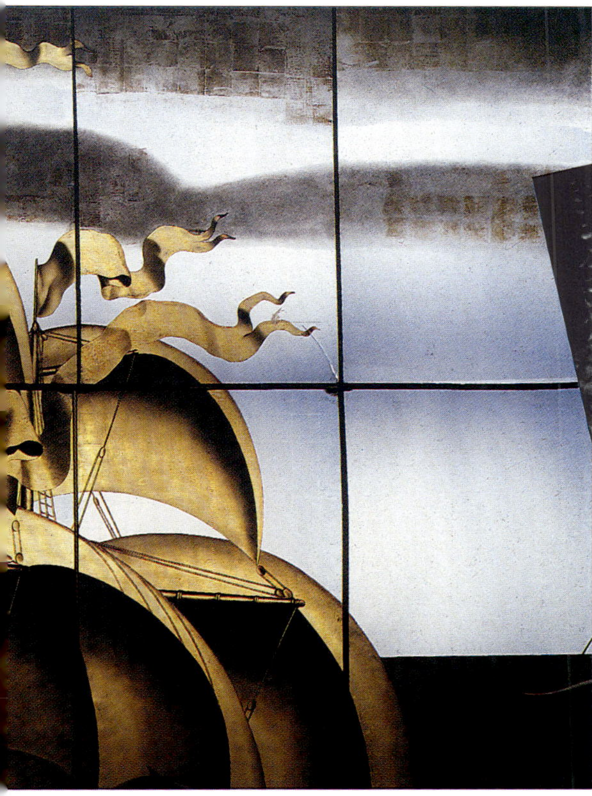

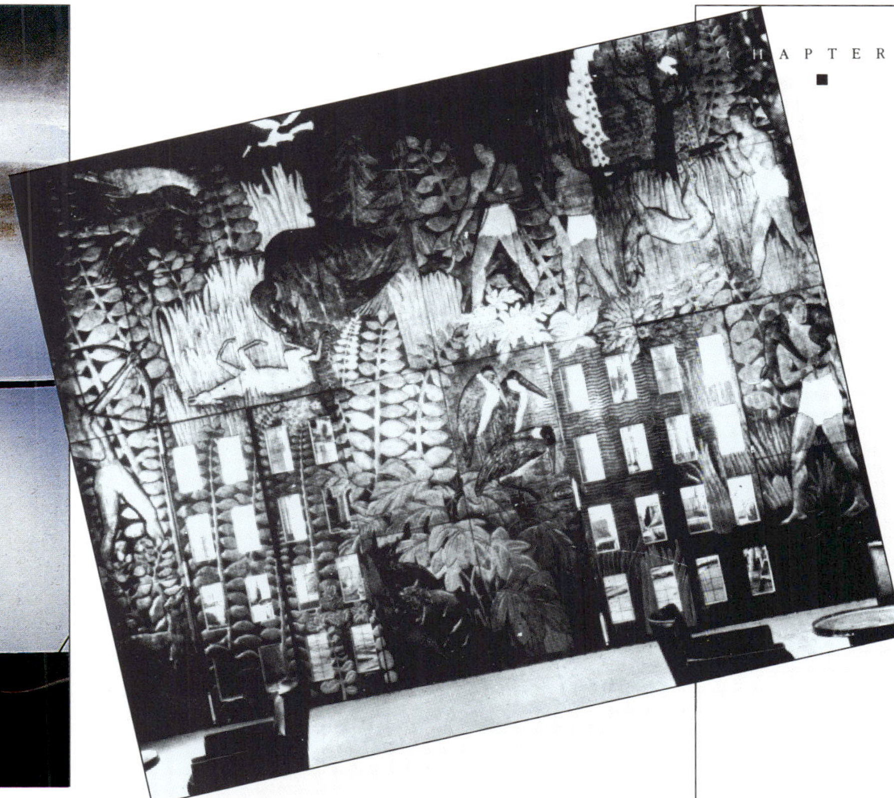

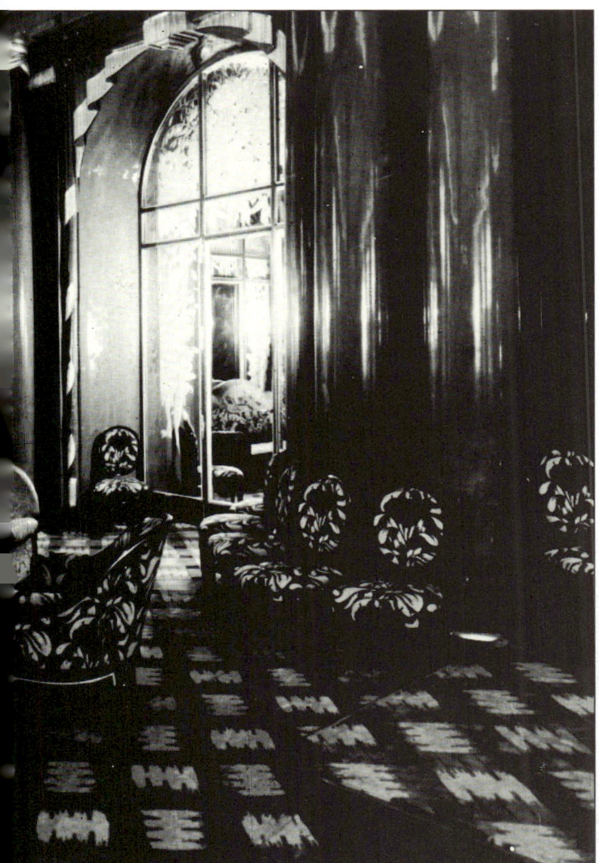

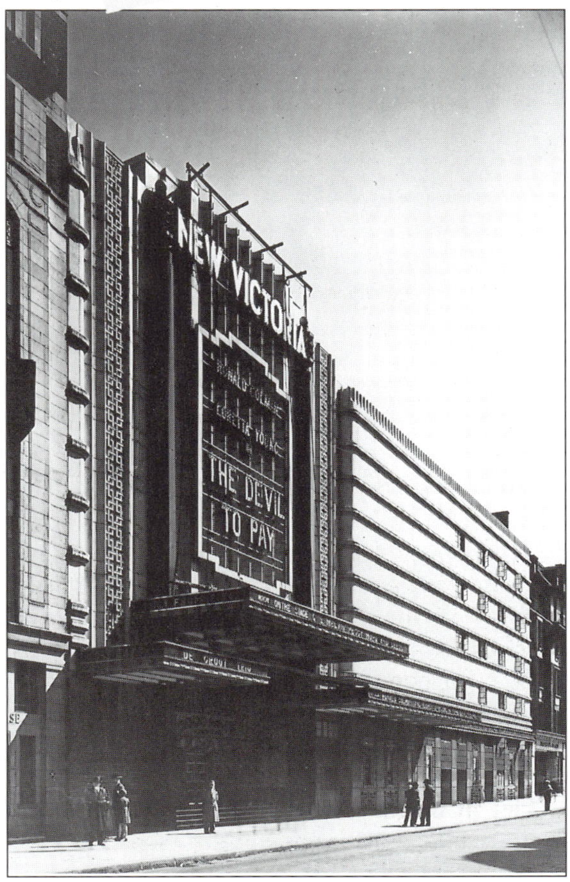
NEW VICTORIA
THE DEVIL
TO PAY

RIGHT Interior of the Odeon, Muswell Hill, London, England, a splendid example of an Art Deco cinema (movie theater) interior. Particularly interesting is the octagonal clock with 'The Odeon' on its face, of which there are very few examples still in existence.

FAR RIGHT View of the Odeon cinema (movie theater), Woolwich, near London, England, looking down across the River Thames to the London docks. The brickwork entrance is set at a right angle to the auditorium.

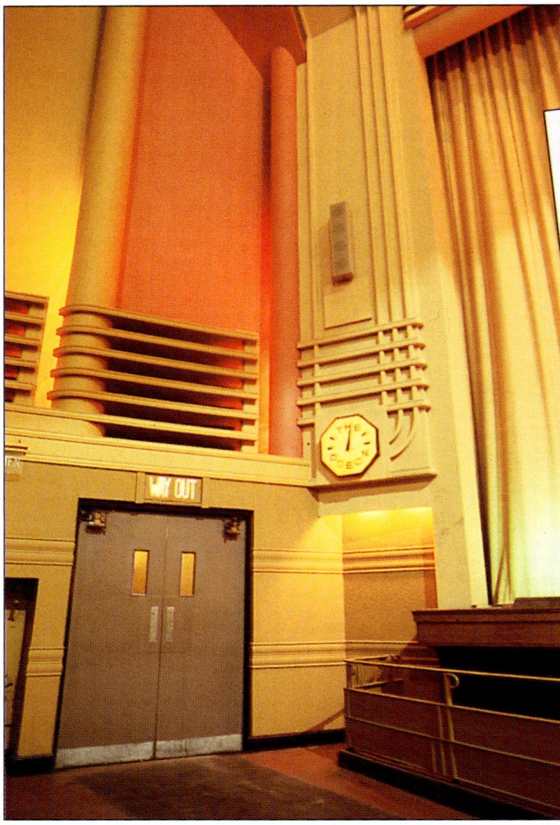

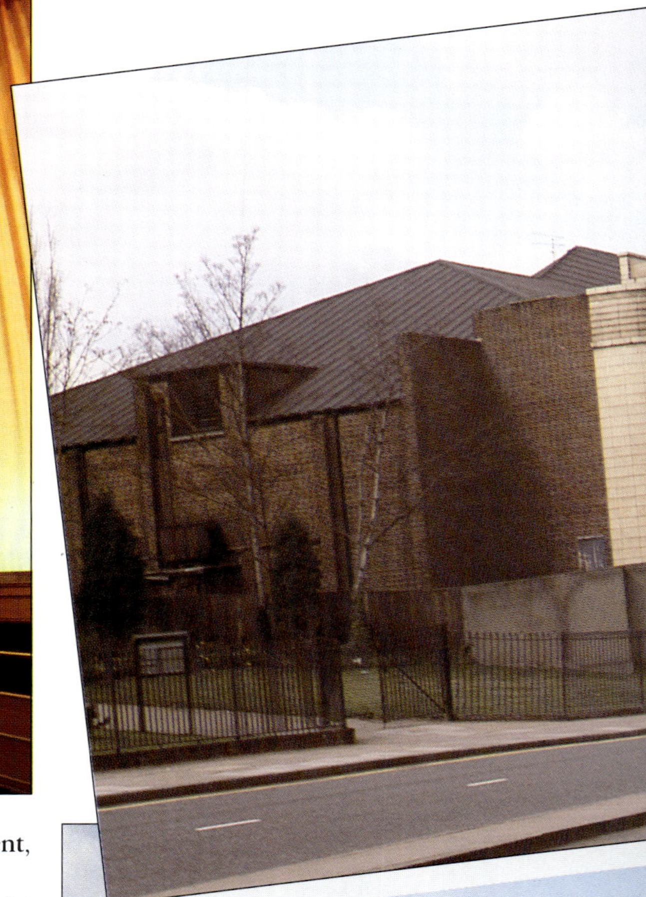

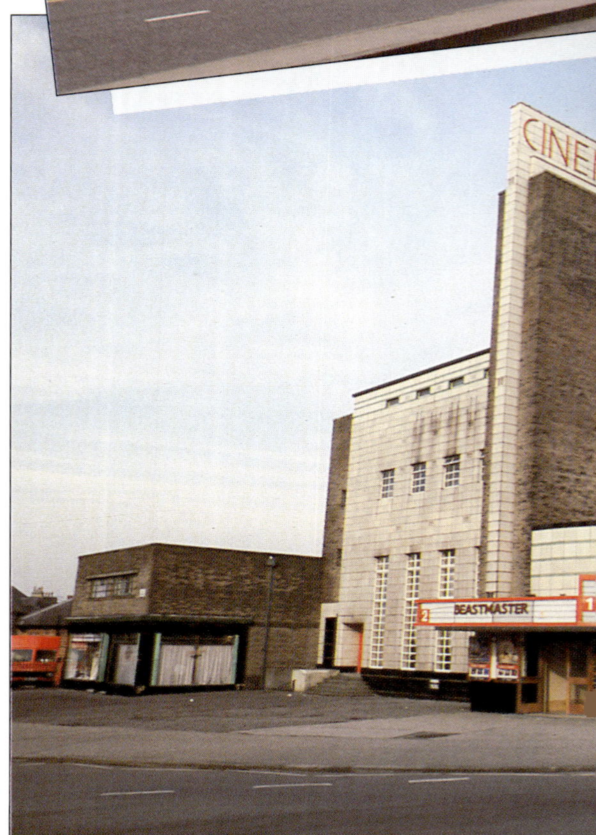

but, particularly for the Art Deco movement, almost impossible to emulate.

The introduction of new materials brought new problems, and the search for a new style demanded a new approach to the large commission or project. What was needed was co-operation between all the mastercraftsmen. The example of Modernism which stressed a need to reappraise all given ideas promoted an atmosphere in which interchange between different disciplines was encouraged and promoted. Why bother to learn to weld, inlay wood, work with lacquer, bend chrome, blow glass, mould plastics, cast bakelite, when all you needed to do was seek out the relevant craftsman? Art Deco was revolutionary in that it promoted the concept of the designer. The designer could be at worst a dilettante or mediocre amateur, at best a brilliant innovator and promoter of the possibilities created by other people's expertise.

Although Art Deco is best known to us through its smaller objects, such as posters, textiles and ceramics, it is the large commissions which display the full possibilities of the style. The Exposition des Arts Décoratifs et Industriels, the magnificent French ocean liner, the *Normandie*,

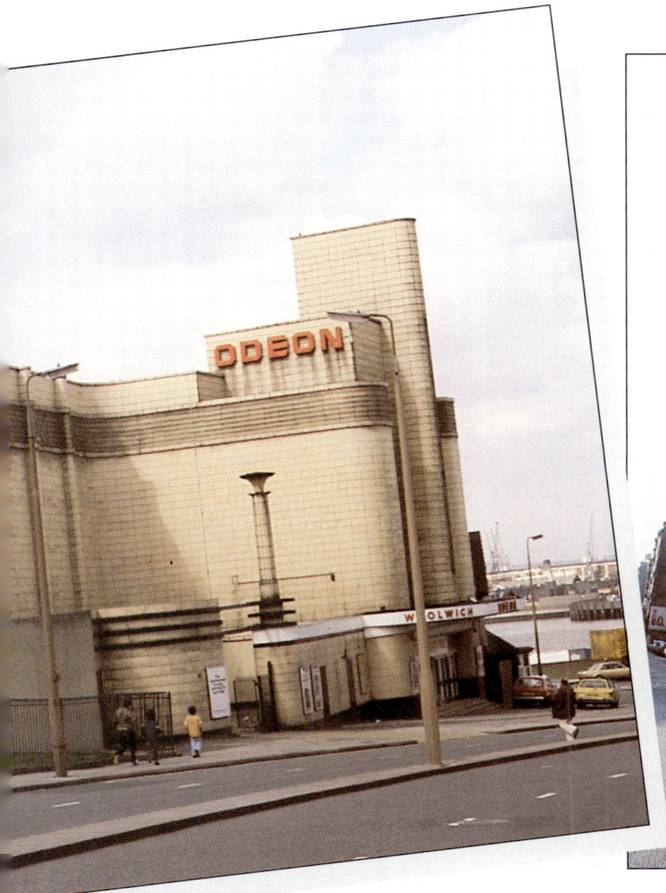

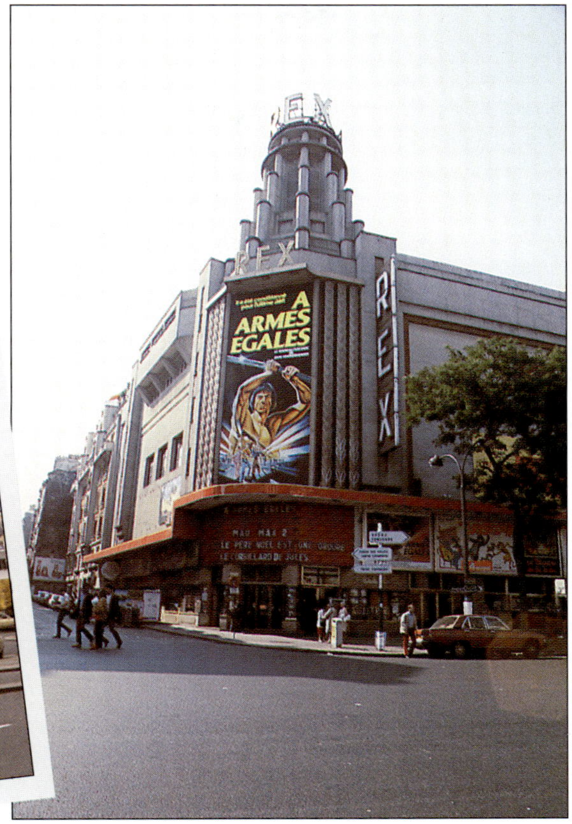

LEFT Exterior view of the corner tower of the Rex cinema (movie theater).

BELOW LEFT The Harrogate Odeon cinema (movie theater), England. This view highlights the contrast between the faïence tiling and the plain and patterned brickwork. It still has the original corner tower with the neon cinema sign as advertisement.

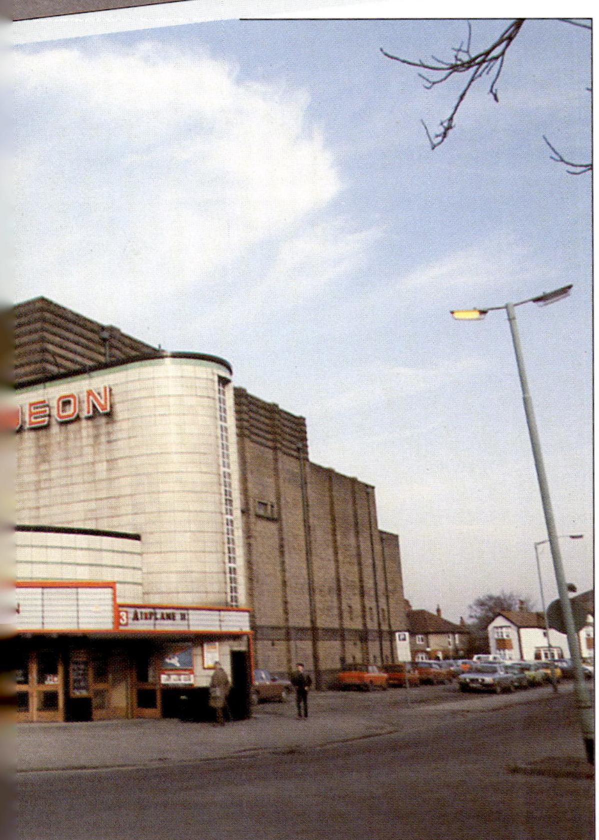

the glass entrance to the Strand Palace Hotel, now in the Victoria and Albert Museum, London, the preserved splendours of the ballroom in London's Park Lane Hotel, and New York's Radio City Music Hall, or the stylized elegance of the Hoover factory in England, marooned on the A40 London to Oxford road or, more spectacularly, the dizzying, skyscraping summit of the Chrysler building are just some examples of Art Deco at its most ambitious and successful.

The massive scale of the Exposition des Arts Décoratifs et Industriels has already been discussed, but what needs further explanation is the detail of some of the best pavilions. Perhaps the most remarkable of all was the pavilion for the Au Bon Marché store designed by the house of Pomone, specifically by Louis Boileau. The squat aspect, like that of most of the pavilions, was dictated probably as much by necessity and other practical considerations as it was by any aesthetic. Huge doors, like those of some gigantic tomb, adorned the frontage. From the outside it looked severe, each layer of the building echoing the entrance steps divided by low hedging, forcing the eye upward to the flat roof. All the flat surfaces of the walls were decorated with

RIGHT The massive scale of the Normandie is seen in this photo of the building of the ship at Saint Nazaire, France.

BELOW RIGHT The Grand Staircase on the Normandie leads the passengers up to Baudry's sculpture *La Normandie*.

abstract patterns and, in keeping with many of the other pavilions, leaded windows were employed wherever possible to lighten the effect. At night, these windows were spectacularly transformed. As light poured through the coloured glass, the Pavilion Au Bon Marché became fragile and glowing. Another particularly striking pavilion was that of the Diamond Dealers, designed by Lambert, Sacke and Bailly. Using very little floor space, its elegance relied on the high oval roof with its shallow rectangular planes. Like a massive Fabergé egg, or vast precious stone, this alerted the viewer to its purpose, the promotion of the diamond industry. The simplicity and clear lines of many of the pavilions were countered by the opulence of the Ruhlmann Group's pavilion, Hôtel d'un Collectionneur. Emile-Jacques Ruhlmann, the prince of modern furniture, imbued this with a panache and sophistication that even he would react

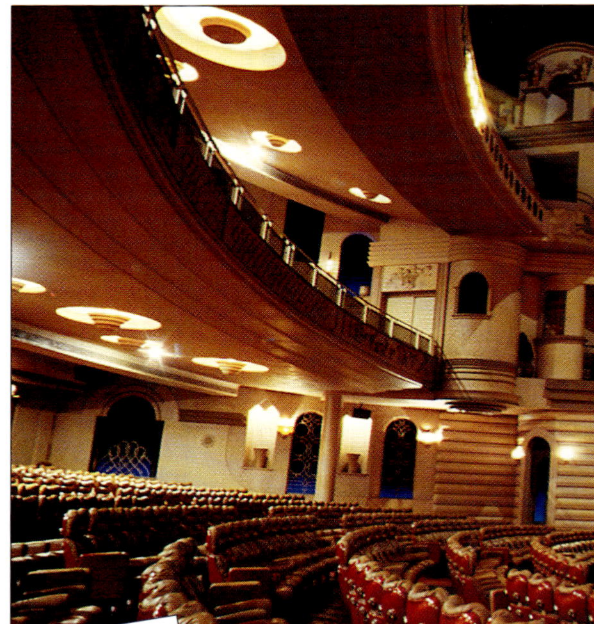

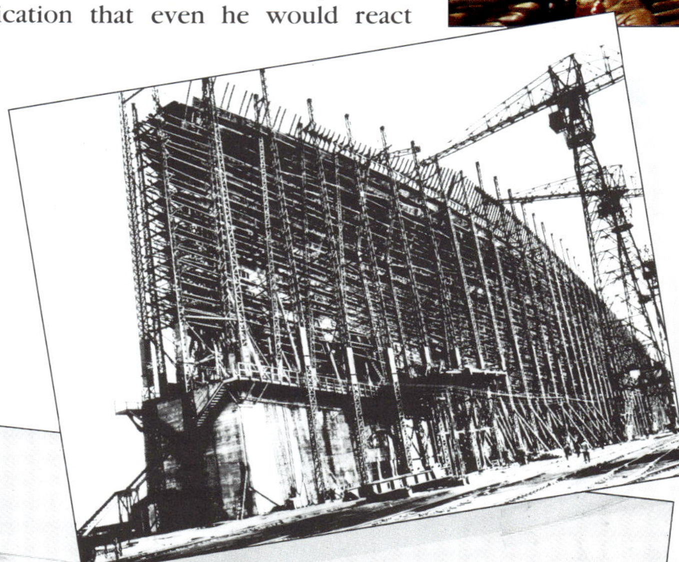

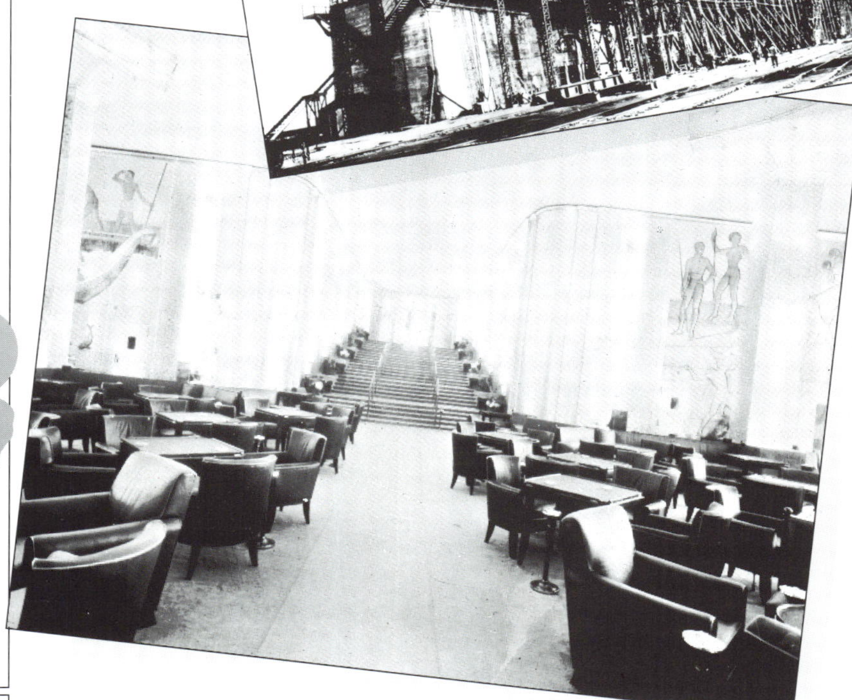

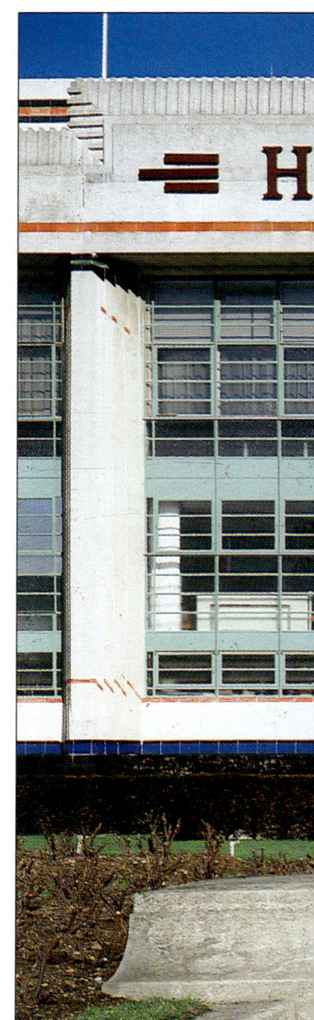

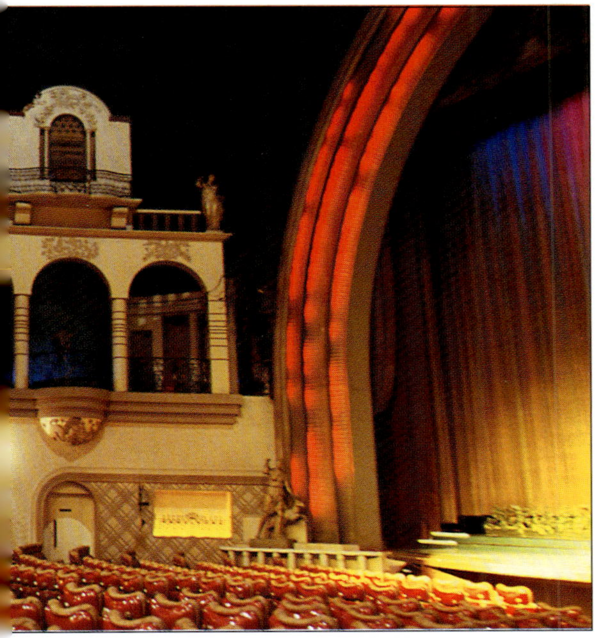

against in favour of the modern Deco style. The diversity of the exhibition was reflected in its scale, which was enormous. It was a showcase for the world, but was dismantled as quickly as it was constructed. If the French needed a more permanent display for their craftsmen they very soon found a solution.

In 1932, the ship *Normandie* slid into the [redacted] water at the St Nazaire dock. Run by La [redacted] pagnie Générale Transatlantique, the [redacted] project enjoyed the sponsorship of a [redacted] who had wisely recognized that [redacted] showcase of the decorative arts, in [redacted] passengers would be a captive [redacted] least four or five days, would [redacted] prestige abroad. The success of the [redacted] had as much to do with the latest [redacted] it did with the luxury aboard. It [redacted] maiden voyage from Le Havre on [redacted] arriving at New York on 3 June, having [redacted]

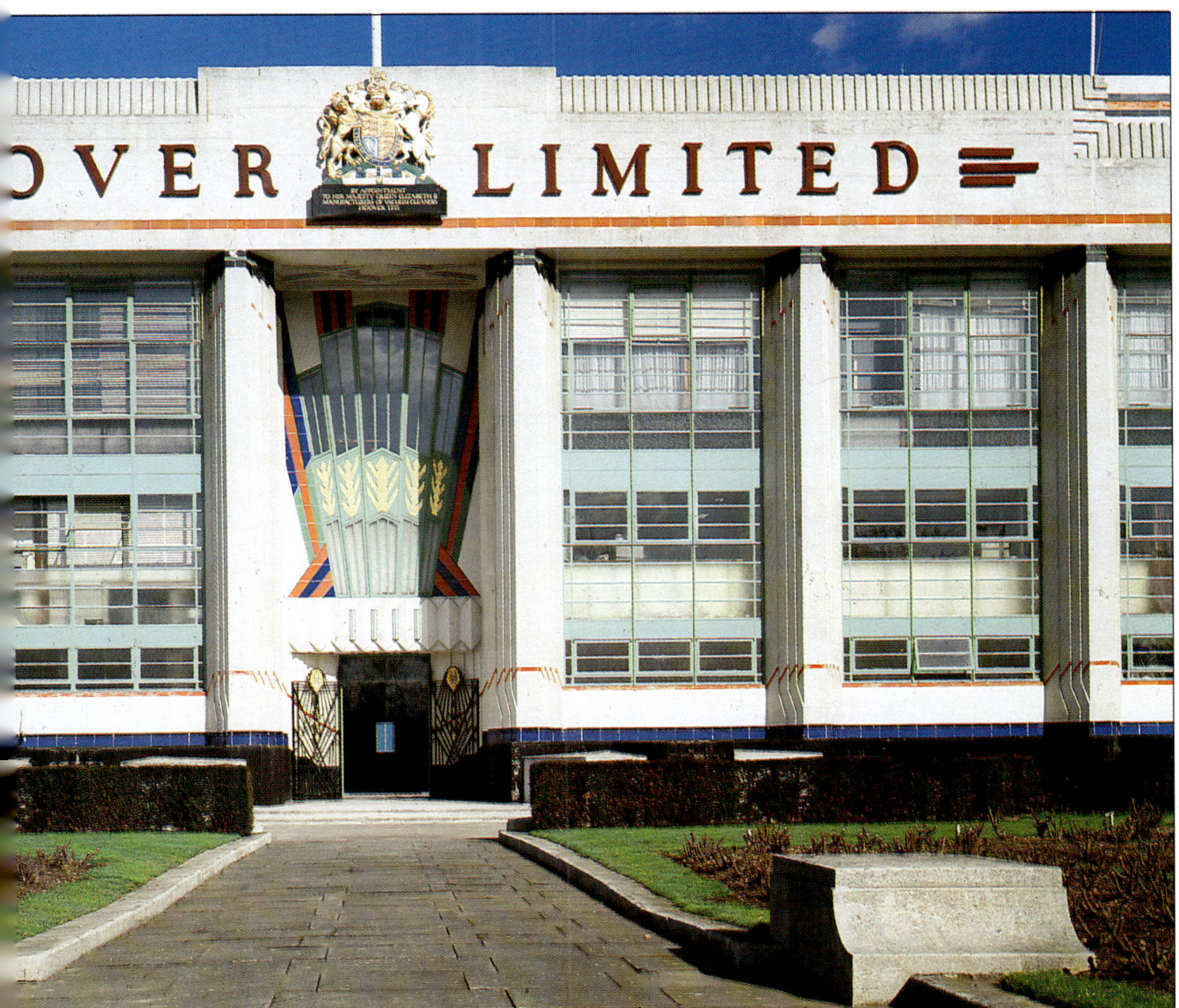

LEFT Interior view of a Paris cinema (movie theater), the Rex. [redacted]

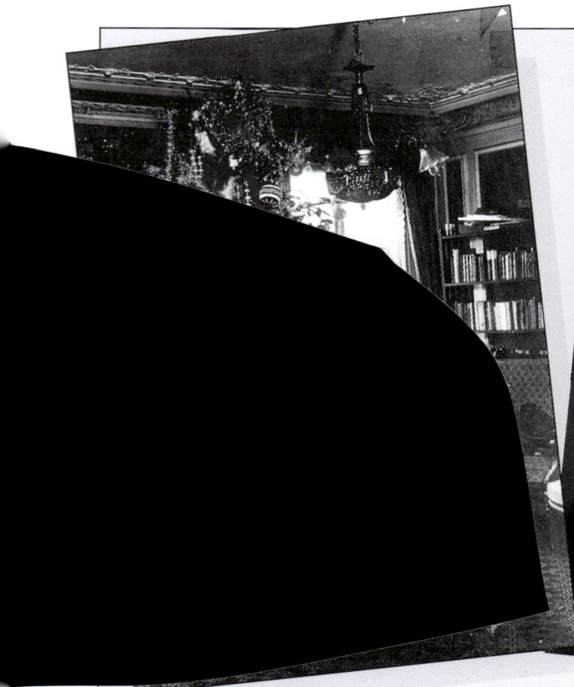

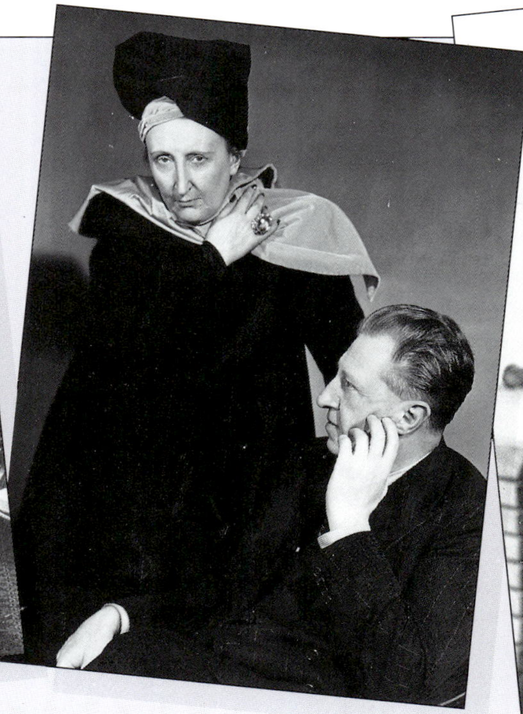

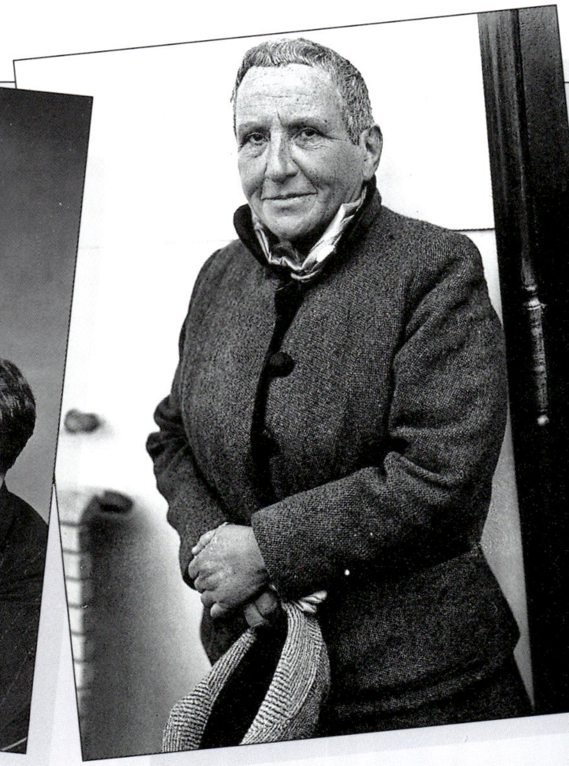

AMERICANS IN PARIS

"If you are lucky enough to have lived in Paris as a young man, then wherever you go for the rest of your life it stays with you, for Paris is a moveable feast."

Ernest Hemingway

For architects, designers and craftsmen in Paris 1925 meant the demands of meeting deadlines for the Exposition de La Société des Arts Décoratifs et Industriels. For the Americans in Paris, the capital of Bohemia, that year was more aptly described by Scott Fitzgerald, of *The Great Gatsby* fame, as "the summer of a thousand parties".

The hordes of young American men and women who had come eight years previously to save a sinking Europe, and had confronted the bloody horrors of the war to end all wars, also discovered the unique romance of Paris. Paris, the lovers' city, was also the cultural centre of the world. It was where intellectual Americans had to come and test themselves against the competition and come into contact with the avant garde. Although the move to Paris was often disguised behind the heavy veils of cultural exchange, the reality was more prosaic. For those with an independent income from generous relatives or inherited wealth, the strength of the dollar, cheap accommodation, good food and, following the introduction of Prohibition in January 1920, legal access to cheap alcohol, made Paris a happy and exciting experience. If they came for literature and art they got a lot more besides.

Scott Fitzgerald and his wife Zelda moved to Paris in 1925, where he was to write *Tender is the Night*. Arriving there, he found a milieu of fellow writers and artists among which, during the 1920s were the Americans Djuna Barnes, Robert McAlmon, William Carlos Williams, Henry Miller (*Tropic of Cancer*), the photographers Berenice Abbott and Man Ray, Ernest Hemingway, who was busy writing *The Sun Also Rises* and *Fiesta*, and Sherwood Anderson, as well as the wealthy publishers Harry and Caresse Crosby (Black Sun Press), the modern dancer Isadora Duncan, and the poets T S Eliot and Ezra Pound. Travelling between Paris and Antibes in the South of France throughout the summer of 1925, the Fitzgeralds united the heady world of Hollywood and its Rudolf Valentinos, the French aristocracy, and the Bohemian writers. The Americans had come to lie on the beaches, worship the sun, and sit at the feet of the muse of European art.

Writers such as Hemingway, Fitzgerald and Malcom Cowley, had come to a Paris that other Americans had already annexed before them. More than 20 years earlier, the Sybil of Montparnasse, Gertrude Stein, and her companion Alice B Toklas had been central to all that was advanced in art. Gertrude Stein, famous for the enigmatic phrase "A rose is a rose is a rose", had also claimed that if America was her country, Paris was her home. This Laurel and Hardy of the art world had patronized and collected the work of, among others, Pablo Picasso, Georges Braque, Henri Matisse and the Delaunays, from as early as 1906. Not overburdened with humility, and quite, quite assured of her genius as a writer, Gertrude Stein effected a bridg-

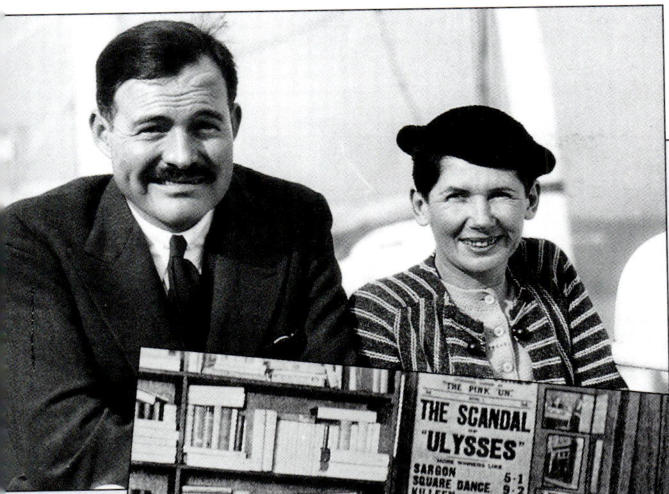

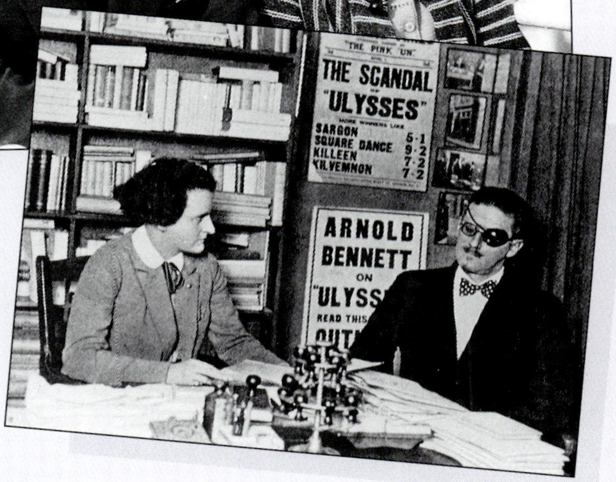

ABOVE LEFT Ernest Hemingway, the macho Nobel prizewinning action man of American letters, pictured here with his second wife (he had four), Pauline Pfeiffer. One of the founding fathers of modern literature, Hemingway was the acknowledged leader of the emigré bohemians who congregated in Paris in the 1920s. His posthumously-published *A Moveable Feast*, claims 'If you are lucky enough to have lived in Paris . . . then wherever you go for the rest of your life, it stays with you, for Paris is a moveable feast'.

BELOW LEFT Sylvia Beach, owner of the Shakespeare and Company bookshop, and publisher of James Joyce's *Ulysses*, pictured with Joyce in her shop.

FAR LEFT F. Scott Fitzgerald, his writings and his tragic marriage, are symbols of the glamorous and fated Jazz Age. This photo of Scott Fitzgerald's family was sent as a belated Christmas card to friends. Taken in their hotel room in Paris at Christmas 1925, at the end of the 'summer of a thousand parties', the glamorous trio are pictured at the height of their happiness and contentment.

CENTRE Brother and sister, Osbert and Edith Sitwell, represented the aristocratic and fashionable extreme of the Modernist movement in writing. Stylishly eccentric, they were closely allied to other writers of notoriety, such as Ezra Pound and James Joyce, and gave readings of their work at Sylvia Beach's bookshop, Shakespeare and Co., on Paris's Left Bank.

LEFT Gertrude Stein the writer, Svengali of modern literature and the arts. Through cajoling, bullying, encouraging, and by her own example, Gertrude Stein, from her salon at Rue de Fleurus in Paris, sponsored and assisted the talents of the soon-to-be-famous Picasso, Matisse and the ingrate Hemingway.

ing between the worlds of French culture and the English-speaking peoples.

If Gertrude Stein was the severe autocrat of the visual arts and writer supreme, Americans in Paris would find a warmer welcome at Shakespeare and Co., the bookdealers and publishers, on the rue Odéon. The informality of the bookshop, which also acted as a post office for emigré Americans and a lending library, disguised a solid pioneering support for the most advanced in literature. Its gentle and sensitive founder, the ever-patient Sylvia Beach, ran a haphazard business on a shoestring and a large quantity of goodwill. Her publishing of James Joyce's *Ulysses* won her notoriety and customers. Written about in American newspapers, Sylvia Beach was one of the best possible ambassadors that France could have called on. American reporters quipped, "Grab your towel and let's go down to Sylvia Beach." If painters and writers came because of her, so too did the designers, and what they saw was Art Deco.

Of course many who came had little or no interest in the more *recherché* areas of modern art. They ate, drank, and enjoyed themselves as all tourists do. What they did was to boost demand for consumer items; Deco jewellery for their relations back home and other examples of French chic as gifts. In rare cases whole interiors from cutlery to curtains made their way across the ocean to America. In 1927, the wealthy American, Templeton Crocker, well in advance of the taste of his peers, commissioned Jean Michel Frank to design his San Francisco apartment in the French Art Deco style.

The tide flowed both ways. While Americans discovered and became attached to a rich European cultural heritage, Parisians discovered Walt Whitman, watched the gauche and wistful cinematic comedy of Charlie Chaplin, admired the vitality and eroticism of Josephine Baker's dancing and listened to the deep, resonant singing of Paul Robeson.

Importantly for the development of Art Deco, the showcase of the Exposition des Arts Décoratifs et Industriels displayed to Americans the possibility of making high-quality furniture, jewellery and porcelain, in good, innovative design. The Metropolitan Museum of New York would only take a few years to realize the sense of putting money aside to invest in the best examples of Art Deco objects. The beginnings of the migration of Art Deco to America were assured. A year later Mina Loy, backed by Peggy Guggenheim's millions, opened an art gallery in Paris selling, among other things, American design.

Few autobiographies, collections of letters, diaries of American men and women of letters of that period fail to mention Jimmy the barman at Dingo's, Kiki of Mont parnasse, argumentative, drunken evenings around the tables and at the bars of the Dôme, the Rotonde, the Clôserie des Lilas, or La Coupole, the Brasserie Lipp and the Café Flore, and the inevitable reconciliations the next day. Many tourists today find their way straight to the Left bank to sit outside the Deux Magots, where Hemingway sat, order a kir, and breathe in the nostalgia, conjuring in their mind's eye the myth of Paris in the '20s.

RIGHT Auditorium of the New Victoria cinema (movie theater), London, England. Note particularly the wonderful design for the Safety Curtain.

more than 30 knots per hour. If its efficiency was the main attraction for transatlantic travellers, the *Normandie*'s decor was the icing on the cake.

The *Normandie* was the latest of the great French liners, double the tonnage of its predecessor, the *Ile de France*. An important innovation in ship design, it increased the luxurious accommodation for passengers by dividing the funnel uptakes to the three characteristic red chimneys, thus providing a long sweep of massive reception rooms, one after the other, down its length. The main dining-room alone measured more than 300 ft, and could seat 700 people for dinner. The scale of the boat and the massive investment in it allowed for an unrivalled decorative commission.

The list of craftsmen who worked on various aspects of the *Normandie* reads like a catalogue of the cream of Art Deco. Few of the leading French designers of the time passed up the chance to display their talents, but for all of them the eventual glory and fame they derived from working on the commission was tragically short-lived. In 1941, the ship was commandeered by the United States government to be used as a troop carrier. While stripping the ship of its decorations in order to modify it for its new role a workman accidentally set fire to the ship that boasted it was 100 per cent fire proof. Most of the greatest works of Art Deco ended up at the bottom of New York harbour.

In creating the *Normandie* its sponsors deliberately chose to be as modern as possible. Not only was it a chance to promote the French decorative arts, but it was also used as a vehicle to display the extent and glory of the French Empire. Shamed by the defeat of the First World War, a whole movement in literature and arts arose that chose to look beyond the confines of mainland France toward the French colonies. Many of the designs were of an exotic nature, both oriental and African in flavour. The most famous single commission for the ship were the four panels designed for the main lounge by Jean Dupas on the theme of the History of Navigation. Each panel measured 50 by 22 feet, and the whole ensemble stretched round the two walls. Of the four panels only one survived, and can be seen at the Metropolitan Museum in New York. Working in reverse, the glass panels were both painted and etched on the back by the craftsman Charles Champigneulle, using a method known as *verre églomise*. It was typical of the Art Deco

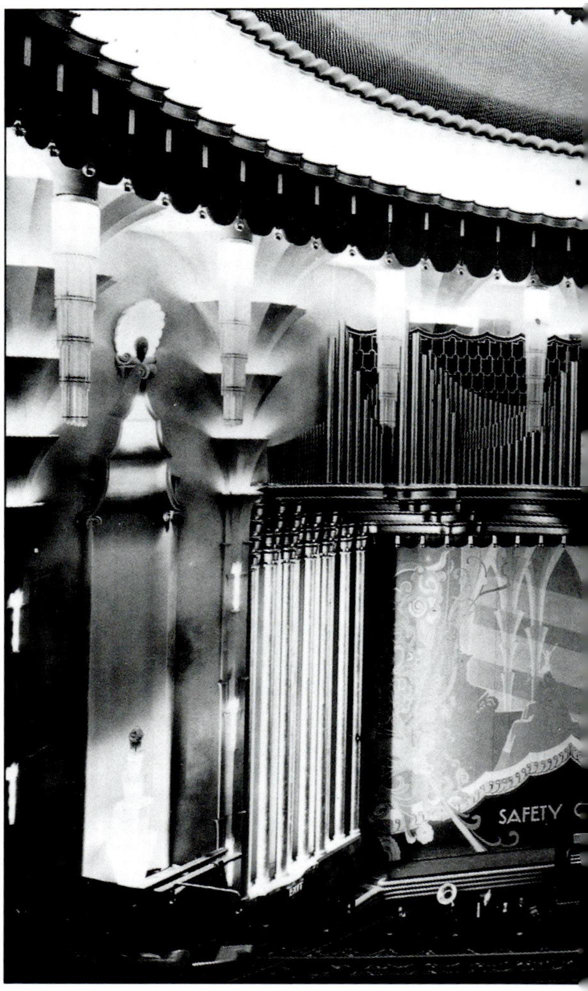

attitude prevalent at the time that craftsmen revived and invented working methods as well as experimenting with new materials. Traditional industries like the Sèvres porcelain works designed the service for the *salon de thé*, and the Aubusson tapestry studios were given a boost by commissions for the stateroom "Trouville" by the designer and cabinetmaker Jules Leleu. Other staterooms named after French départements or cities gave ample opportunity for new designers to create unique work. Pierre-Paul Montagnac, the President of the Société des Artistes Décoratifs, executed the "Caen" suite. The decorating firm of Dominique, which had previously won the prestigious commission to decorate the Paris private residence of that most quintessentially Art Deco of designers, Jean Puiforcat, created the four rooms of the stateroom the "Rouen".

Some of the designers, like René Prou, specialized almost exclusively in commissions on

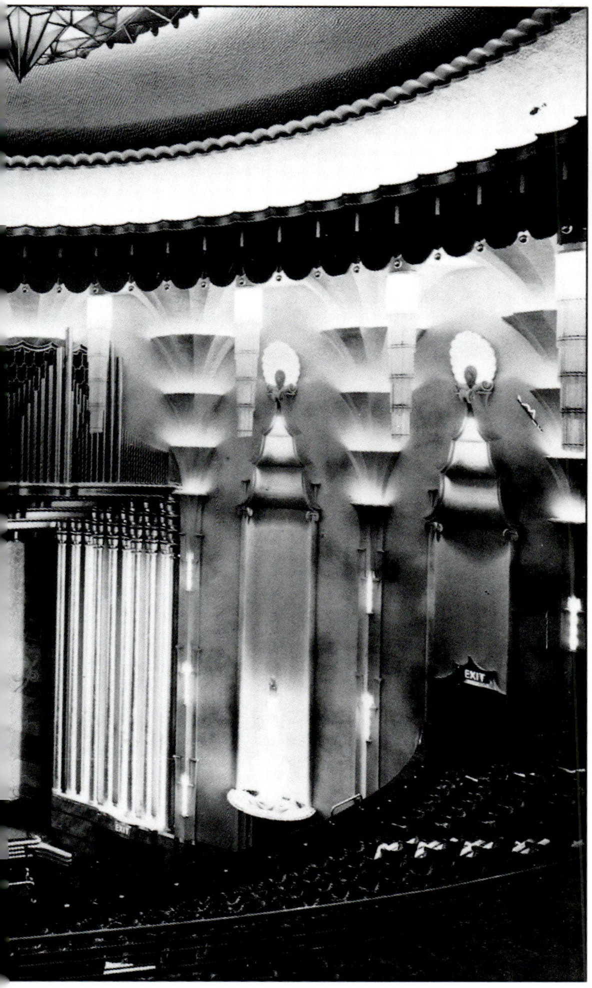

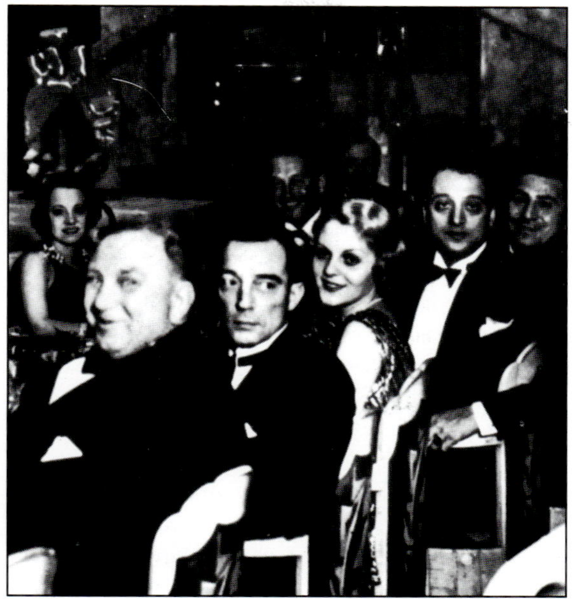

LEFT Hollywood Greats: Buster Keaton and other show business personalities aboard the Ile de France.

the scale of the *Normandie*. Prou also executed work for the first-class carriages on the French railways.

Although it has been suggested that the furniture in some rooms was designed by Emile-Jacques Ruhlmann, his premature death in 1933 robbed the *Normandie* of one of its most inspired designers. The metal furniture attributed to Ruhlmann in two large staterooms, harmonizing with the metal-clad walls, must have been designed very early on in the *Normandie*'s decorative scheme. Blanche J. Klotz worked on very similar lines to Ruhlmann, also using metal, but Ruhlmann's innovative capacity would surely have been stretched by such a demanding and lavish commission.

Another great loss, as a result of the stripping of the *Normandie* in preparation for its wartime role, was the disappearance of much of the metalwork. At least three of France's greatest specialists worked on the commission: Adelbert Szabo, Edgar Brandt and Raymond Henri Subes. Presumably, because metal is one of the easiest materials to melt down and recast for use in the armaments industry, most of the more basic design elements such as the sweeping handrails and doors which added the practical and finishing touches to the ship's design were lost forever. Adelbert Szabo had created doors for the first class dining room, and Edgar Brandt was also commissioned to design doors and gates. Raymond Henri Subes, who worked both in wrought iron and later in steel lacquered in Duco varnish, was, in collaboration with the architects Patout and Pacon, one of the few people to display his designs for elements of the *Normandie* at the Salons des Artistes Décorateurs in 1933 and 1935, also in Paris. Along with all the press photographs, and the famous poster by Cassandre, these must have given those who had neither the money nor the desire to travel on the *Normandie* an idea of the style and chic aboard the boat. The influence of the *Normandie* commission spread through all branches of the decorative arts. It is tragic that so little has survived to the present day.

If premature decline was to be expected of the large liners, very few of which are still in service, superseded by the speedier aeroplane, this was less the case with large building commissions for hotels, cinemas and factories, but even these projects were always in danger from the elements, changing taste and rebuilding schemes.

Conservation departments all over the world

RIGHT The staircase of the Strand Palace Hotel, Westminster, London, 1930. A fine example of an Art Deco interior in a public building employing a sophisticated use of abstract design.

BELOW RIGHT The manicure saloon of the Strand Palace Hotel, London, England.

have taught the public that there are always examples of taste that are in continuous danger from the necessity to maximize the use of land in urban centres, and modernization. Yet the generation that grew up with Art Deco also grew out of it into other styles. For them it was a retrogressive step to hold onto something that was passé. It is only with the advantage of hindsight – and the foresight of some great collectors – that Art Deco has been saved, in its grander, more elaborate manifestations. Not long ago the quiet, serene design of the Hoover factory seemed laughably out-of-date. With its survival now almost completely assured, the public have an opportunity to see Art Deco in its application to industry. Technological advance would undoubtedly have necessitated improvements inside the factory were it to remain competitive, but the neo-Egyptian exterior is still a pleasure to the eye.

No one can deny that New York's skyline would be hugely impoverished by the loss of the Chrysler building. Its steep, rapier-like point adds a unique quality to what is after all just a high-rise block, of which hundreds and thousands are to be seen in capital cities all over the world. The gradual and gentle half circles that edge the eye smoothly up to that final rapid sweep are typically Deco. The inset darts on those half circles are a motif that recur again and again, on anything from cigarette lighters to large pieces of furniture. These "sun rays" tell a great deal about Art Deco's optimistic and joyous quality – even at its most cumbersome it also has details expressing lightness. If the Chrysler building is the cathedral of Art Deco then its holy shrine is without a doubt Radio City Music Hall in the same city. It is along the length of America's Eastern seaboard, from New York right down to Miami, that fine examples of Art Deco buildings

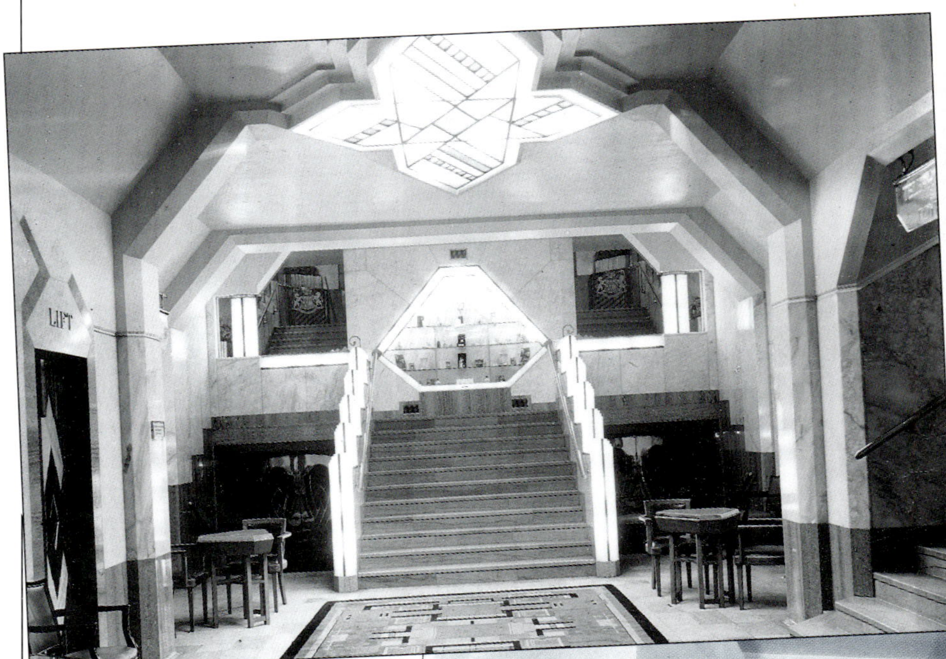

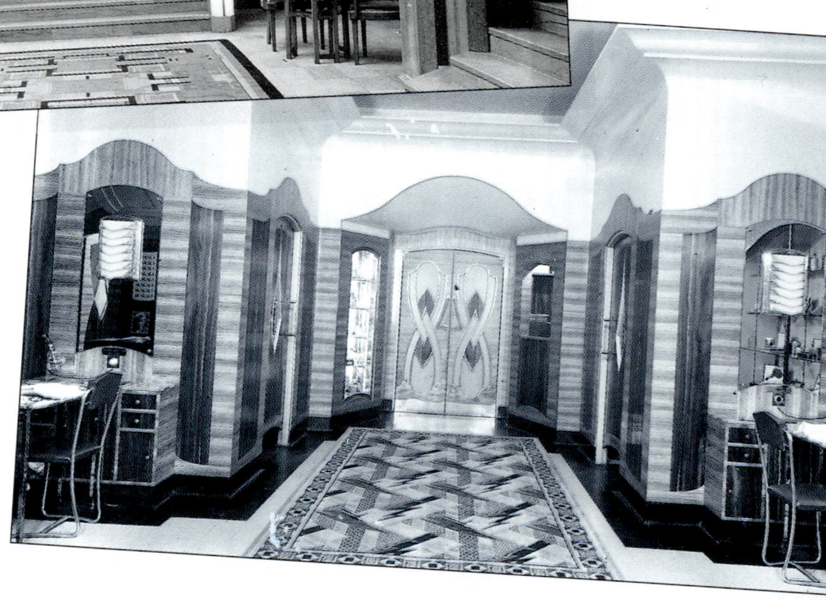

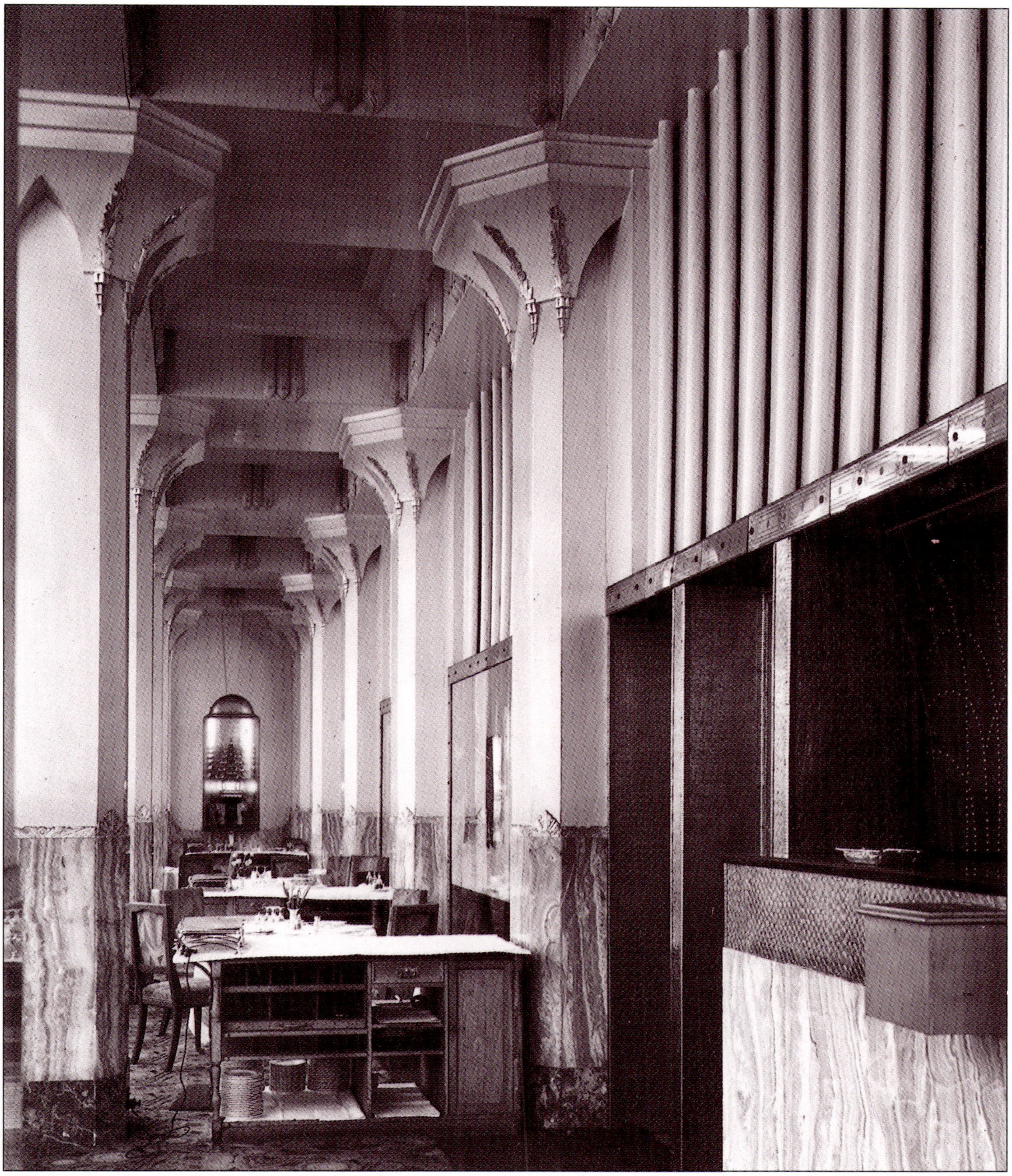

CHAPTER 3

LEFT The interior of the famous Claridges Hotel, London, England.

still survive in the most unlikely of places.

For serious students of Art Deco and lovers of the style, the small suburban cinemas surrounding the heart of London, England still give an accurate indication of Art Deco's application to public buildings. The cinema has always been the setting for an evening out, an occasion for escaping into another world, and the interior of, for example, the Odeon Cinema, Camberwell (a London suburb), with its elegant curves, spacious carpeted halls, and potted palms, treads that difficult dividing line between discreet and calming elegance, and a sense of occasion.

Without the examples of the Park Lane Hotel ballroom, the Muswell Hill Odeon, the Coca-Cola bottling plant in Los Angeles, or the Grand Hotel, Dax, in France, Art Deco would seem to the onlooker from the end of the 20th century merely a style of the domestic interior and of small objects.

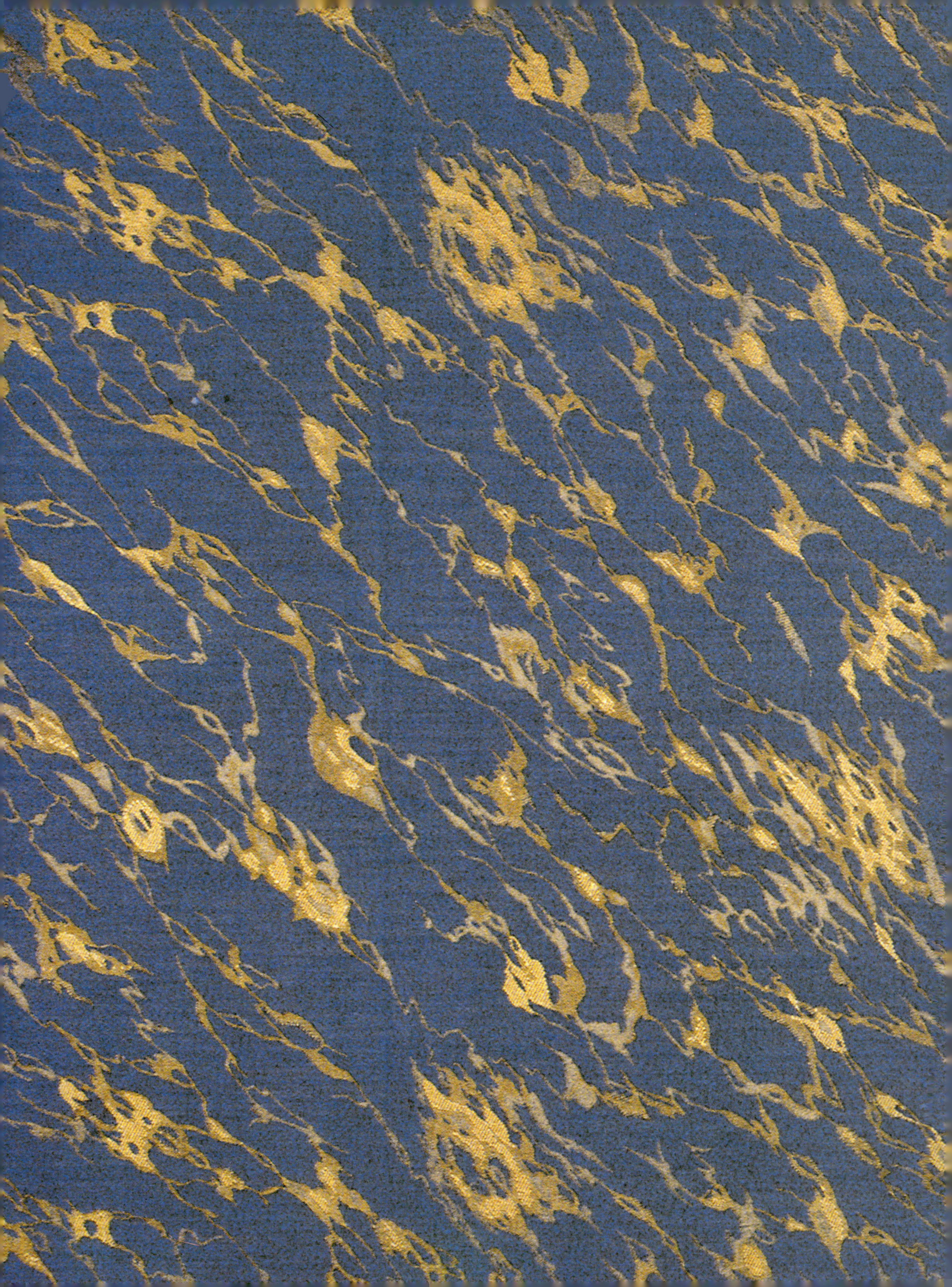

CHAPTER FOUR

FURNITURE

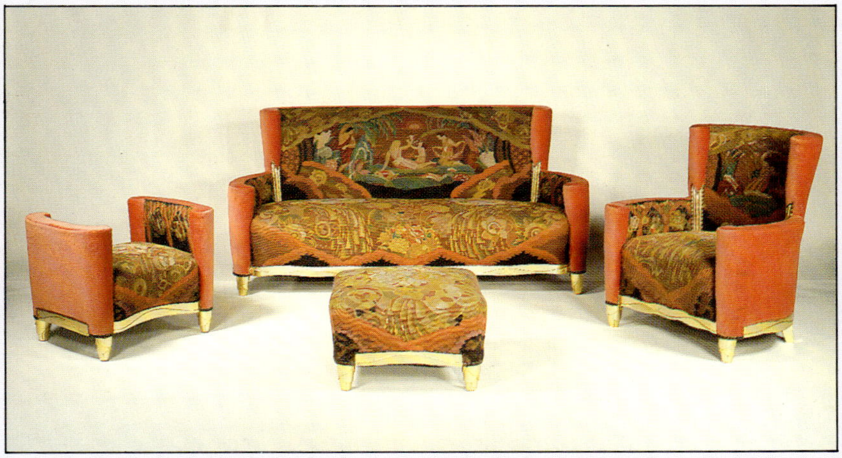

ABOVE Five-piece giltwood and Beauvais tapestry drawing room suite by Maurice Dufrene. This type of application of tapestry to furniture, by no means unique, provided a boost to an ailing industry. Note in particular the giltwood layering down the stubby feet.

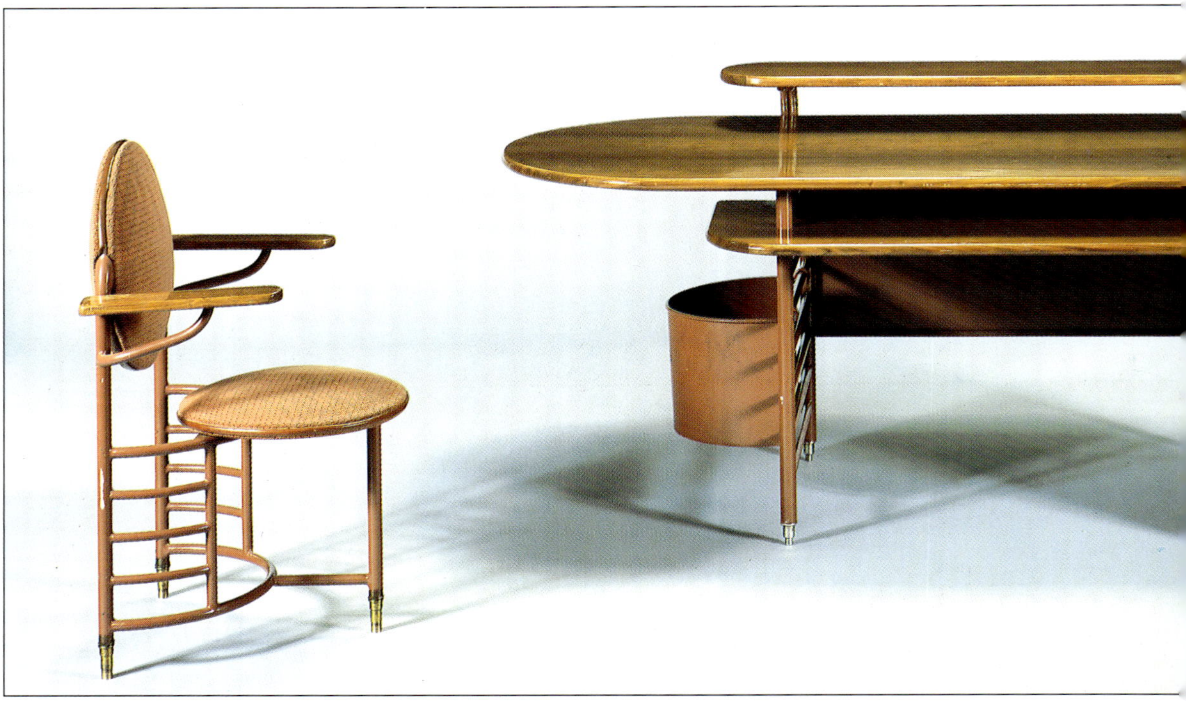

RIGHT Desk and chair (1936–9) by the American genius of architecture Frank Lloyd Wright. This set, called 'Cherokee Red', made from enamelled steel, American walnut and brass-plated metal, was designed for the S. C. Johnson & Son Administration Building in Racine, Wisconsin. The designs represent the saner, rational and more utilitarian attitudes to modern furniture design. Not necessarily inexpensive, the desks and chairs could at least be mass-produced.

If anyone nowadays were to start collecting Art Deco the most difficult thing of all to obtain would be Art Deco furniture. Most pieces of any sophistication are in the Musée des Arts Décoratifs in Paris, or New York's Metropolitan Museum. A few other museums around the world have examples, and a few private collectors like Alain Lesieutre, Felix Marcilhac, and Mr and Mrs Peter M Brant have substantial collections. Scarcity is one of the obvious difficulties facing a new collector, but price is even more prohibitive. For a piece of furniture by Jean Dunand, Emile-Jacques Ruhlmann, or Pierre Legrain the price would now be in the hundreds of thousands. Art Deco furniture is certainly one of the most interesting and inspired applications of the style. The high prices nowadays are certainly due to its rarity, but they also reflect another factor, that of the value of quality craftsmanship. Even when Emile-Jacques Ruhlmann sold his furniture in the 1920s, such pieces were only affordable by the wealthiest of wealthy clients, such as maharajahs and princes. If his work commanded such prices, it was not because of commercial greed but because of the months and months of skilled labour and the use of the most expensive materials as expressions of his genius. If such a piece of furniture were to be copied today it would be next to impossible to find a cabinetmaker capable of producing it. What men like Ruskin and William Morris had feared, the loss of the crafts due to industrialization, had become a reality. The 1920s and '30s witnessed, among so many things, the dying of the old crafts. Skills like French polishing and marquetry had been passed down from father to son, and the apprentice system protected and maintained expertise. Even today, craftsmen jealously guard their secrets, and find it difficult to pass on the experience that comes from years of perfect co-ordination between hand and eye.

Art Deco furniture, therefore, more than any other expression of that style deserves preservation. It is the final chapter in the craft of cabinetmaking.

Within Art Deco furniture design, there were two distinct trends. On the one hand, there were the early experiments in what we have now come to recognize as modern furniture, using metals and plastics in forms which could lead to eventual mass production, and on the other the high-quality craftsmanship of which Ruhlmann was the greatest exponent. Purists would say that Art Deco furniture is truly only that of the highest quality of production.

At the turn of the century, most quality furniture that was built to last was in the Louis XVI or Empire styles. Solid it might have been, but in no way was it modern. The achievement of

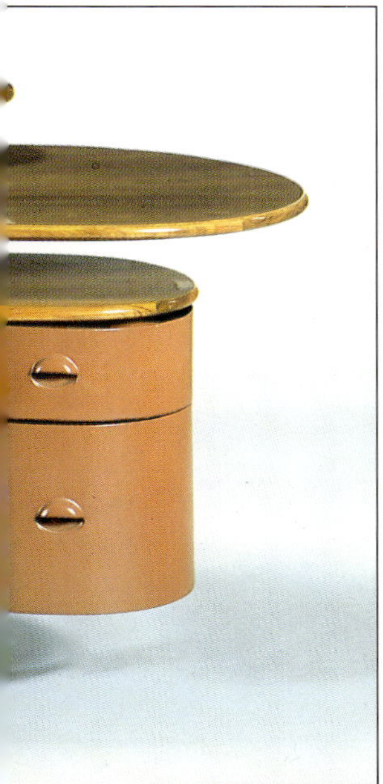

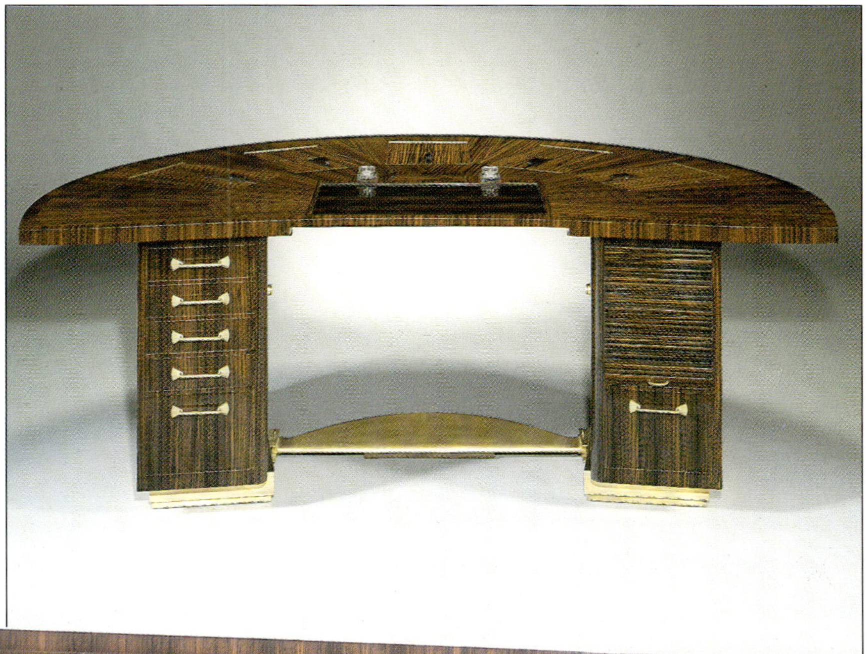

LEFT Fan-shaped Macassar ebony and gilt bronze desk of 1929 by Emile Jacques Ruhlmann. Note how the grain on the left-hand side continues without interruption up across the drawers, and the exquisite coupling of the luxury materials. Masterpieces like this desk justly place Ruhlmann amongst the best of all cabinetmaker-designers.

BELOW LEFT Delicate and decorative wardrobe by Jules Leleu, with mother-of-pearl and ebony inlay.

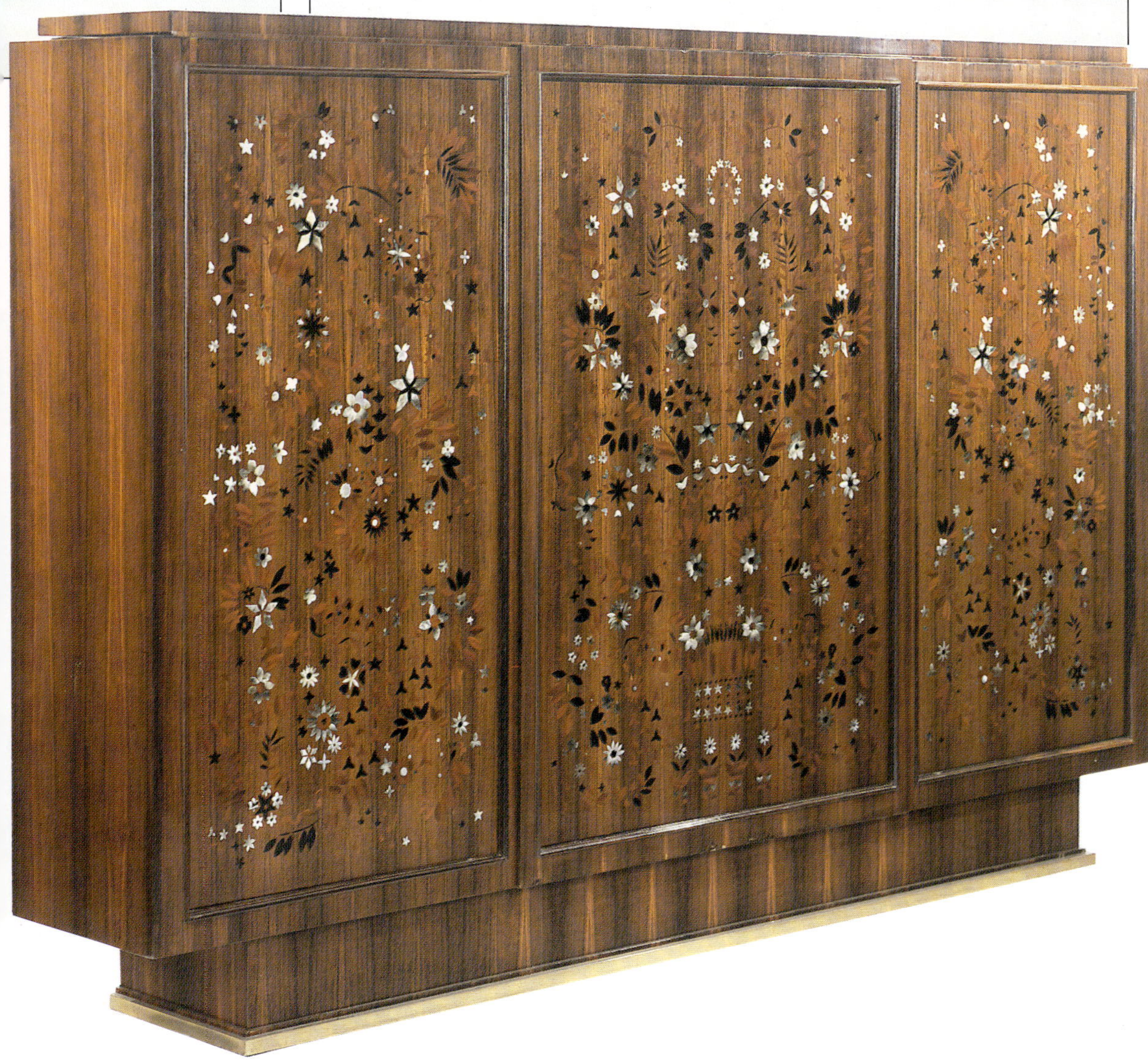

ART DECO

RIGHT Inlaid secretaire by Süe et Mare that capitalises fully on the grain and character of the wood, in contrast to the delicate ivory detailing round the keyholes and the theatrical yet precise geometry of the lid.

Ruhlmann, Süe et Mare, Jean Dunand and others, was to re-evaluate the furniture styles, take the best and subtly alter and revamp them. Many of the people responsible for furniture design, including those just mentioned, were not themselves great craftsmen, but they were capable of running large workshops, and using the talents of their own and other studios' craftsmen to the best effect. They were virtuoso performers, and they showed off their abilities to the utmost. The materials they used were equal to their skills. France's vast empire provided them with the most exotic of materials: macassar ebony, mother-of-pearl, abalone, ivory, tortoiseshell, amboyna wood, burr walnut, palmwood, silver and gold and the inspiration of oriental techniques such as chinoiserie and lacquerwork.

Expensive and élitist as the luxury trade undoubtedly was, its resurgence depended on other factors. Apart from a few specialist shops, the outlet for contemporary furniture was limited. When the new department stores realized that design could be of great use to them, the situation altered. Au Printemps set up its Studio Primavera, Le Louvre set up Studium Louvre, Au Bon Marché set up Pomone, and Galeries Lafayette set up La Maîtrise. Customers soon realized that at these shops they could buy the most modern furniture at a reasonable price. The further advantage of the studio system was that craftsmen were also allowed to accept private customers, as long as this did not interfere with the studio's work.

The whole furniture industry had a surprising openness of attitude, and ideas and skills were generously shared. In Ruhlmann's "Hôtel d'un Collectionneur" at the 1925 Exposition des Arts Décoratifs et Industriels, he included the work of sculptor Antoine Bourdelle, animal sculptor François Pompon, Jean Dupas, metalworker Edgar Brandt, silver designer Jean Puiforcat, lacquer expert Jean Dunand, and Pierre Legrain. It was an act of consolidation, an appeal for unity, which must also have displayed Ruhlmann's talents as an interior designer.

There are two matching Ruhlmann cabinets dating from 1925 in the Metropolitan Museum of Art in New York and in the Musée des Arts Decoratifs in Paris which show an absolute synthesis of his ideas at work and amply demonstrate his absolute mastery of the medium. Made from rosewood, the cabinets are inlaid with macassar ebony and ivory. The floral display on the front is highly reminiscent of Art Nouveau, yet the strictly spartan lines of the vase containing the flowers displays a sensibility well in advance of the turn-of-the-century style. It is in all the detailing around the edges of the pieces

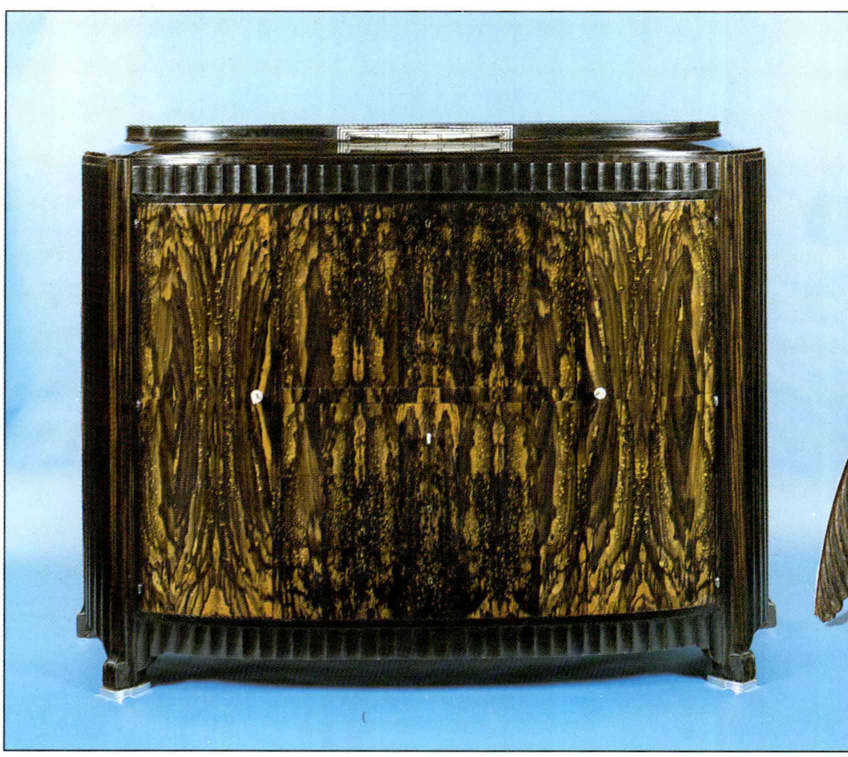

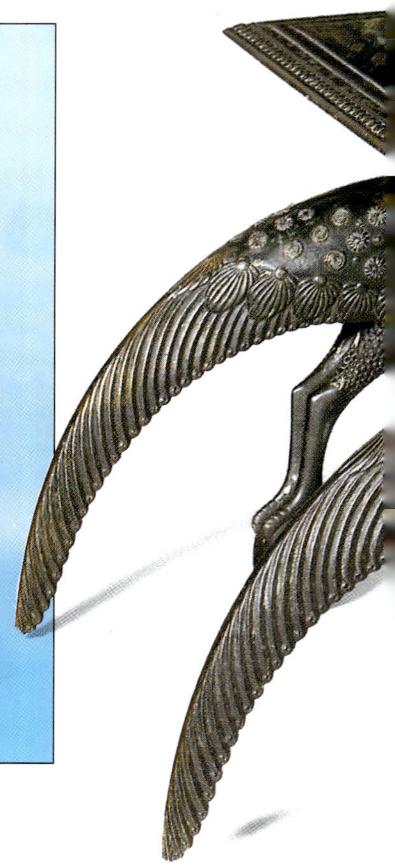

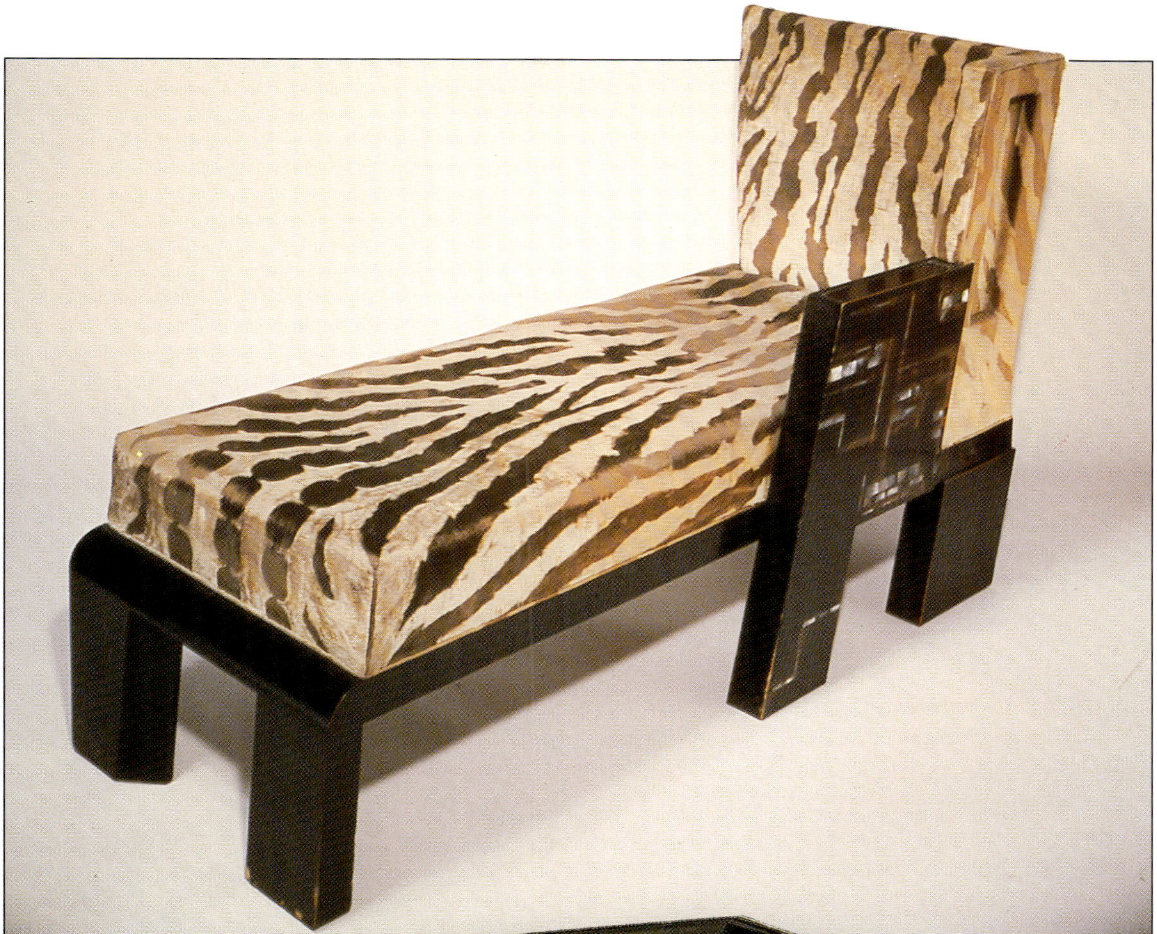

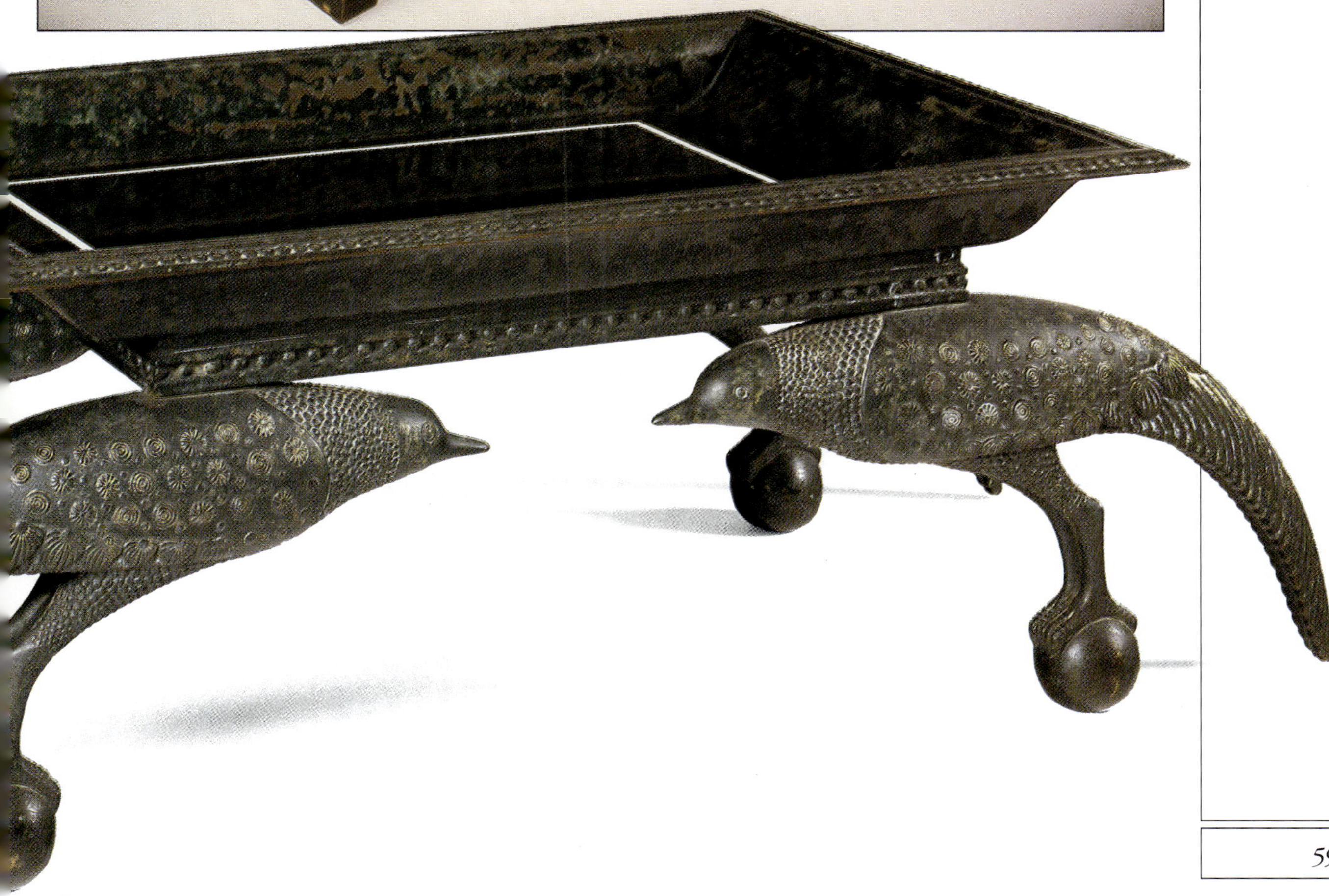

LEFT The famous Zebra chaise-longue in black lacquer by Pierre Legrain of 1925.

BELOW LEFT Bizarre bronze and marble table by Armand J. Rateau, with four encrusted stylized birds used as supports.

RIGHT Elegant mahogany and inlaid ivory petit armoire in the style of Emile Jacques Ruhlmann, with the characteristic splayed sword legs, geometric inlay and piano key motif on the top of the cabinet.

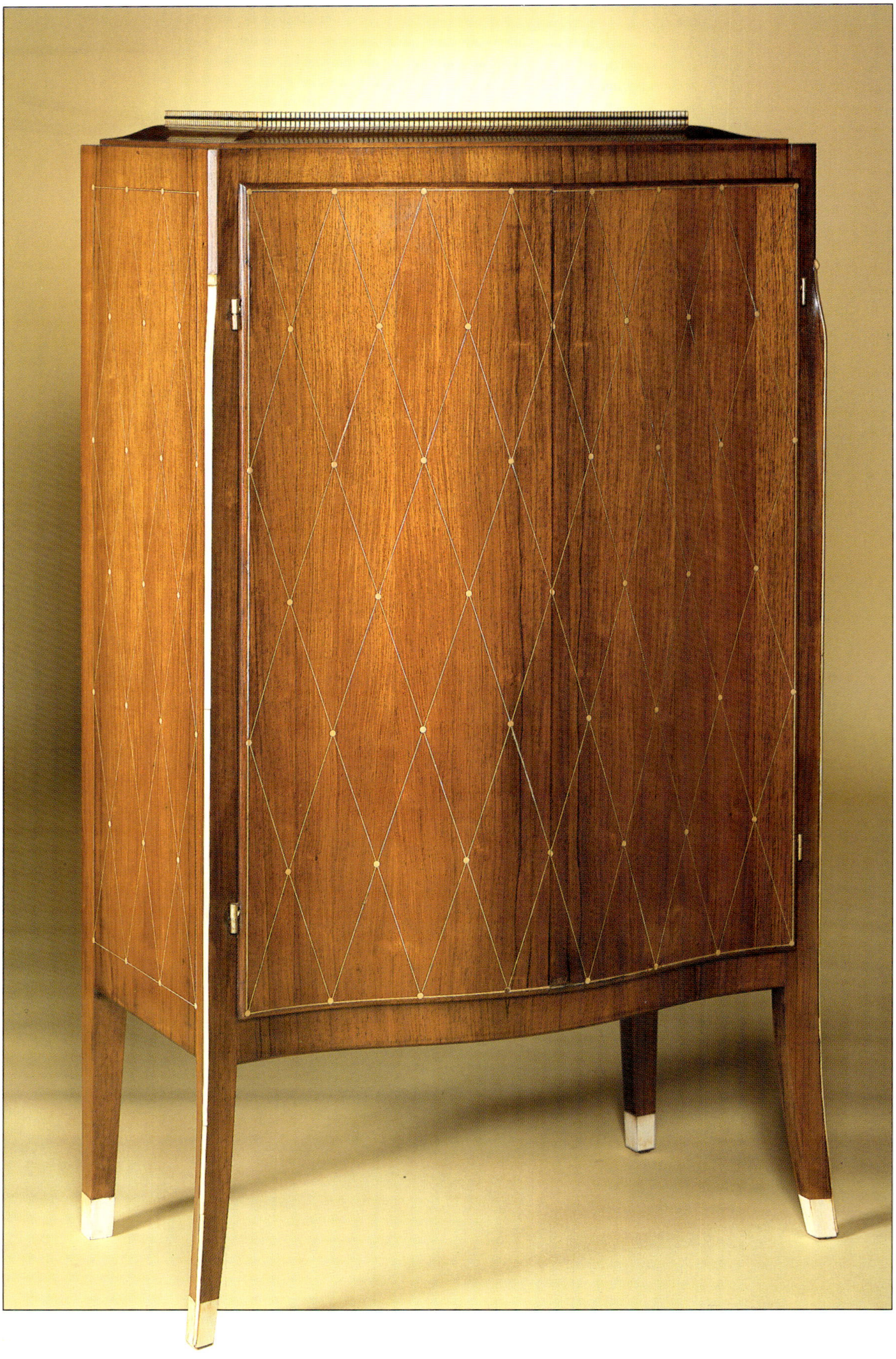

that the Art Deco spirit comes to the fore. On the top edge, the ivory keys set into the macassar ebony suggest a modernized Greek decoration, or even a piano. The pieces are quite classical but in a modern vein. The slightly-offset and angled edging strips that run from the short legs to the white top edge are carefully finished with a small strip of ivory. The back legs, double the width of those at the front, are squared off, while the front legs taper elegantly down hexagonally. The pin-prick detailing on the front in ebony works as an open edge, marking out the floral pattern, but at the same time allowing the character of the rose-wood grain to show through. It is the detailing on the front legs that exemplifies Ruhlmann at his best. The legs are clearly supports, but the scrolls stand proud of the cabinet and are also inlaid with ivory. They are pure ornament, extraneous to the functionality of the cabinet, decorative yet discreet. The cabinet in the Félix Marcilhac collection in Paris also reveals Ruhlmann's ingenuity. As a complete object there is little novelty in the piece. It is a classical bombe shape, a form perhaps perfected by 18th

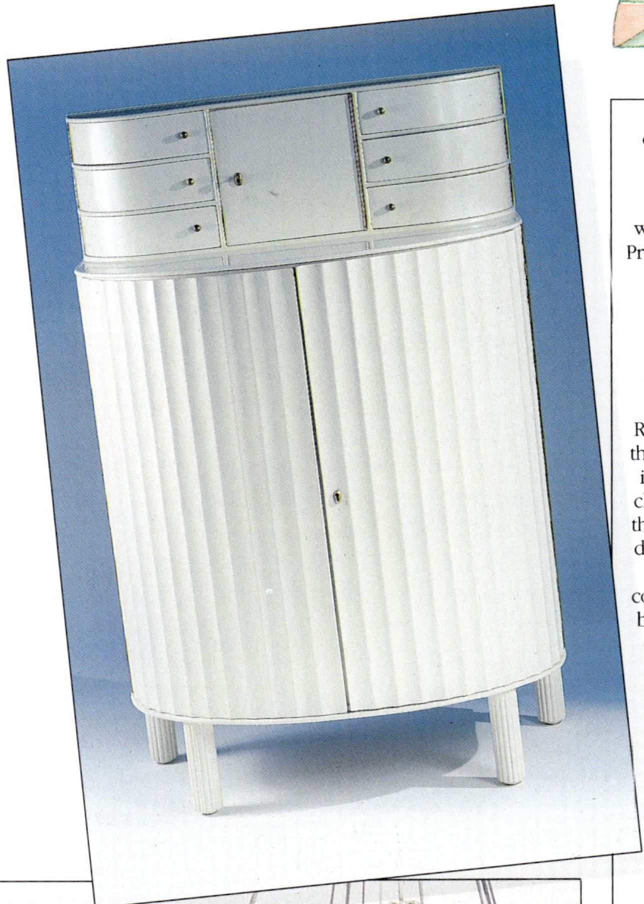

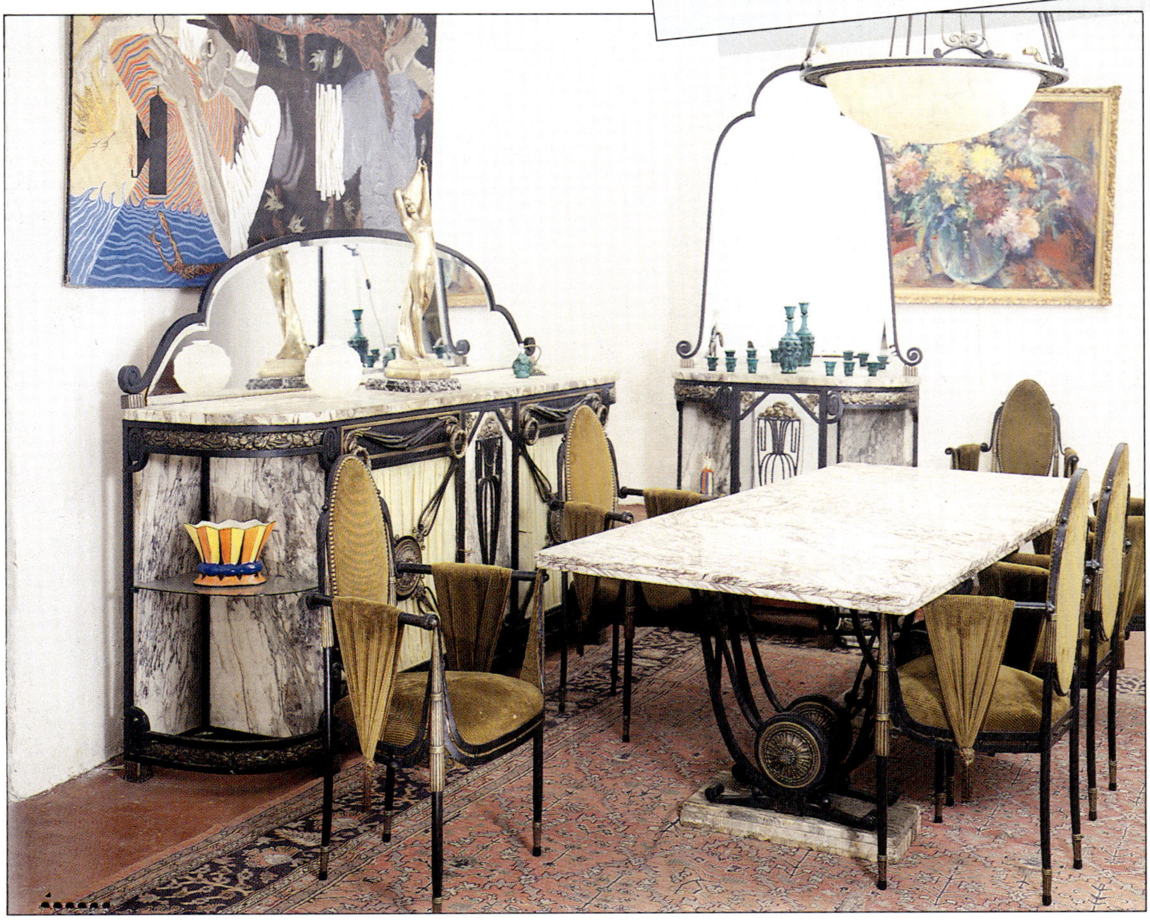

LEFT Painted wooden cabinet by Otto Prutscher, restrained in its simple, sophisticated elegance.

BELOW LEFT Suite of furniture in bronze, marble, wrought iron, corduroy and silk by Raymond Subes. A detail that is particularly unique is the swag in corduroy cloth over the armrest of the chair, which is purely decorative. Note also the gentle sweeping arch containing the tall mirror behind the table, and its echo in reverse on the table legs.

ART DECO

RIGHT Pair of chairs from 1927 by the architect Robert Mallet Stevens. The use of wood and fabric is a clever rethinking of the deckchair concept.

century Dutch cabinet makers, and works on the same lines as most French Louis XVI furniture. The framework of the cabinet is hidden behind sensual tortoiseshell squares – the surface is all-important. The shaping is curved and voluptuous, with only the key plate and the toes on the feet projecting. Ruhlmann's furniture always allows for an uncomplicated appreciation of the qualities of each material. If not necessarily a strict follower of the truth to material ethic, his best pieces never disguise themselves. In this way his work was very different from the eccentricities of Pierre Legrain, who made the African chairs for Mme Tachard.

Born in 1887, Legrain initially made his mark as a designer of book covers for his wealthy patron Jacques Doucet. Legrain was like many of the other Art Deco designers in that he seemed to be able to apply himself with equal success to designing for a wide range of craft disciplines. It is important to stress again the value of having access to experts in many different fields, which set designers like Legrain free to experiment at will. One of Legrain's most famous pieces of furniture was the "Zebra" chair, or chaise longue. His clear affinity to all things African could hardly be more explicit than in this piece made in 1925. Compared to such representations of the opposite extreme of Art Deco as Eileen Gray's experiments in metals or, more directly, Le Corbusier's own chaise longue, Legrain's is nothing short of bizarre. The zebra skin is imitated in velvet, the armrest which logic tells you should be against a wall is decorated on the reverse with abstract patterns, expensively executed in mother of pearl. The overall design is almost crude, appearing both clumsy and uncomfortable, the exact opposite to the Le Corbusier chair, which is probably the most comfortable piece of furniture ever invented. The arm rest is left open from the front in order to house a small shelf whose purpose could be nothing more than aesthetic. The whole chair exudes a feeling of gratuitous luxury and

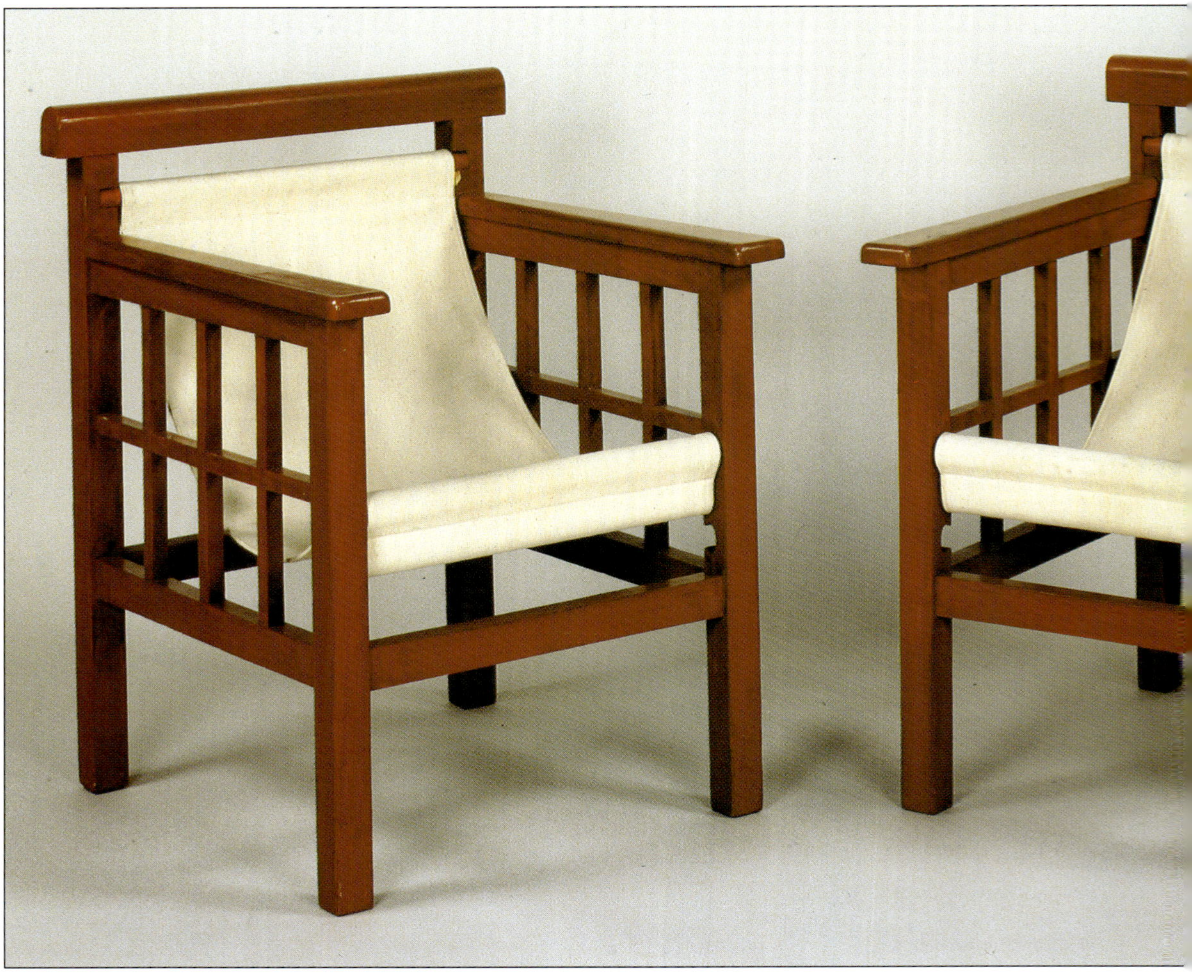

decadence, the kind of chaise longue that Nancy Cunard or some other wealthy aesthete might have possessed, on which to lie back elegantly while puffing on an opium pipe.

Another equally eccentric furniture designer and one who was often used by others for his designs incorporating lacquer work was Jean Dunand. Both Dunand and Eileen Gray used the talents of the Japanese lacquer master Sougawara. Dunand was another of the designers who executed major commissions for the liners *Ile de France* and *Normandie*. His most famous single piece, however, was a bed made in 1930 for Mme Bertholet, in lacquer and mother-of-pearl. It is a beautiful yet almost completely absurd object. So beautiful, in fact, that it verges on the hideous. The actual construction must have been a nightmare of intricate modelling and shaping. There is no sense here of truth to material, yet curiously enough lacquer is one of the very few materials that would work successfully. Inlaid wood would have lifted in any centrally-heated house, while paint would have cracked and chipped. The small fish bubbling away at the foot end are almost comical compared with the serene still life of water lilies on the curved headboard, derived no doubt from Monet's water lily paintings, or oriental examples.

Following Art Deco furniture to its other extreme, it is worth noting the great influence of Frank Lloyd Wright, Hoffman, the Dutchman Gerrit Rietveld, and the Bauhaus School. The strong move against unnecessary ornament, and the desire to provide functional furniture, were inseparable from the need to provide new forms in the most economical way at the cheapest possible price. Designers like Eliel Saarinen, famous for Dulles Airport, Washington DC, Alvar Aalto and the Americans Donald Deskey, the architect of Radio City Music Hall, and Ken Weber, all pushed the design of furniture in a more "rational" direction using stark, uncluttered streamlining that also left its stamp on the Art Deco age.

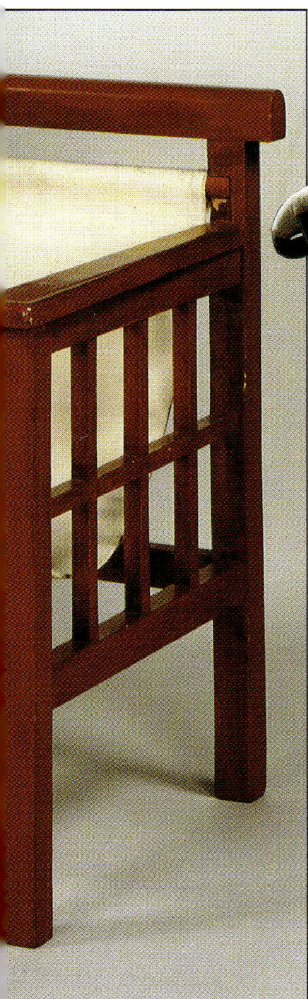

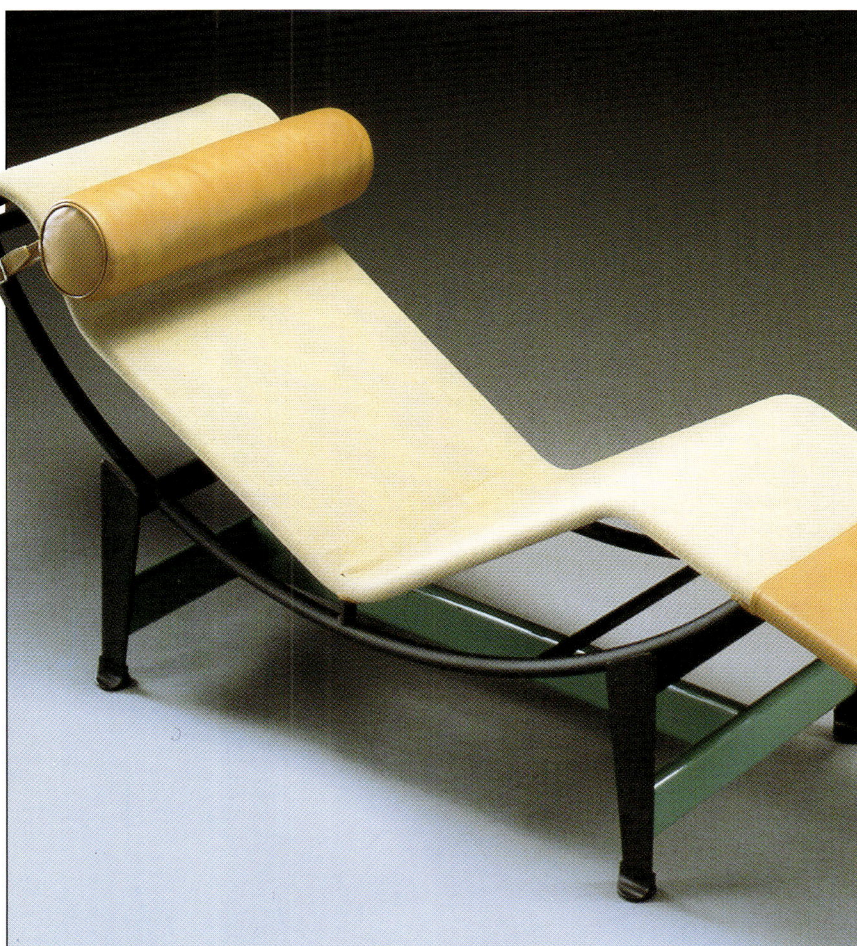

LEFT Reproduction by Cassina of the famous chaise-longue by Le Corbusier. This chair is the absolute ultimate in luxury and comfort.

RIGHT Sycamore sideboard by Jacques Adnet. The heaviness is lightened and relieved only by the chrome fittings, and by the drawers which look as if they were somehow magically held in suspension.

BELOW RIGHT One of the most exquisite and sensational examples in the whole canon of Art Deco furniture, this lacquered bed by Jean Dunand is the ultimate in design for luxury living between the two great wars.

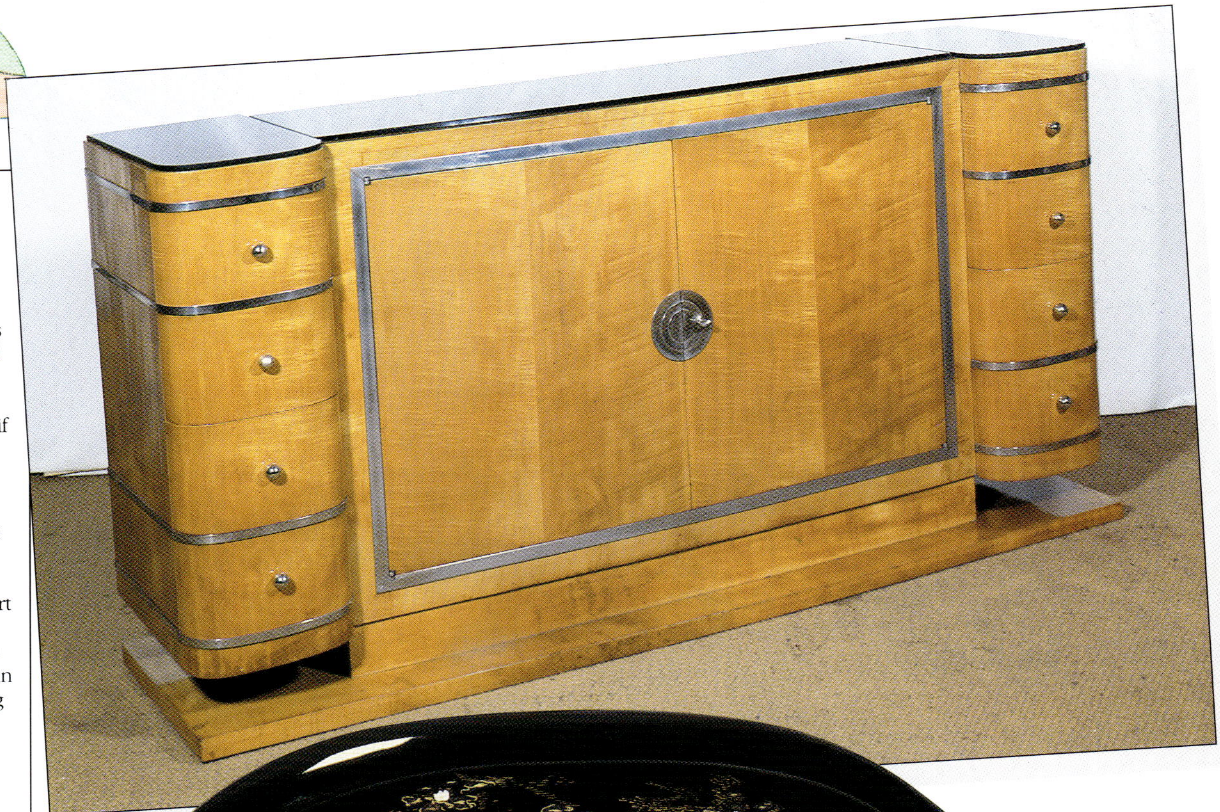

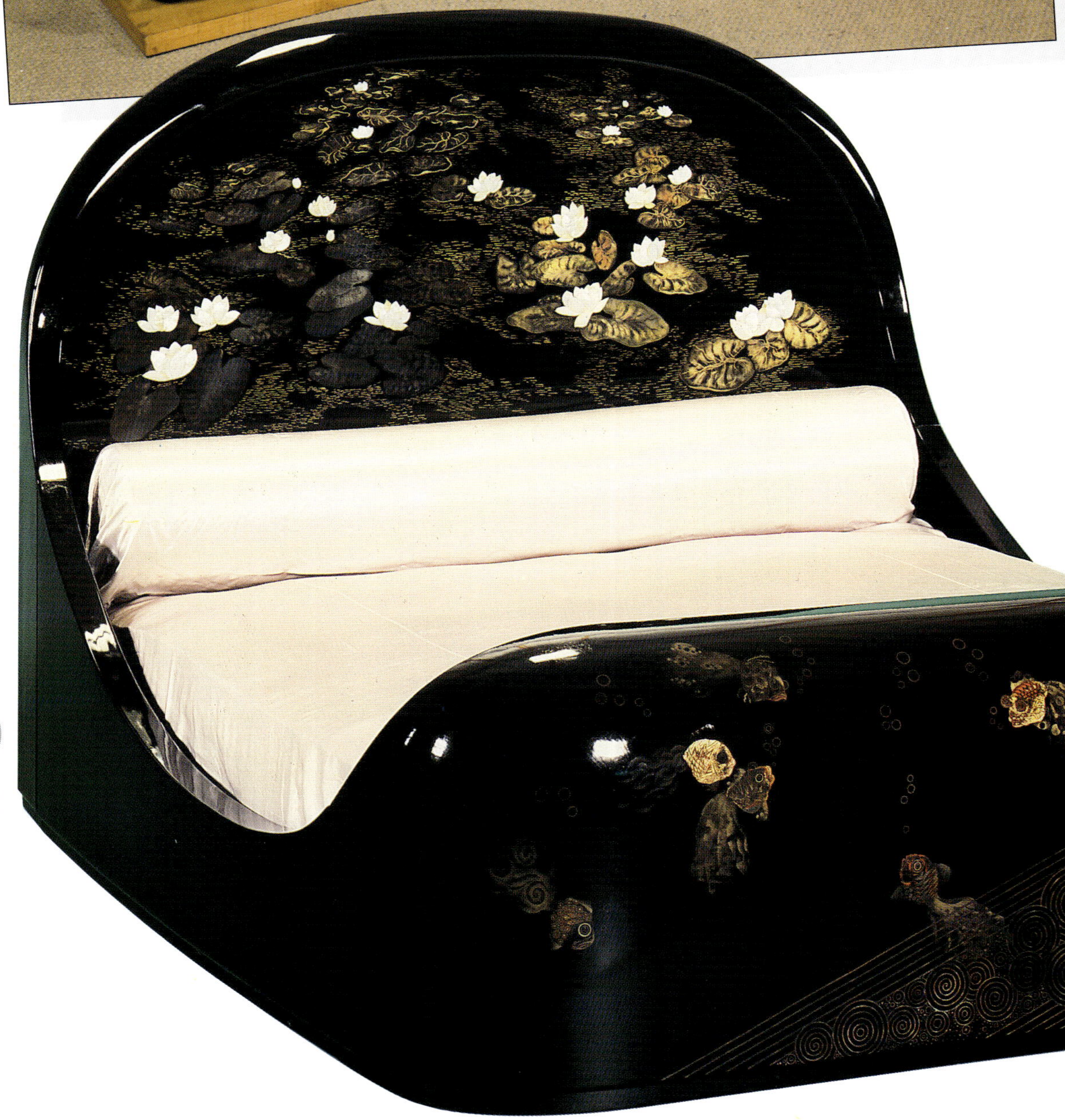

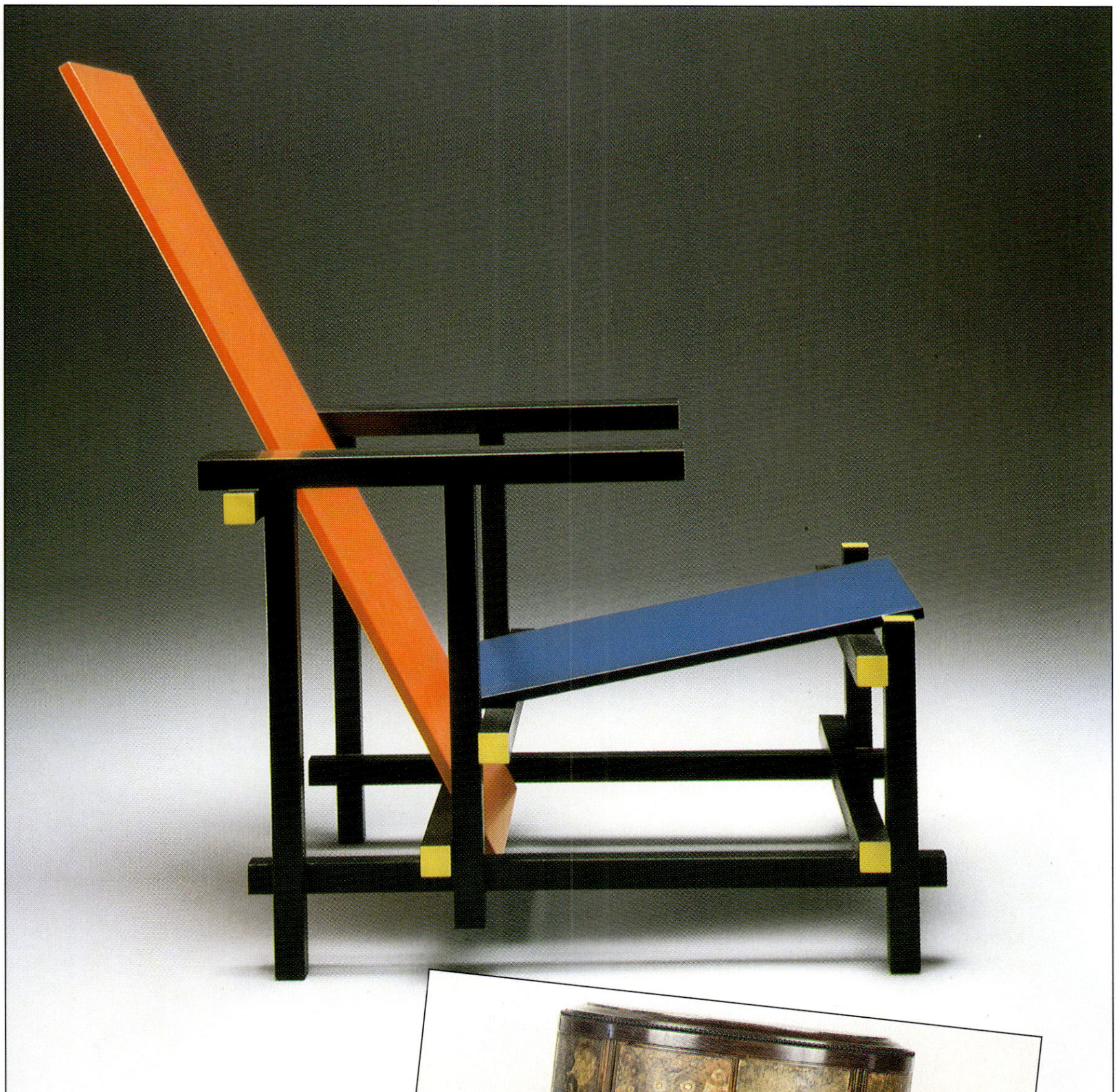

LEFT Reproduction by Cassina of the original Red-Blue Chair of 1918 by the Dutch *de Stijl* architect-craftsman Gerrit Rietveld. If there is one piece of furniture in the history of modern art that can be said to have had an influence beyond the discipline of furniture-making, then it must be Rietveld's chair.

BELOW LEFT Unusual decorated cabinet bombe in japoniste style by Clément Mère, partner in the Süe et Mare collaboration.

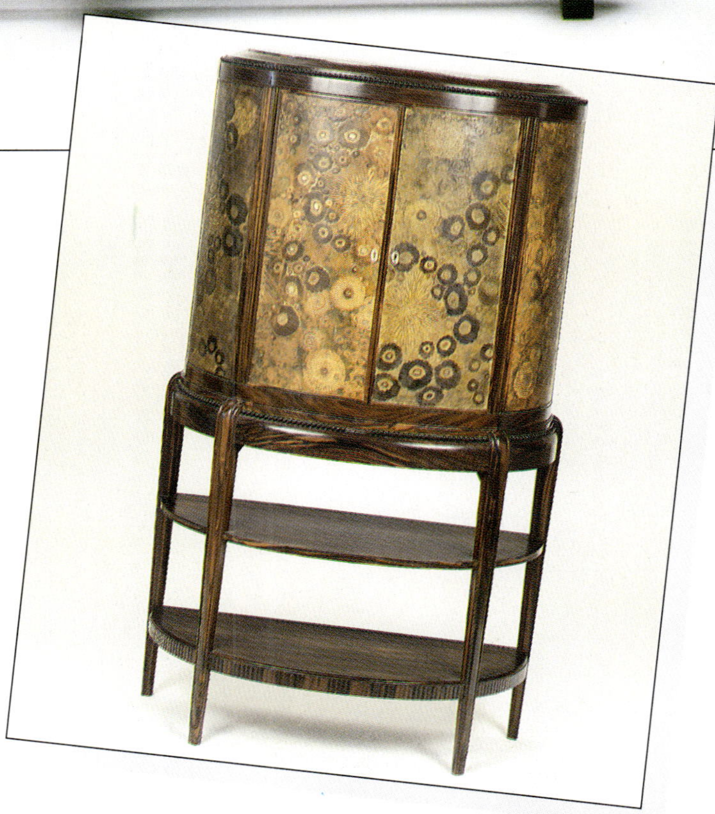

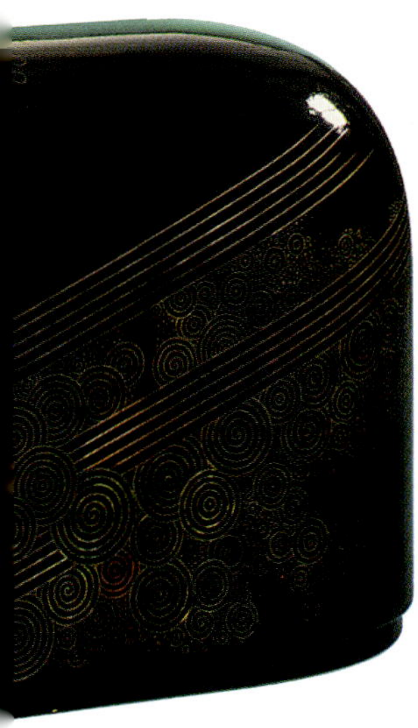

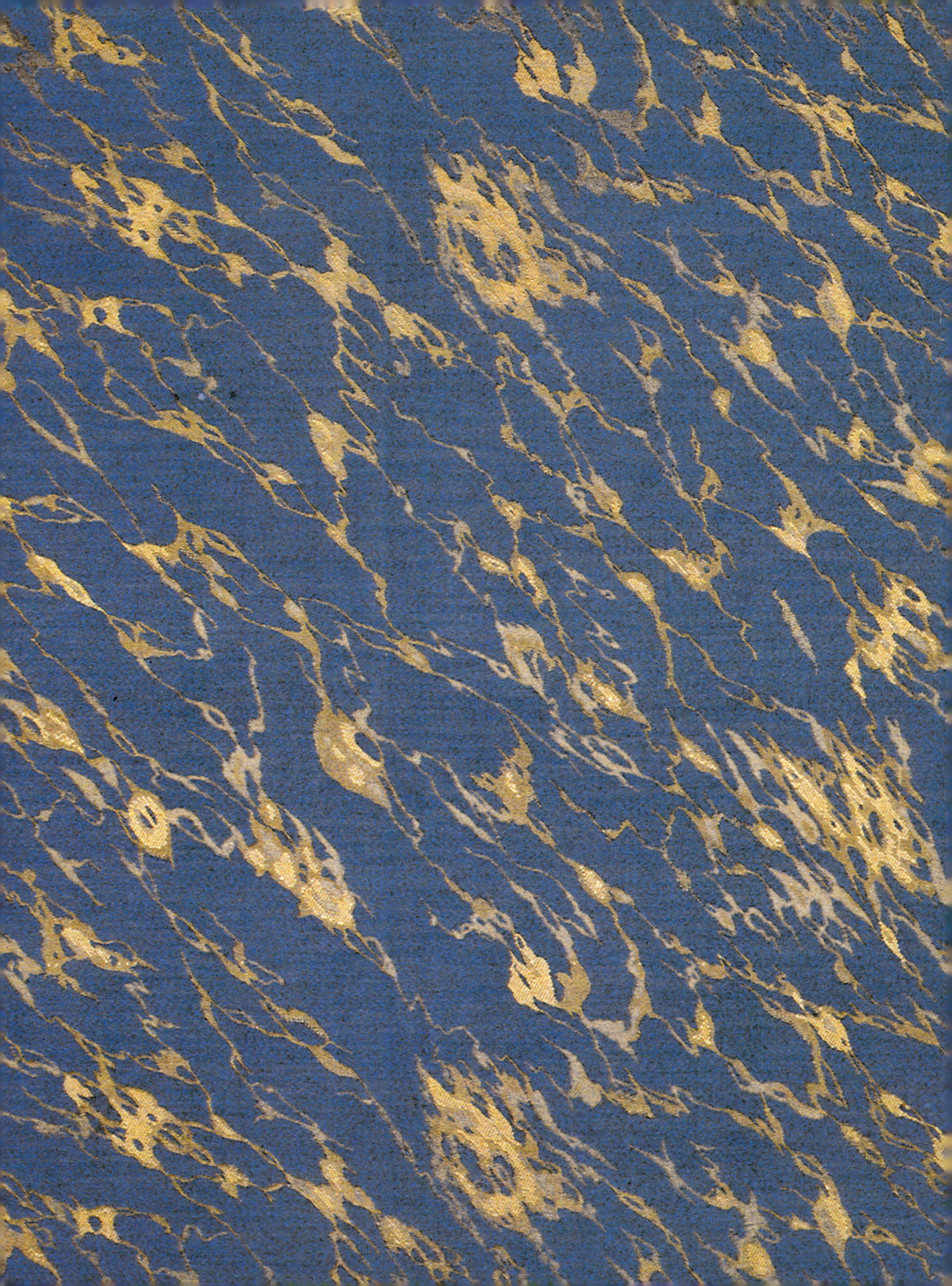

CHAPTER FIVE

METALWORK

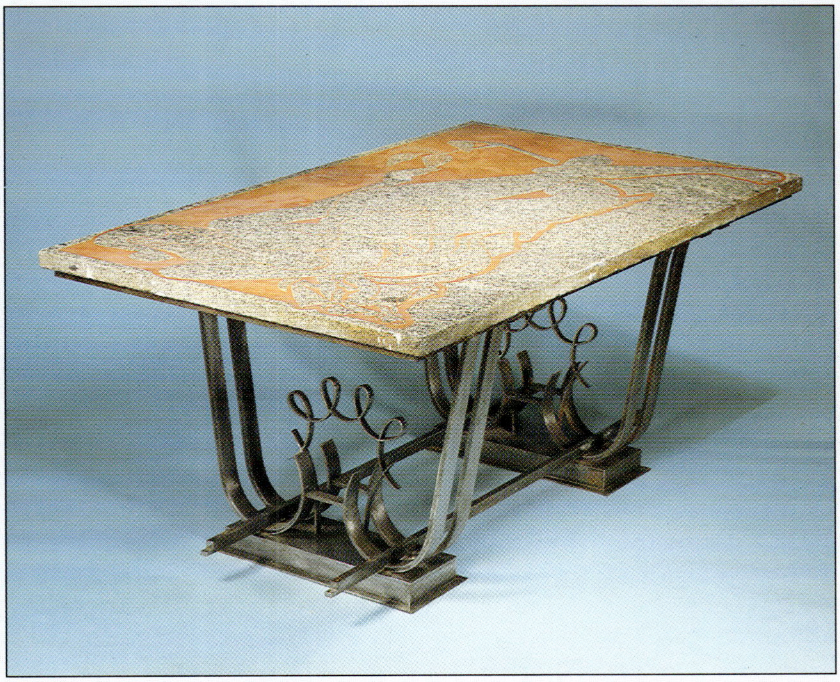

A wrought iron and grey granite centre table by Raymond Subes, 1925, which fully utilises the flexible strength and malleability of the material. The image on the surface, a nude with fruit bowl, is highlighted in reverse in red ochre.

RIGHT Pair of bronze jardinières with cobras by Edgar Brandt.

CENTRE Rustic 1920s marriage between glass and wrought iron. The wrought ironwork is by Majorelle and the glass bowl by the firm of Daum, Nancy.

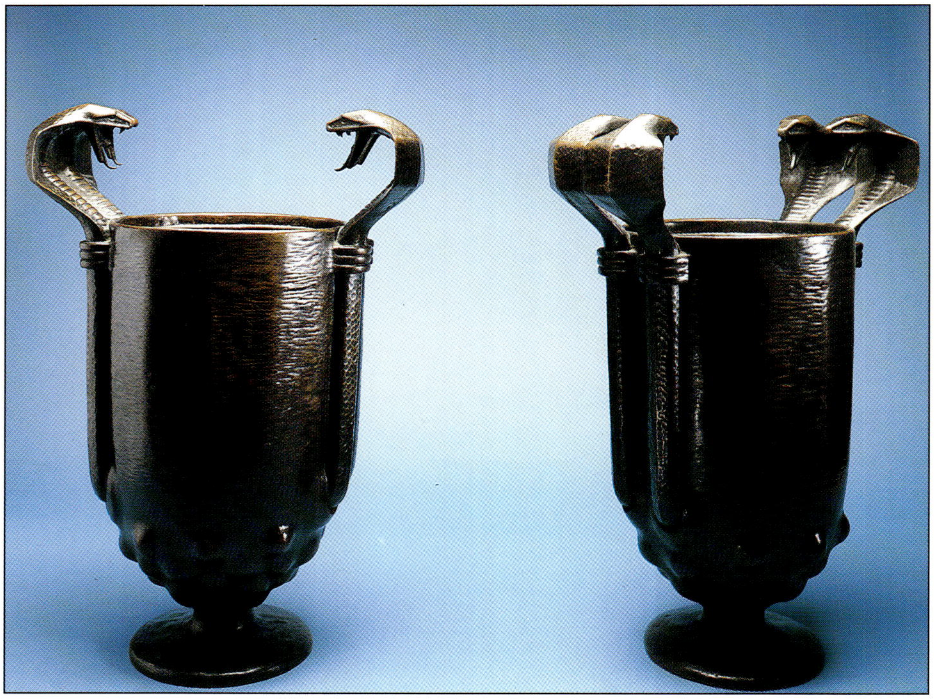

Adaptability and inventiveness flourished in Art Deco metalwork. Metal was often used on its own for gates and doors, but it could also be employed in conjunction with almost any of the other favoured materials. The history of Art Deco metalwork is also the history of changing materials. The 1920s was the period of wrought iron, bronze and copper. By the early 1930s these had not been completely replaced, but designers favoured the more modern aluminium, steel and chrome. The '30s were remarkable, not for any single colour preference, but for the lack of any colour at all. Glass and shiny metals complemented each other; both were reflecting and anonymous, sparkling and transparent. The typical '30s room had mirrored walls, with discreet metal borders, repeated in the bent metal furniture. It was stark, and ideally suited to university professors in pursuit of the pleasures of the mind. There were no distractions, except for their own reflections, twice or even ten times at the corners where the mirrors met. Such ideas were a long way from those involved in the initial resurgence of metalcraft, promoted most notably by the craftsman Edgar Brandt.

Walking round any Victorian square in London, as in many other cities, the uniformity of the cast ironwork and plaster mouldings is one of the most striking aspects of the period style. Houses had to be built quickly and cheaply to meet the needs of a growing population, and mass-produced, hastily constructed housing spread across urban areas; detailing and ornament were still preferred, but the result for the metalwork trade was an almost complete poverty of design. Builders used pattern manuals provided by the foundries that picked out the required effect and repeated it. In effect, the skilled craftsman had become almost entirely redundant. Into this vacuum stepped men like Edgar Brandt, Armand Albert Rateau, Raymond Henri Subes, Jacques Adnet, Louis Sognot, Adelbert Szabo and Paul Kiss.

As wrought iron has few limitations beyond that of the craftsman's skill, it broke through the confines of use in one specific area. Art Deco Metalwork pieces ranged from the intimacy of a commemorative medallion or a small mantelpiece clock, to the huge entrance gates for the Exposition des Arts Décoratifs et Industriels. Almost all these outstanding craftsmen/designers worked across this wide range, spreading their time and creativity between all the possible applications of the material.

Edgar Brandt was born in Paris in 1880 and, through his father's involvement in an engineering firm, he very early on developed an interest in working with metal. Most of his early work came from direct commissions by

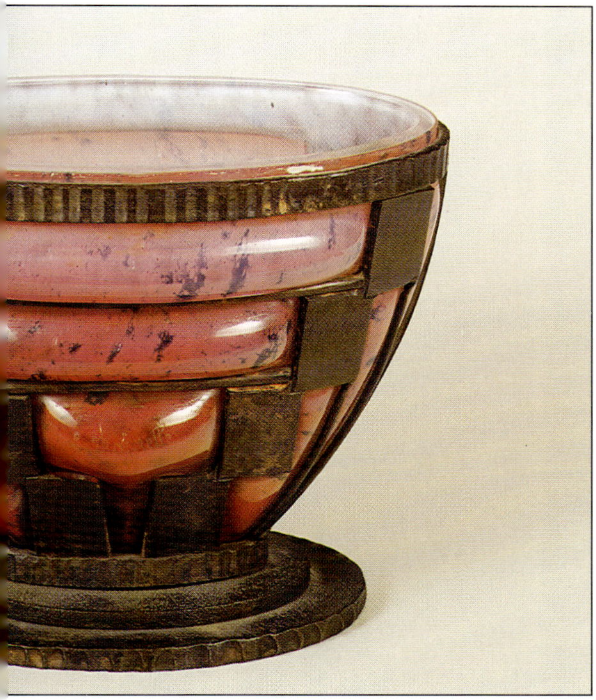

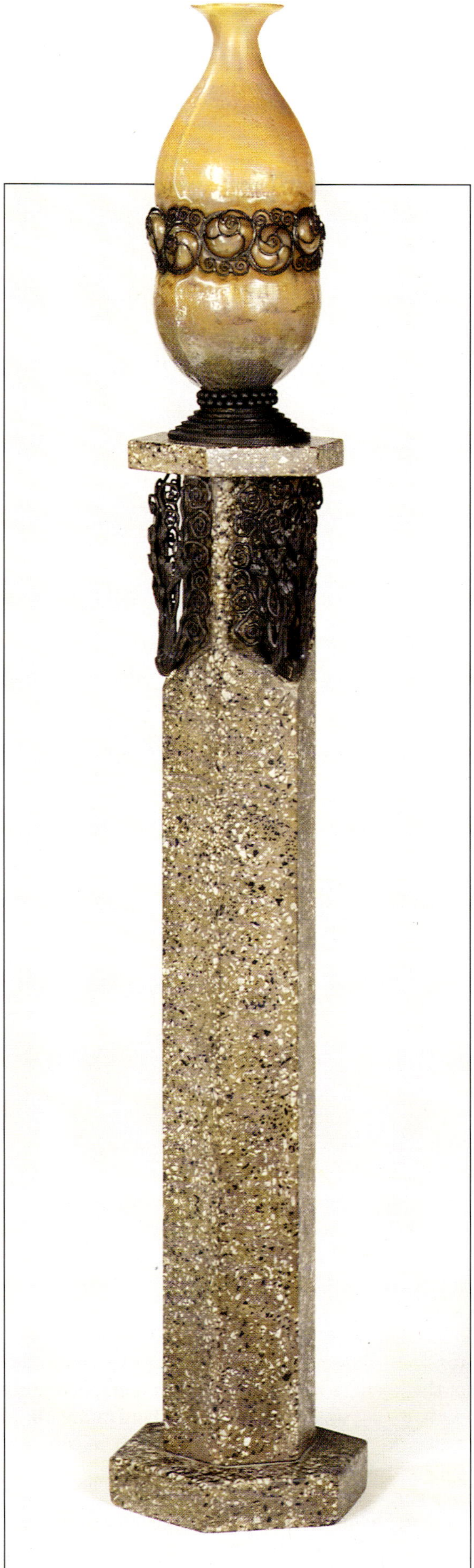

LEFT Stone and wrought iron column supporting a glass vase and a wrought iron vase by Edgar Brandt and Daum, Nancy.

architects, who needed metal fixtures for private houses and hotels. Brandt never lost that willingness to work with others, and his best work was almost always the result of direct collaboration. Many of his commissions demanded a highly developed sense of detail and the ability to work to a very strict set of limitations. At the same time as sets of monumental doors, or wrought iron staircases for the liners *Paris, Ile de France* and *Normandie*, Brandt would be designing more mundane work: grilles for indoor heating, radiator covers and other everyday objects. Some of his finest work was with the glass expert Antoine Daum. Standard lamps of great elegance came out of this partnership. The most famous lamp, the "Cobra", showed Brandt's genius at its most quirky, bizarre and stylish. In contrast to Art Nouveau, Art Deco used animal themes far more readily. The "Cobra" lamp is the most powerful and vibrant of Brandt's creations. Brandt has caught and frozen the image at its highest point of potential. The snake is ready to lunge forward and strike; its head and coiled body cradle the alabaster shade. Stylistically and technically, Brandt continually invented and reinvented his ideas. The "Cobra" lamp was almost only possible as a structure because of the malleability and strength of bronze; in wood, or other materials, the snake would have been unable to support its

RIGHT Chrome hatstand in the shape of a woman's head by the Italian designer Bazzi. Note the contemporary, marcel-waved hairstyle which fixes it irrevocably in the 1930s era.

CENTRE RIGHT Elevator door of the Chrysler Building, by William van Alen, the most distinctively Art Deco of the New York skyscrapers. Recently threatened with destruction, the building has passed through several hands, including those of a religious cult, but is now the subject of a preservation order.

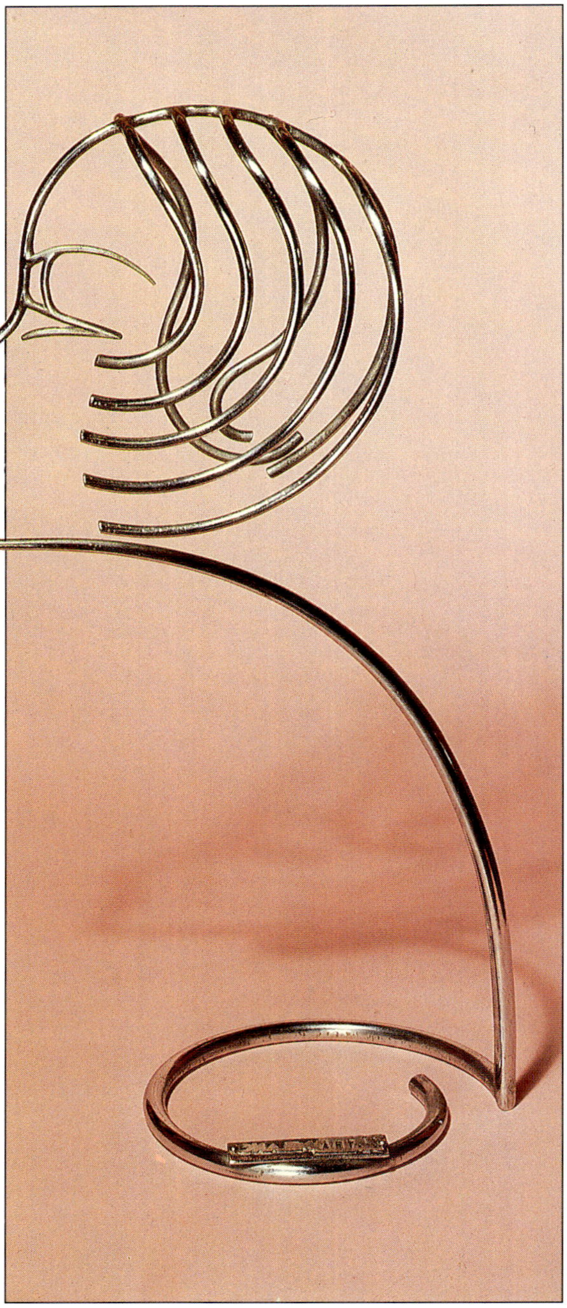

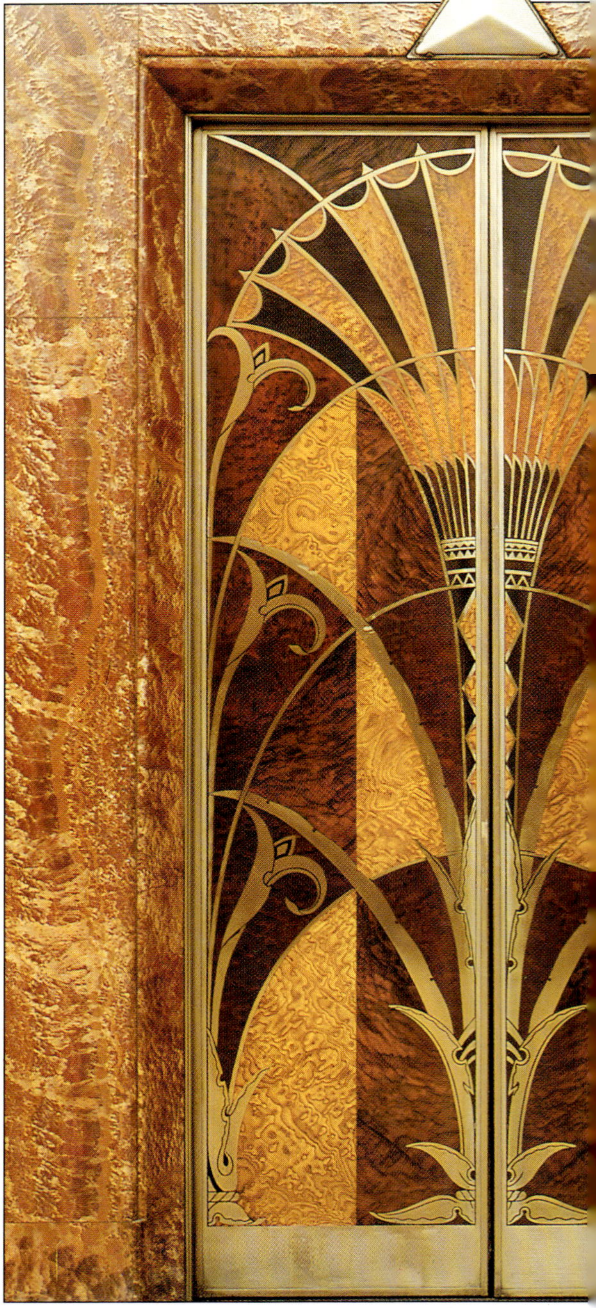

own weight, let alone that of the shade. In the same way, Brandt exploited the tensile strengths of the material he used when designing furniture. Console tables, instead of standing solidly on four squat legs, could be treated more as open sculptures. Legs could be opened out with delicate filigree mouldings of fans and thistles filling the gaps, yet still have enough strength to support the heavy weight of a thick slab of marble. Fire screens and doors could be reinterpreted to look almost like drawings suspended in air. Curling lines and leaves in door fronts seemed exquisitely delicate but had a strength and solidity fit for the purpose. Brandt also collaborated with Henri Favier on a series of screens for which he provided the framework.

Although Brandt was clearly the leader of the more traditional metal workers, men like Subes, Adnet, Kiss, Rateau, and Szabo produced work of great beauty. The most eccentric of this group by far was Armand Albert Rateau. He constructed a bronze chaise longue for Jeanne Lanvin's boudoir

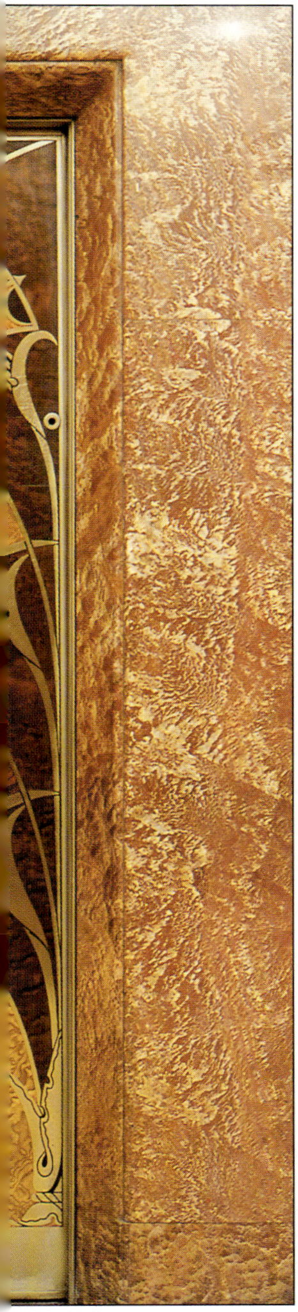

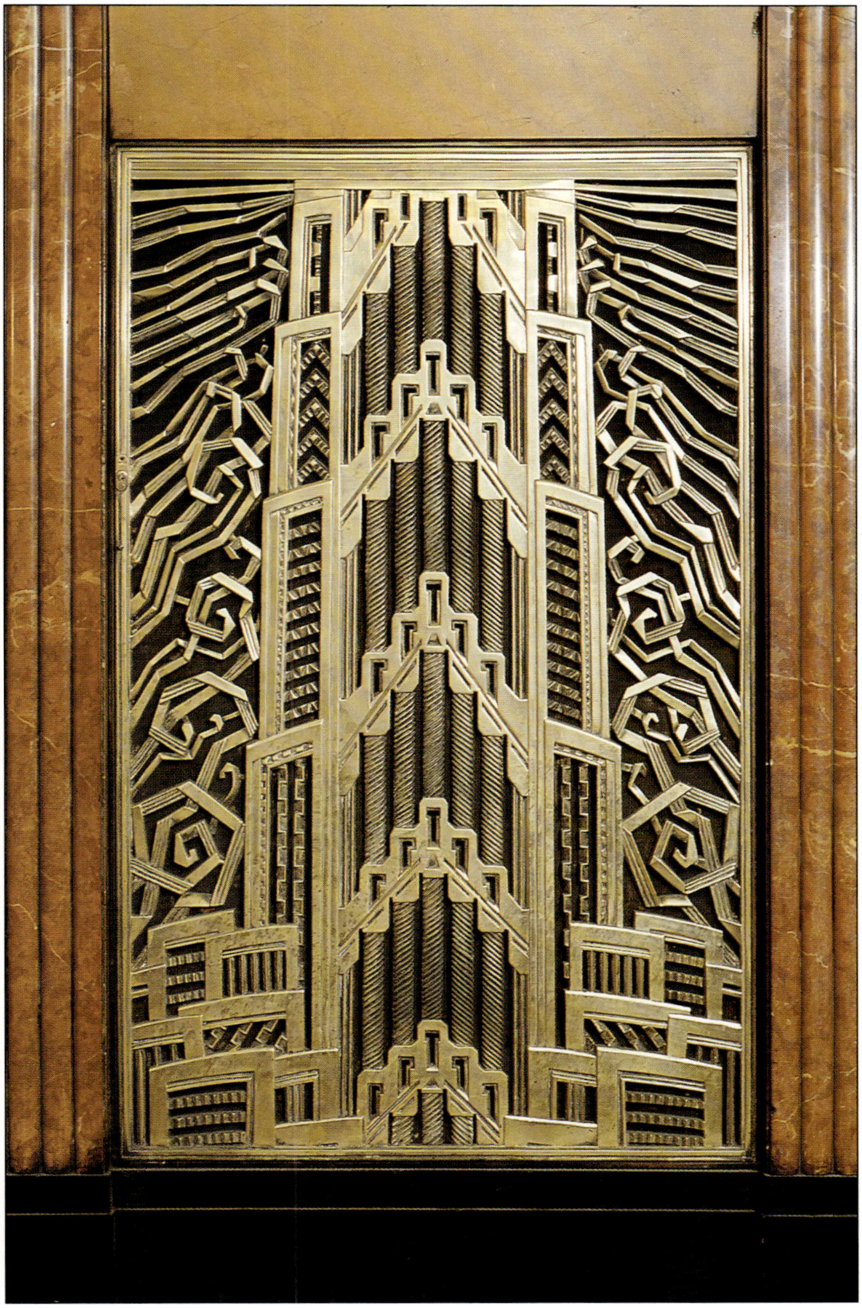

LEFT Radiator grille reproducing the exterior of the building in brass by Jacques Delamane, for the Chanin Building, New York, 1929.

that rested, almost comically, on the backs of four deer. A washstand and mirror was modelled from two peacocks standing back to back, their two heads holding the mirror. With metal, anything was possible, but the bizarre examples of Rateau were way out of keeping with the clean and practical furniture of Le Corbusier or the Irish designer Eileen Gray.

Elegance was not just the domain of the intricate foliage of a Brandt screen, a Kiss cabinet, or a Subes mantelpiece clock: it could be seen to even greater effect in an oak table top supported by just two sheets of bent metal by Louis Sognot. It was minimal, reduced to the contrast between the two materials used; the shiny cold metal, and the rich patina and grain of the wood.

The battle between a revamped French traditional approach to metalwork and the modernist tendency was short-lived. It started and finished with Art Deco, which, for a brief moment, managed to contain both opposing forces. The modernists, however, won the day.

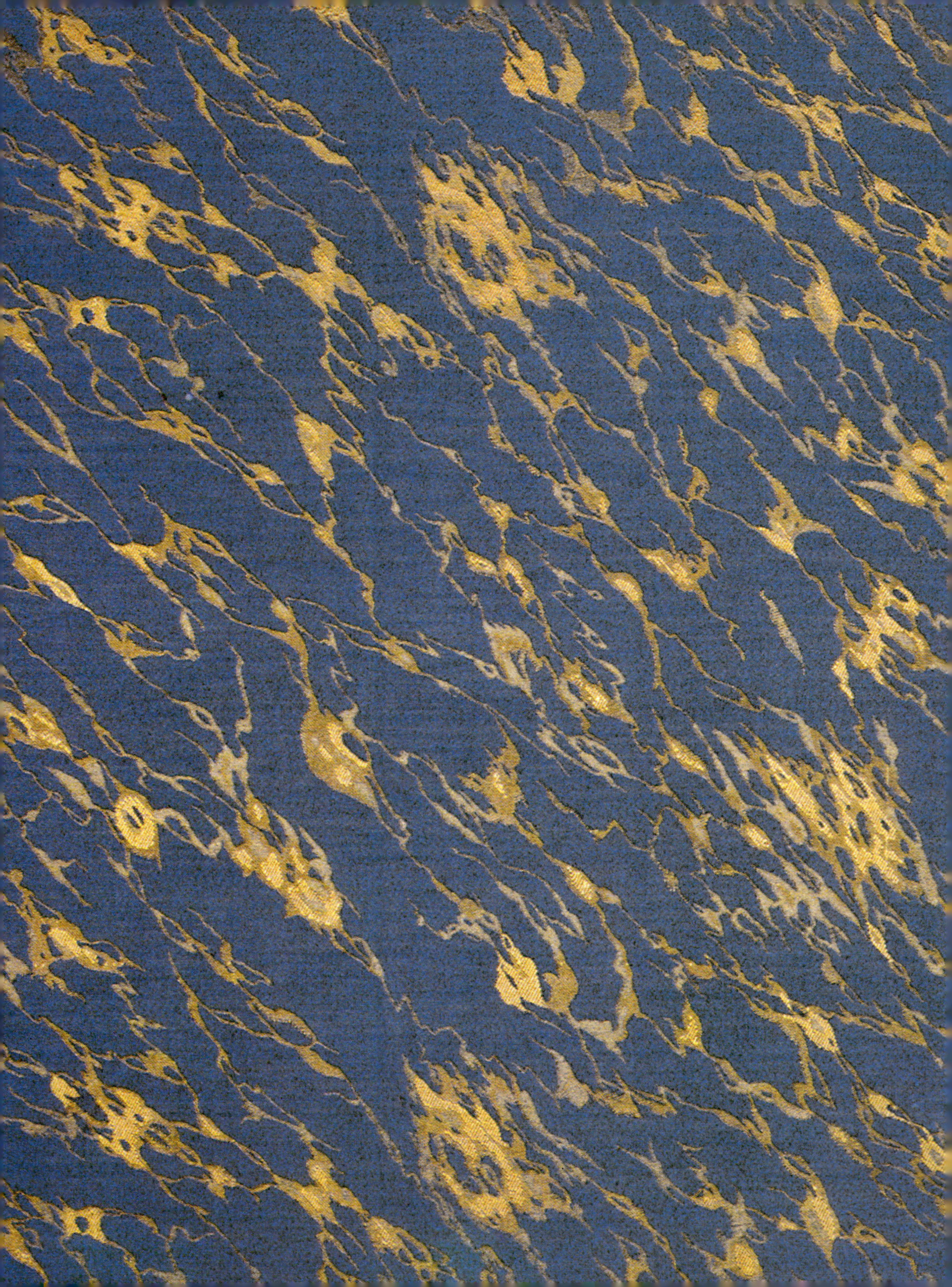

CHAPTER SIX

TABLEWARE, CERAMICS AND GLASS

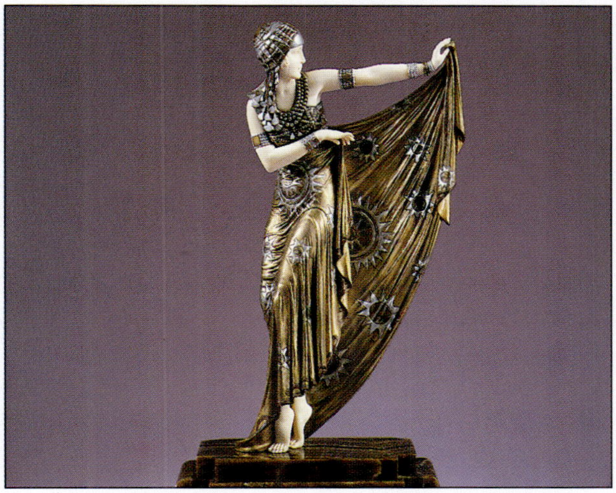

'Sunburst' by Demetre Chiparus in cold painted bronze and ivory. The sun symbol is often used in Art Deco design, and here sits boldly on the sheet of drapery falling from the woman's outstretched arm.

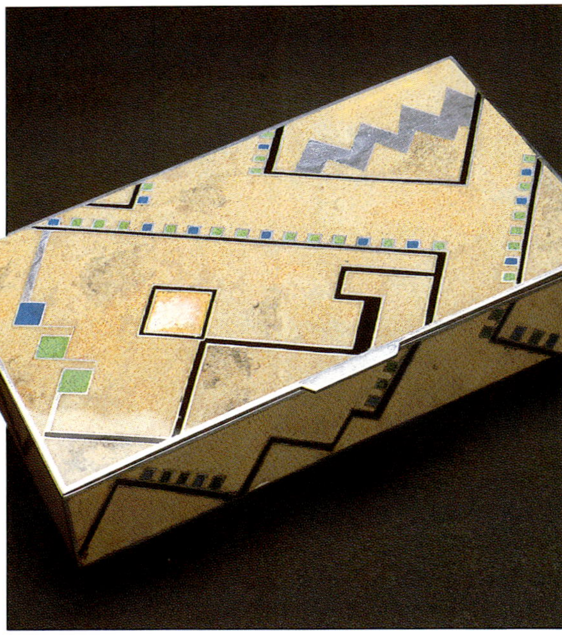

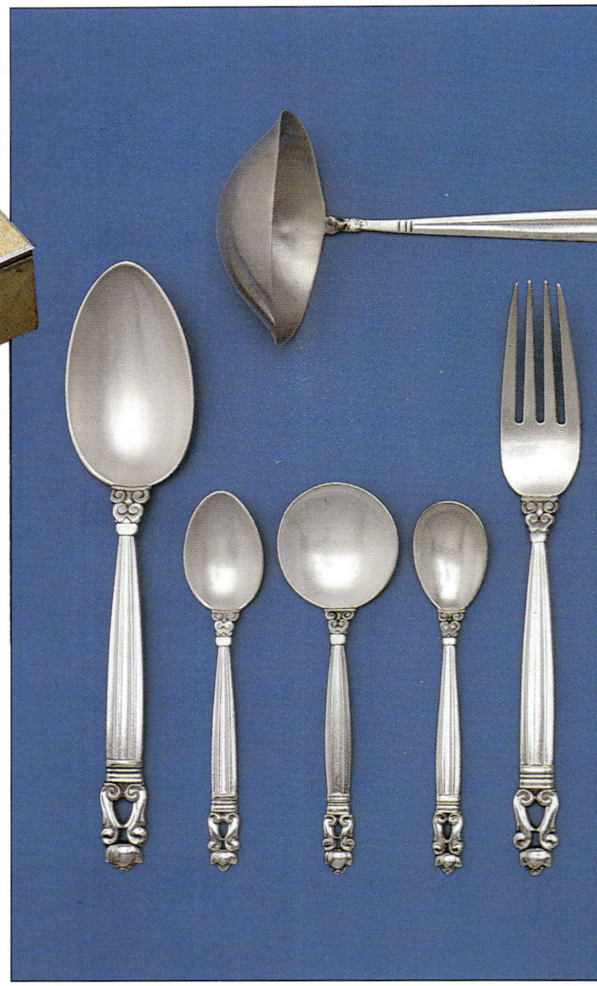

RIGHT A delicate enamelled silver box produced in 1928 by the master Jean Goulden, combines elements of Russian constructivism and French abstract art. The lustre of enamel works particularly well with the sharp and snappy demarcation lines inset in silver.

CENTRE Designed in 1915 by Johan Rohde, this 180-piece 'Acorn' pattern table service was manufactured by the Danish firm of Georg Jensen based in Copenhagen, proving that not all good things or even the best designs originate in France.

Tableware and objets d'art in the Art Deco style were designed for a far larger market than its furniture or high-class metalwork could hope to reach. Tableware consists of tea or coffee services, dishes, salt-cellars and cutlery (flatware), while objets d'art include clocks, ornaments, statuettes, boxes, candlesticks, ice buckets, cocktail shakers, some vases, ashtrays, fans, travelling sets, vanity cases, table lamps and scent bottles.

If any single area of Art Deco could be said to have been responsible for the spreading of the style, then the honours should go to objets d'art. Today, these everyday items can still be found in flea markets and antique fairs, and at a price that does not involve notifying the bank manager in advance. Art Deco ashtrays, pin-boxes and powder compacts were produced in their hundreds of thousands. Ten years ago, these items were deemed almost worthless; even now they are well within the range of all amateur collectors. One of the main reasons for this is mass production, but it also has a great deal to do with the materials that were used.

The 1930s, in particular, saw the emergence of new materials like Bakelite, Vitrolite, Vitroflex, urea formaldehyde, phenolic resin and other plastics. Cheap and manmade, these had a flexibility which particularly suited them to the small everyday object. Later forms of plastics had the added advantage that they were no longer brittle, and were thus almost unbreakable. This is why so much has survived.

A further reason for their proliferation in Art Deco style was the novelty of the material. Initially, manufacturers were worried about their use for such consumer items as food and cosmetics containers; but, as soon as fears proved unfounded, whole industries turned toward their use. Mass production and the use of innovative designers do not always go hand in hand. What happened was that plastics producers merely copied the style of the day, taking its designs second hand. Purists would say that examples of such mass production were clearly second rate, but it is because of these applications that Art Deco became available to all. This is why it became such a universal style. Design, it must be remembered, is not necessarily debased by multiplication. Moreover, within the area of the plastic or resin pieces, there are oddities that are original in themselves, yet are typical, encapsulating the period. The "Tennis Ball"

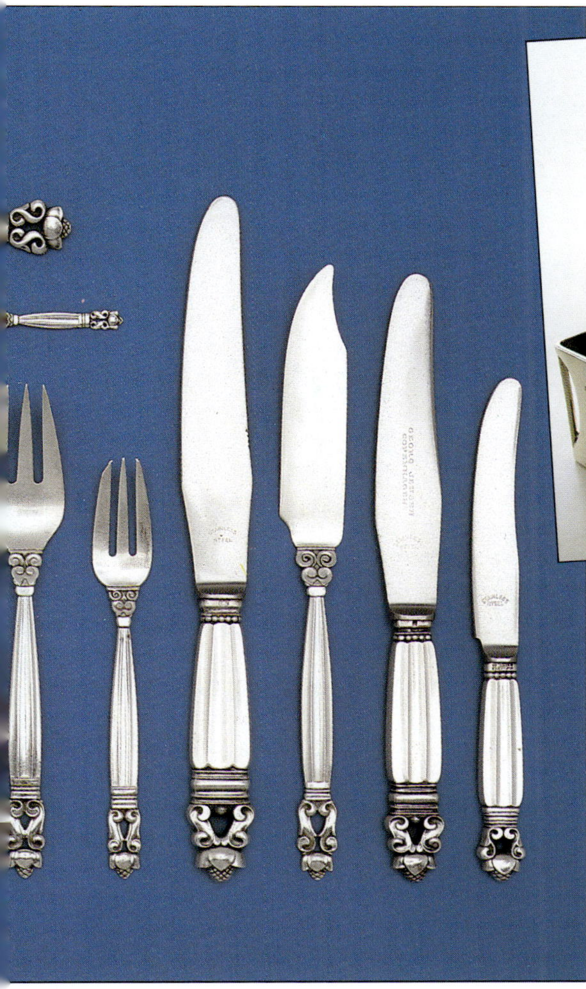

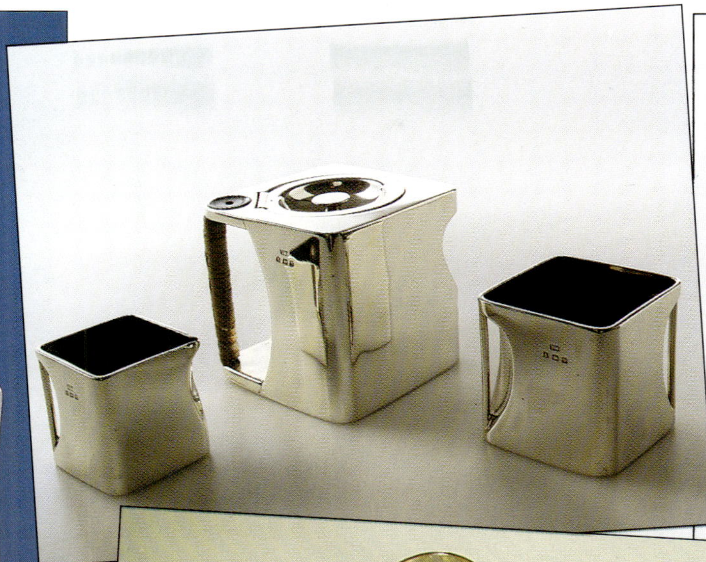

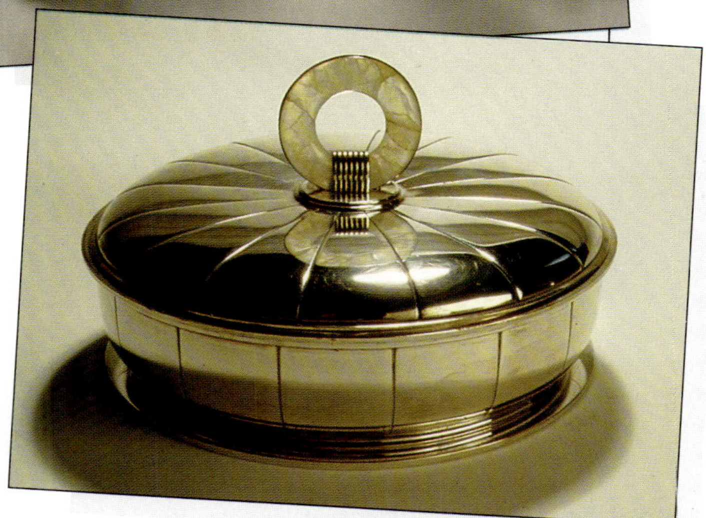

LEFT Stylish but somehow impractical cubist tea set in silver from the 1930s.

BELOW LEFT A 1925 simple and stylish silver dish by Jean Puiforcat.

ashtray, made for the Dunlop company from phenolic resin with a lead weight insert in the base, is both witty and practical. Plastic allowed for the invention and production of many such items which are both tacky and vulgar that are representative of the humour of the time. Not necessarily beautiful, or crafted to a superb finish, they are unmistakably Art Deco. Plastic has become so much *the* material of the second half of the 20th century, used for anything from car bumpers to furniture, that it is forgotten that there is a history of style revealed in its uses. Deco began it all.

While the potential of plastics was explored for household objects, luxury materials were used in display items and ornaments. Perhaps the most representative of the luxury items were the Chryselephantine statuettes by artists like Gerdago, Otto Poerzl, Josef Lorenzl, Alexandre Kelety, Demetre Chiparus, and the master of them all, Ferdinand Preiss. Derived from the Greek, 'Chryselephantine' was used to describe a sculpture of gold and ivory. What it meant in Art Deco terms was the combination of many different materials, including not only gold and ivory, but tortoiseshell, lacquerwork, silver and bronze.

The production of these sculptures was not a Parisian monopoly. Ferdinand Preiss set up his partnership with Arthur Kessler in Berlin, and was well enough known. and collected, to work from Germany. His most famous series of sculptures is on the theme of dance. Usually made from cold-painted bronze with tinted ivory, the dancers are little masterpieces of their type. Titles like *Flame Leaper, Charleston Dancer, Autumn Dancer* and *Con Brio*, reveal Preiss's interest both in contemporary dance and sculpture as a vehicle for his talent to depict the female form in action. Semi-erotic, the dancers are elegantly frozen in mid-flight. In these turning hips and shoulders, outstretched arms, figures on

RIGHT 'The Archer' by Ferdinand Preiss in bronze and ivory. The amazonian yet androgynous quality and pose of this updated classical figure is a perfect excuse for showing off technical virtuosity.

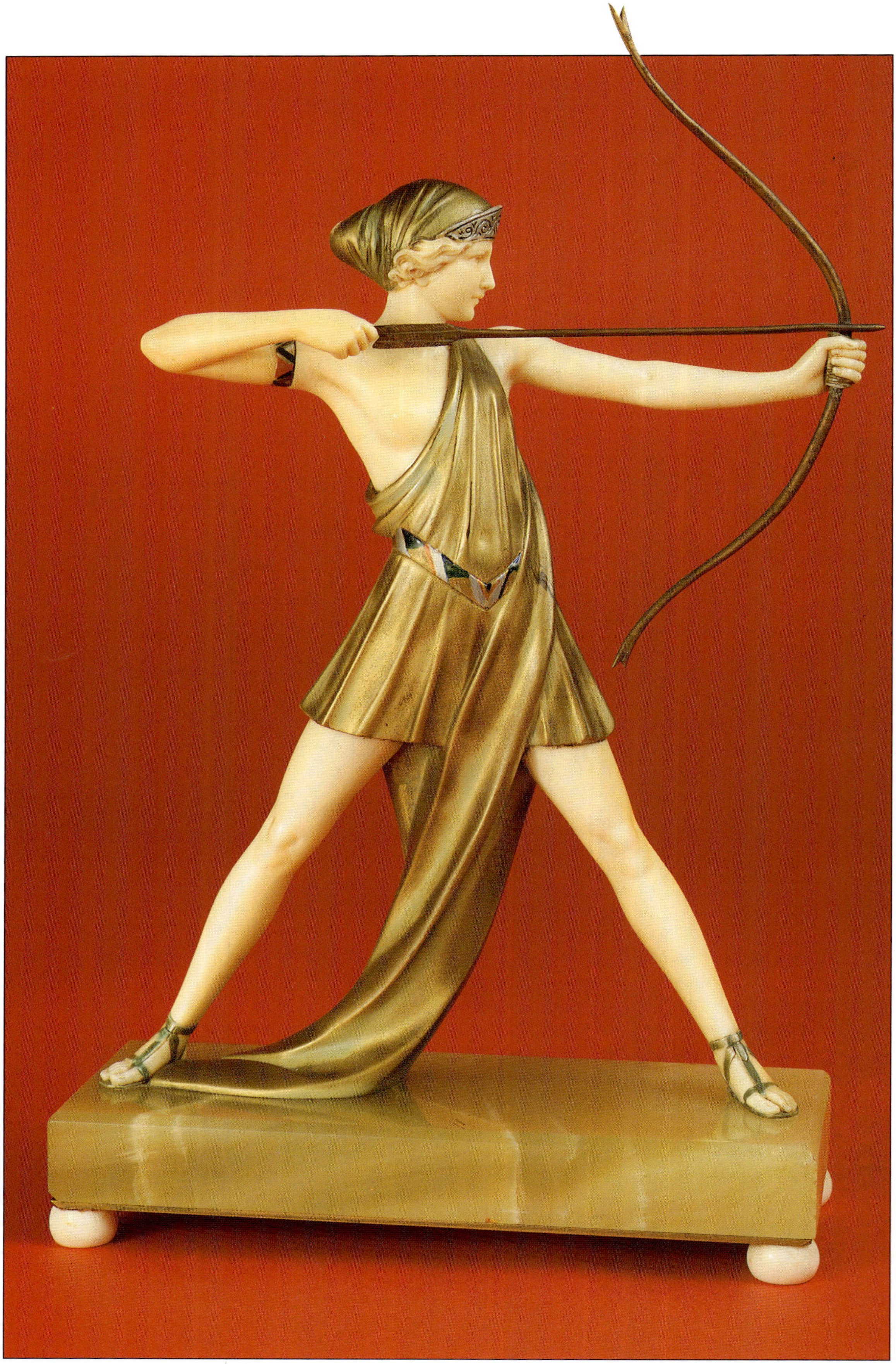

their tip-toes. Preiss used a wealth of new forms that are far distanced from the poses of classical sculpture. The rapt, faraway gaze of these dancers also creates a sense of distance: haughty goddesses so gracefully prancing through their exercises; and Preiss statuettes, as much as any item of fashion, reveal, on idealized figures, the dress that was typical of the day.

Gerdago, Chiparus, Kelety, Lorenzl and Poerzl all distinguished themselves by reinterpreting the female muse, as Preiss had done. Demetre Chiparus, a Rumanian who had settled in Paris, concentrated more on the costume of the dancer. Extending themselves in balletic poses, Chiparus dancers were often covered from head to toe in exotic finery. Using the bronze patina technique, he gave his dancers a far greater sense of texture than those of Preiss. Exotic costumes and poses reflected the great interest that the Ballets Russes provided for designers and craftsman alike. Their sculptures could be theatrical, modern, reflecting what was in vogue, but they did not need to concern themselves with the banalities of everyday life. They were exquisite pieces of escapism that, though not cheap, sold in large quantities in the more select shops in Paris, London, Berlin and New York. Sometimes the work of Kelety or Lorenzl might sink to the level of chocolate box lids, but the craftsmanship could not be faulted. The work of Bruno Zach verged even closer to the level of vulgar camp. The sculptures and statuettes of Art Deco are often misunderstood, because they are judged against serious sculpture that demands rigorous critical standards. These light, entertaining pieces never pretended to be any more or less than that.

In the application of Art Deco to mantelpiece clocks, the craftsman/designer was free to produce objects both entirely functional and as elitist as he wished. There could be no criticism, except in stylistic terms, of rounded off or stepped clocks that hinted at Aztec influences made from the uninspiring, yet immensely useful, phenolic resin. They shared much with the designs for the first wireless sets. Built to contain the latest in technological design, the cases for the radios now look curiously antiquated. Of course they had to be solid and robust to house the valves (tubes) which warmed up slowly, and became very hot. Consequently they also needed ventilation. The design often resembles a car radiator, but that is hardly surprising when car design was developing along parallel lines. If radiators and radios often had those heavy, curved edges that look like comic-strip speed-lines, or force-lines, the designs for electric clocks were more inventive. Flat diamonds or lozenges of brushed steel, with only the hour and minute hand disturbing the reflective beauty, were the very latest in clock design. A clock could also be traditionally round in chromed brass, set on a metal base like a vanity mirror. Perhaps the most typical clocks of the period were those made from stepped marble blocks, surmounted by a reclining nude by a sculptor like Preiss. Using cheap materials, a mass market could be reached; but there were still craftsmen and silversmiths such as Georg Jensen and Albert Cheuret who refused to accept loss of quality, and produced clock designs of distinctive beauty.

Another technique that was used in the 1920s and 30s was the making of vases in beaten copper. Once the copper had been laboriously hand-hammered, it could be decorated with enamel, painted, etched, or left plain. The master of this technique was Jean Dunand, who also created the decorative lacquerwork screens for the *Normandie*. One of his vases employed the

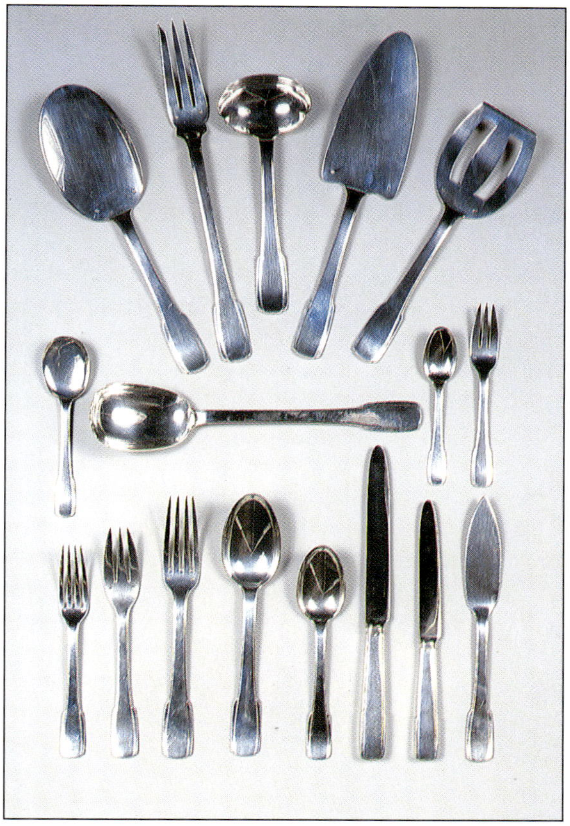

LEFT Examples from a discreetly designed, understated and highly functional silver cutlery service by the Art Deco genius Jean Puiforcat.

RIGHT A selection of table objects in the latest synthetics: Open-and-close cigarette dispenser in Bakelite by Rolinx Products, England; Bakelite inkwell in the form of an elephant's head by Gummon. On the far right is a two-piece box in Bakelite. The fan-edge motif is typical of Art Deco, and was applied to automobiles, household objects and even buildings. The three Bakelite ashtrays in the foreground were all designed specifically for use on the luxury liner the R.M.S. Queen Mary.

device of snakes wriggling up its side, reminiscent of Edgar Brandt's interest in the motif. Dunand could switch from the realistic and the natural to the completely abstract with relative ease and a high degree of success. Even at their most abstract, Dunand's vases looked Grecian, Etruscan, or Oriental; enveloped by rich patterns, they ignored modern austerity.

Where the modern austerity and the new clean line came into its own was with the art of the silversmith. Since the invention of silverplating in the mid-19th century, the required look could be achieved for a less discerning audience at a more attractive price. Apart from the advantage that electroplating gave to the trade, high quality silverwork is a skill that seems never to have suffered, especially as the demand for jewellery has always kept the craft alive. The greatest of all the silversmiths was Jean Puiforcat who, along with Ruhlmann and Lalique, will be remembered not just as a practitioner of the Art Deco style, but as a true master of his respective crafts. Puiforcat, Georg Jensen, the Danish silversmith, and the American Kem Weber, each in their own way, extended the craft of silversmithing, and the language of Art Deco.

Puiforcat learnt his trade at his father's workshop; through Art Nouveau on to Art Deco, he rapidly outgrew him. The precursors to Puiforcat's mature style were Josef Hoffmann and the other members of the Wiener Werkstätte. He adopted their example of radical austerity and perfected it into a new sensuous simplicity. After having seen the beauty and lustre of a plain sheet of silver, it is difficult to imagine that anything could improve it. Puiforcat recognized this, but also saw that the minimum of sophisticated detailing in another element could enhance the material's outstanding beauty through the power of contrast. The best examples of this were also the most minimal. Puiforcat produced dish after dish that was highlighted just by thick ivory handles, an ebony knob, or a ring-pull made from pale jade. The result was luxurious, made doubly so by the fact that the materials themselves that seemed to do all the work; only seemed, because it was Puiforcat's inherent sense of the correctness of form that made it all possible. He was not just a craftsman but also a highly sensitive aesthete; he believed that, ultimately, some forms are right and others wrong. With his work it is possible to sense that he, above all the other contemporary designers, came the closest to that elusive goal.

Other important craftsmen in silver were promoted in Paris by Christofle goldsmiths, who encouraged, among others, the talents of Cazes, and Süe, of the Süe et Mare workshops. Two outstanding examples in particular are the ice-bucket and champagne cooler modelled by Luc Lanel for the *Normandie*. They are not only superbly functional; they are, quite simply, right.

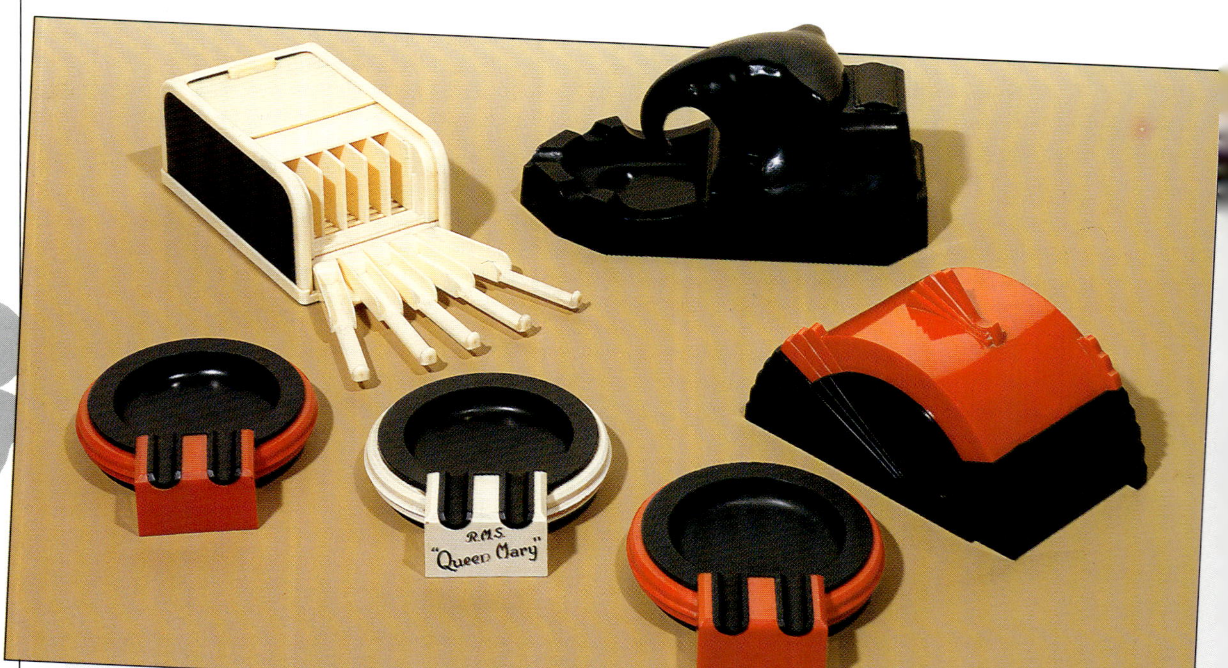

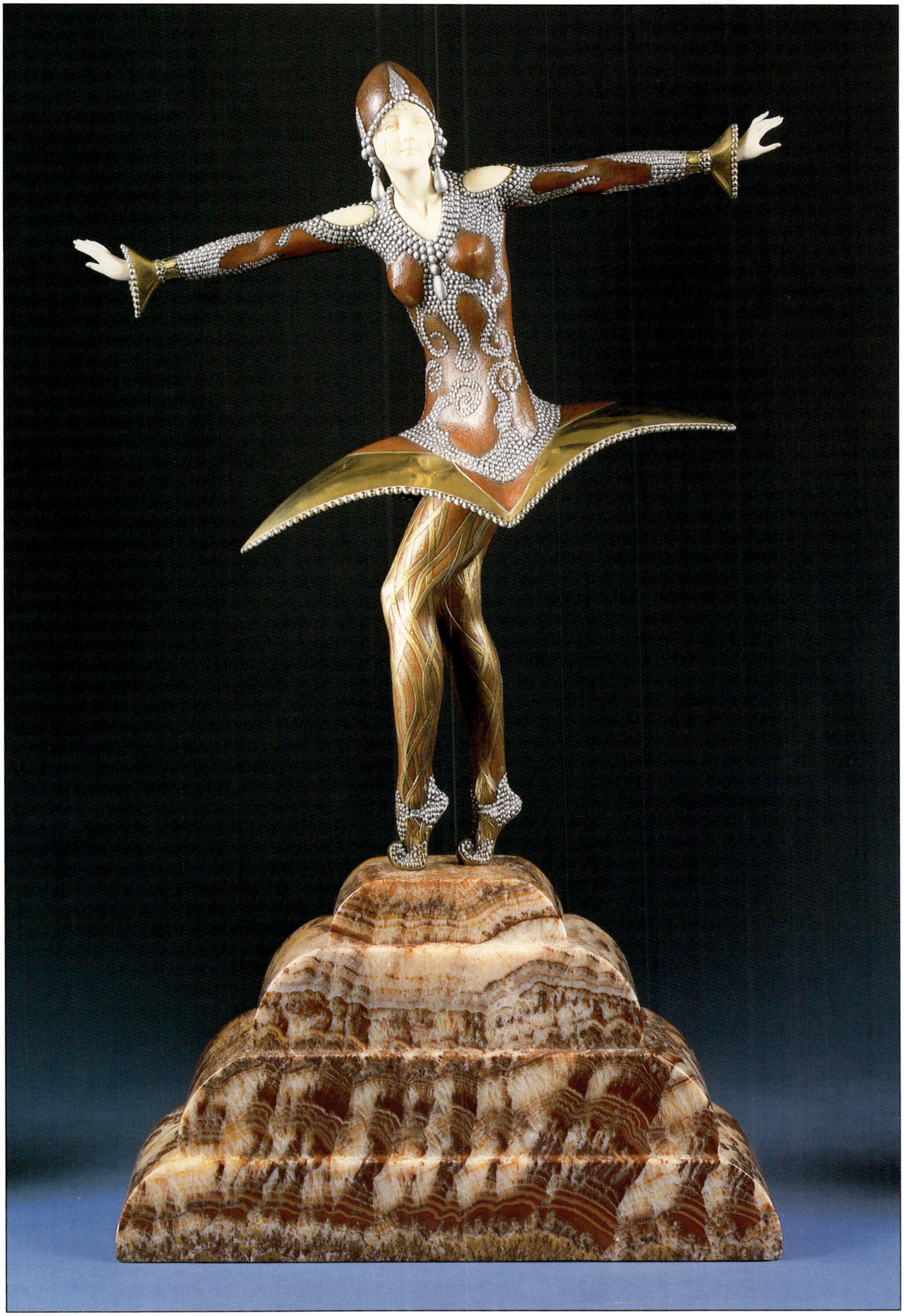

CHAPTER 6

LEFT 'Kora' a gilt and cold painted bronze and ivory figure of an exotic dancer by Demetre Chiparus. His speciality was the heavily-worked detailing of costume that this figure so aptly reveals.

RIGHT Art Deco clock from the firm of Van Cleef and Arpels, Paris. The Japanese temple design is a fine example of 20th century japonaiserie.

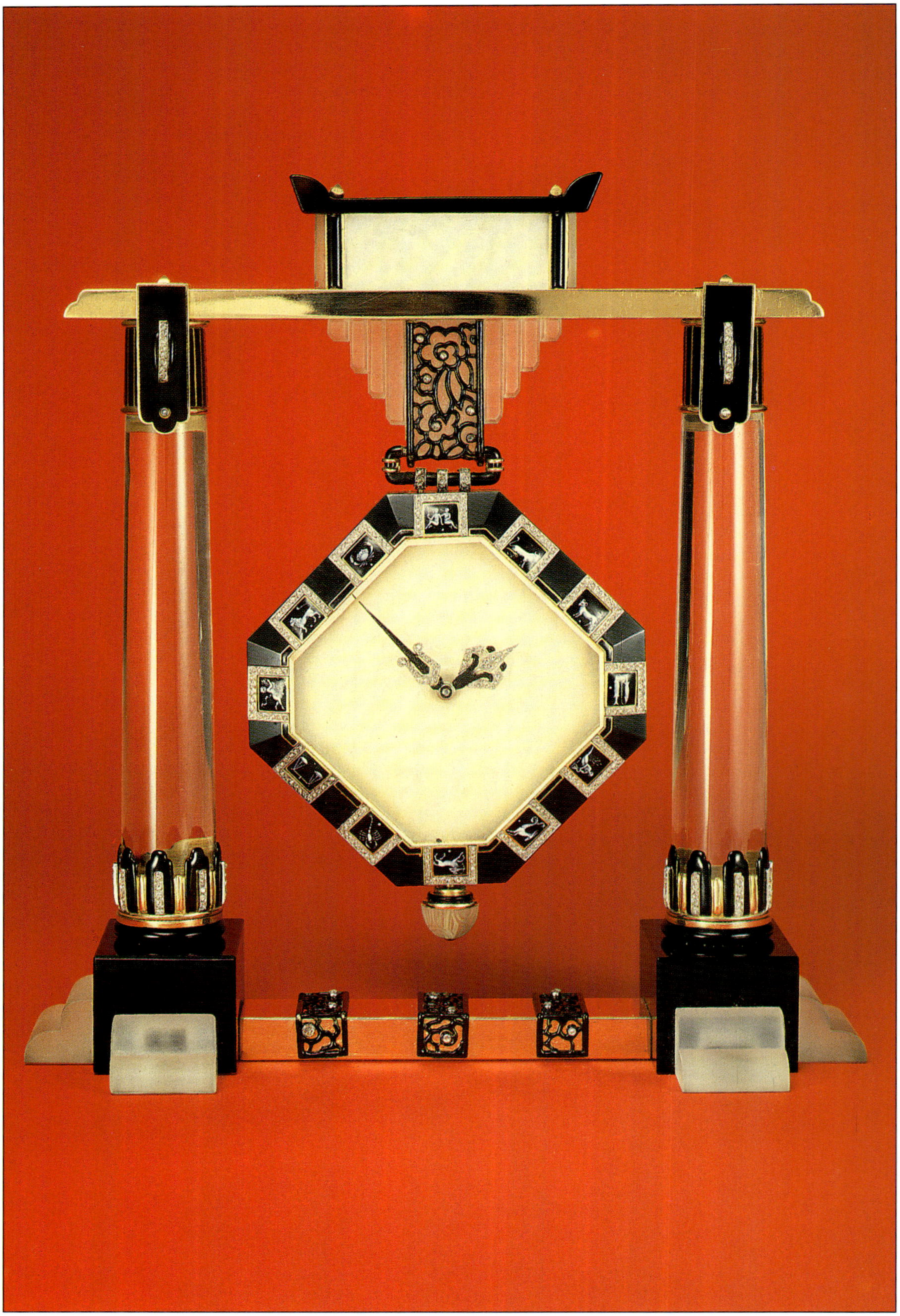

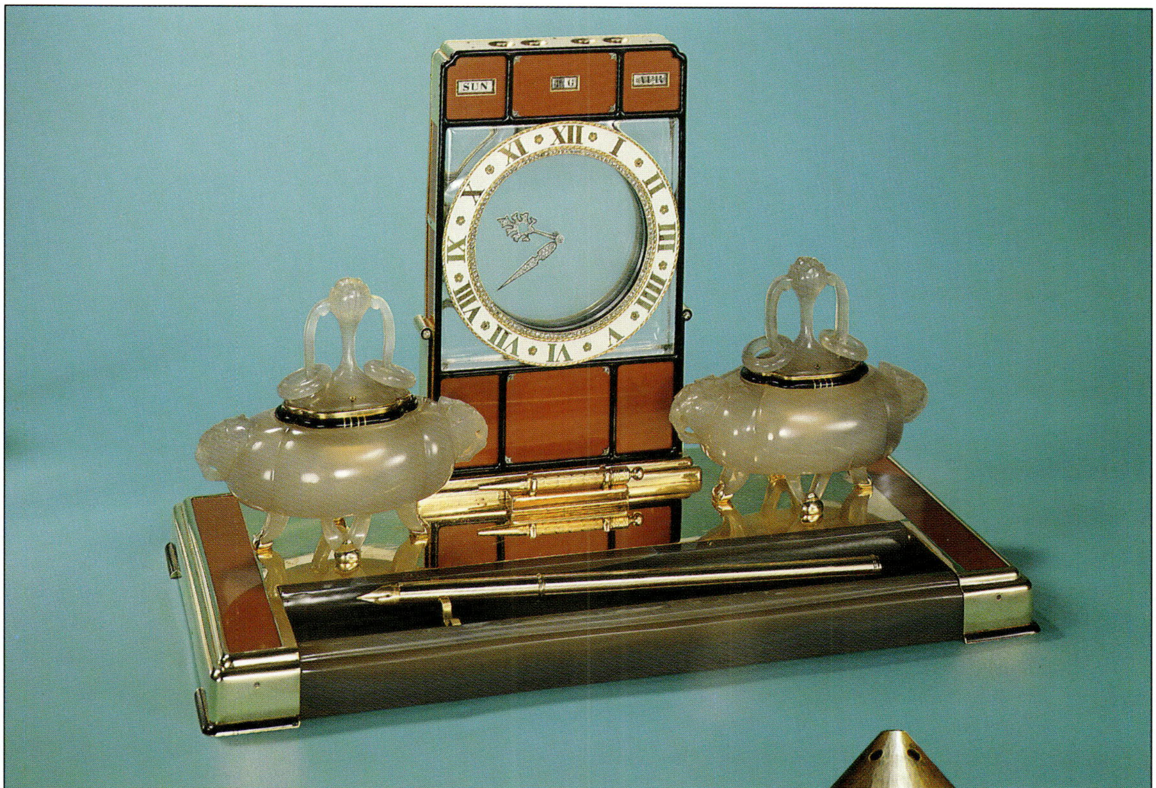

LEFT This 1925 Cartier desk set, mystery clock and calendar on the elephant theme uses jewelled agate, rock crystal, enamel and gold.

BELOW FAR LEFT Lacquered metal bowl dated 1925, by Jean Dunand.

BELOW LEFT Lampshade with beaten metal vase base by Jean Dunand.

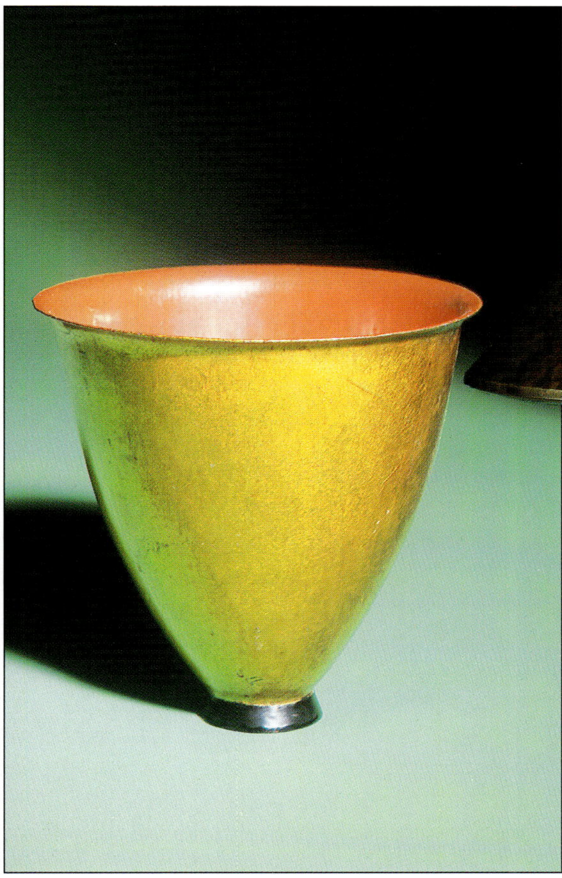

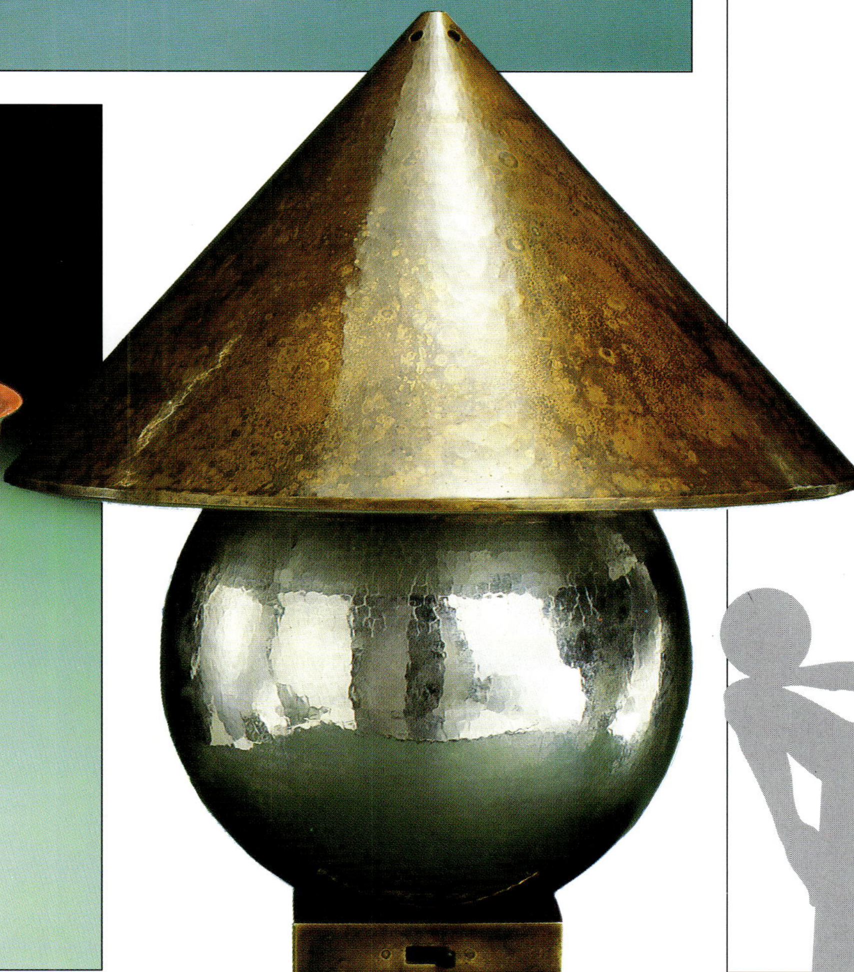

RIGHT Terracotta cup designed by the English craftsman Keith Murray for Wedgwood & Sons in 1935. A pale blue outer glaze is accentuated by the four sets of indented bands that pick out the cream-coloured interior of the cup.

FAR RIGHT Porcelain Art Deco lamp designed by Henri Rapin for production by the Sèvres porcelain works.

BELOW RIGHT Saxbo stoneware vase, c. 1930 from Denmark. The oriental inspiration is evident in the shape and glazing. The return to simple, almost crude, craft pottery was as evident in Scandinavia as it was in Great Britain.

CERAMICS

Of all the applications of Art Deco, ceramics was without a doubt the most widespread. Every country had a pottery or porcelain factory and workshops that at some time in the 1920s or '30s employed some variation on the Art Deco style. The ceramics' place in society had long been central to the question of what role art should play in relation to industry. Apart from the rare instances of studio potters adapting the style, ceramic design was usually an automatic transformation of a design into a mass marketable product. Of course there would always be expensive porcelain statuettes, but even these need not be limited to numbered editions. The production of ceramics, porcelain and plaster models was as vast as it was various. Each country developed its own adaptation of the style and its own speciality.

It may have been that the material qualities of pottery and ceramics were not particularly suited to Art Deco's more rectilinear tendencies, but solutions were quickly found. More often than not, the basic shape of plates, vases, cups and saucers, was left alone. The undecorated object could then be used like an artist's canvas, and novel decorations could be painted or stencilled on. The blank, creamy, off-white surface was an ideal starting point, and for some designers was almost an end in itself.

What manufacturers had discovered of particular significance was that dinner and tea services were as essential to the Art Deco look required by their clients as furniture, glass, clothes, wireless sets, and jewellery. They had to keep up with the changing taste, so that they could provide another addition to the entire Art Deco environment. A set of Clarice Cliff "Bizarre" ware would look as out of place in a Louis Seize room as a Delft Blue plate or Wedgwood tea service would look on an Eileen Gray sidetable. With the ability to transfer design after design onto the same basic form they had always used, the ceramics industry was able to change over to new designs in a matter of weeks, if necessary.

The scale of the ceramics industry in Weimar Germany has already been discussed. In the 1920s a new development in taste had evolved. In 1930, the Berlin State Porcelain Factory held an exhibition in order to discover the preferences of the public. Of the 150 designs from all periods on display the two most popular were plain white pieces. The love of simplicity in Germany may have been out of keeping with the rest of Europe and America, but it was clearly indicative of a trend. The growth of interest in non-Western art forms also had repercussions for the ceramics industry. Examples of Ming porcelain from China and Japanese ceramics had become appreciated for its no-nonsense simplicity, its unique finish. This attitude, when it prevailed, scraped the creative palette back to virtually nothing, and the designer could start all over again, becoming either heavily decorative like Clarice Cliff, or pure and elemental.

The most interesting development of all in modern ceramic design took place in post-revolutionary Russia. Only two months after the Revolution the State Porcelain factory was reorganised completely in order to meet the new requirements of the people. The designer S V Chekhonin played a central part in the renaissance of Russian ceramics, helping to plan the new State works. Not even the most simple and homely of objects could be ignored, as far as its importance to the people was concerned. Even *Pravda*, the communist party newspaper, organized questionnaires on the lines of "What do we require from a plate?" The state wanted all its artists to be involved in production of work that was useful to the masses. Artists of the stature of Tatlin, Puni, Malevich, Suetin and Chasnik readily became involved in meeting the demands of new design. A plate could be appreciated on aesthetic grounds, but it was also beautiful in a political sense. As crockery is something that almost everyone uses it could be adapted to carry a political message. Many of the motifs and symbols that were incorporated into the designs – the hammer and sickle, the cogwheel, the factory worker, the healthy, robust farmworker – suggested that advance could be achieved through hard work and allegiance to the doctrines of the Party. They were ideal propaganda vehicles. Following on from that idea, the concept of mass production was promoted wholeheartedly; design was to be spread as wide as possible, its success measured in part by its popularity. Far from being mass-produced junk, such work equalled French, Dutch and English Art Deco in quality and often surpassed them in its novelty.

Other centres of production around the cities of Moscow and Leningrad concentrated heavily on borrowing the new design ideas of Petrograd

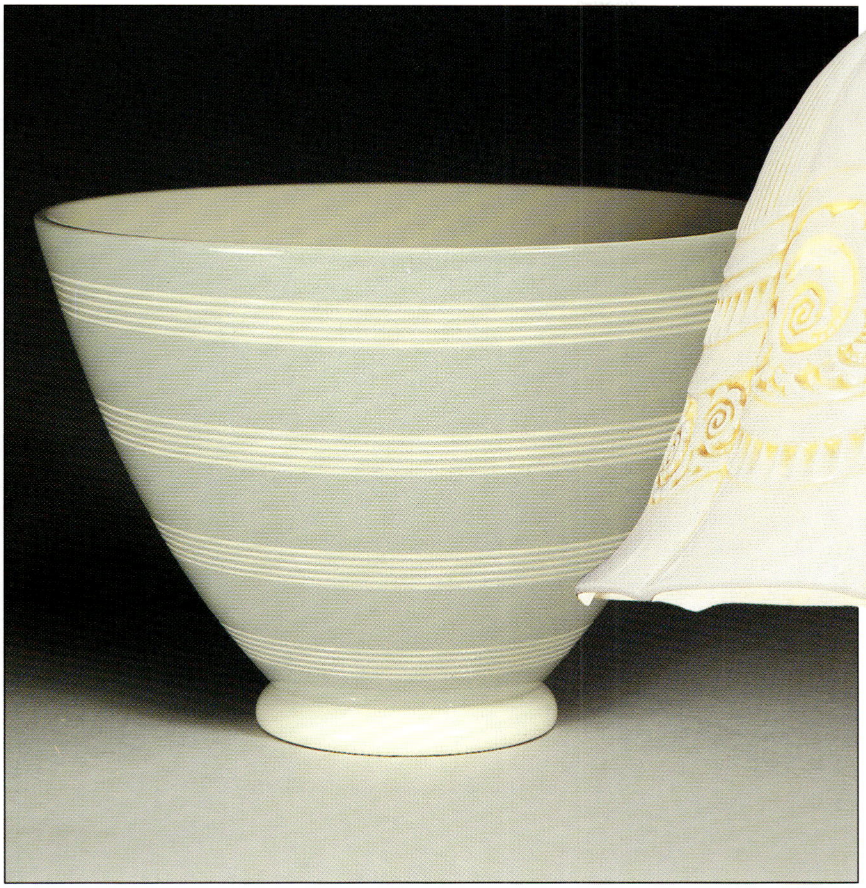

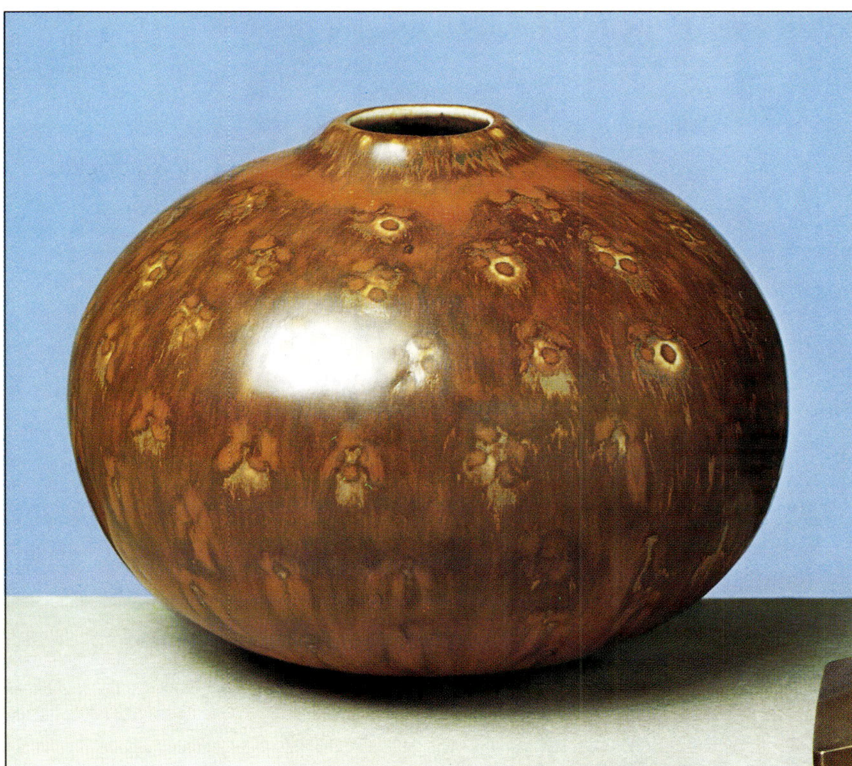

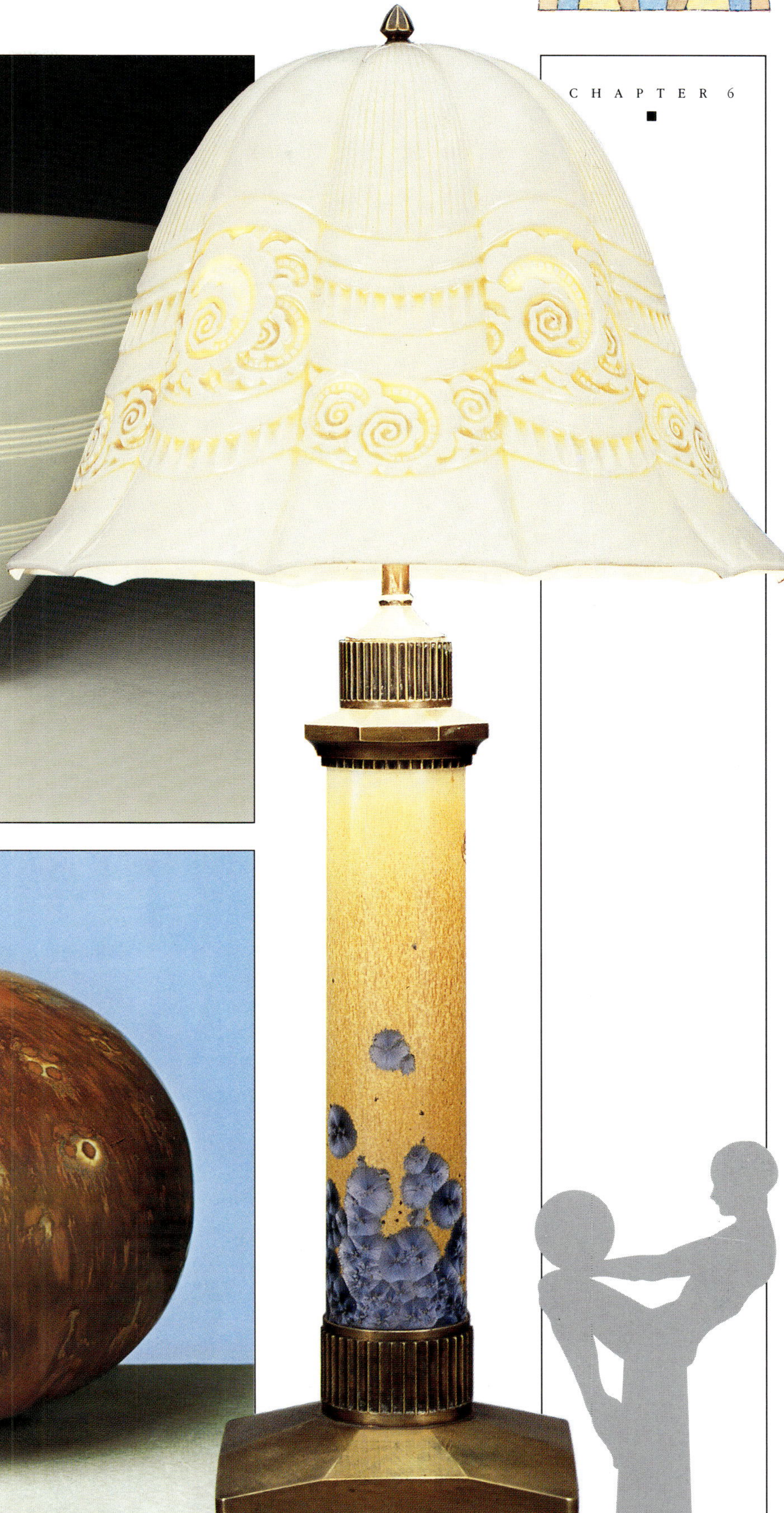

RIGHT A collection of the highly decorative pottery by Clarice Cliff.

BELOW RIGHT Gallé vase that replays the elephant theme so favoured by Deco designers.

and other experimental stations, and churned out vast quantities of plates and cups adorned with the new patterns. The success of the industry was very obvious at the stands in the Russian pavilion at the Exposition des Arts Décoratifs et Industriels. If it had been expected that the political situation in Russia would give rise to a dull uniformity, the opposite was true. Ceramics produced from the designs of the Suprematist group were radically inventive. Futurist vases were displayed that looked as exciting and revolutionary as a Boccione sculpture or Picasso's sculpture of the absinthe glass. Malevich had designed a tea cup that was cut in half and completely solid, thus technically useless. It was nevertheless a response to the questionnaires and discussions on the purpose of ceramics. In spirit, the Russians had come very close to the concerns of the French master Jean Puiforcat, who wished to produce articles that were platonic in their beauty, with an ideal simplicity and elegance. If the advances achieved in Russian industry were stimulated from the top downwards, in Europe the individual designer, working for a factory like Sèvres or Wedgwood, was as much in tune with the new spirit.

In France, the designers responsible for the new style were mainly Suzanne Lalique, the daughter of the glass expert René Lalique, René Buthaud, Jean Luce and Marcel Goupy. It was of course important that factories of the calibre of Sèvres and Limoges involved themselves actively in the new style, and yet again the large Paris stores provided the best outlet for the resulting work. René Buthaud was made the artistic director of the Printemps' Primavera studio works at Tours. Many of the designers mentioned previously in relation to furniture and metalwork also experimented in this medium. Sèvres, which had set up its *faïence* department in 1920, allowed Emile-Jacques Ruhlmann and Jean Dupas to carry out work for them. Another development was the rise in importance of porcelain statuettes and figurines. The advantage of porcelain was that it was particularly suited to creating cheap ornaments for a clientèle that could not afford, or did not appreciate, the finesse of work by Preiss or Gerdago. Ceramic figures also had a different quality to them. Smooth and glossy, they accentuated the glorious, sensual curves of aspects of Art Deco design. People could have a group of ornaments on the mantelpiece or in their display cabinets

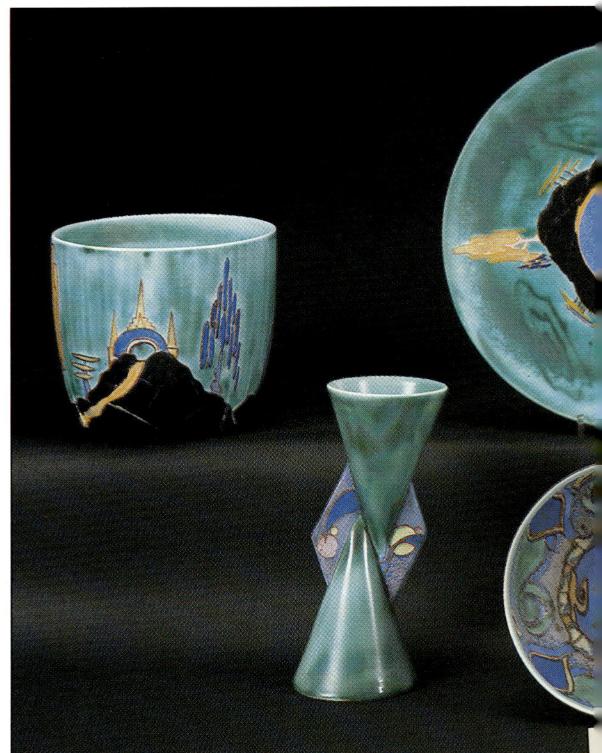

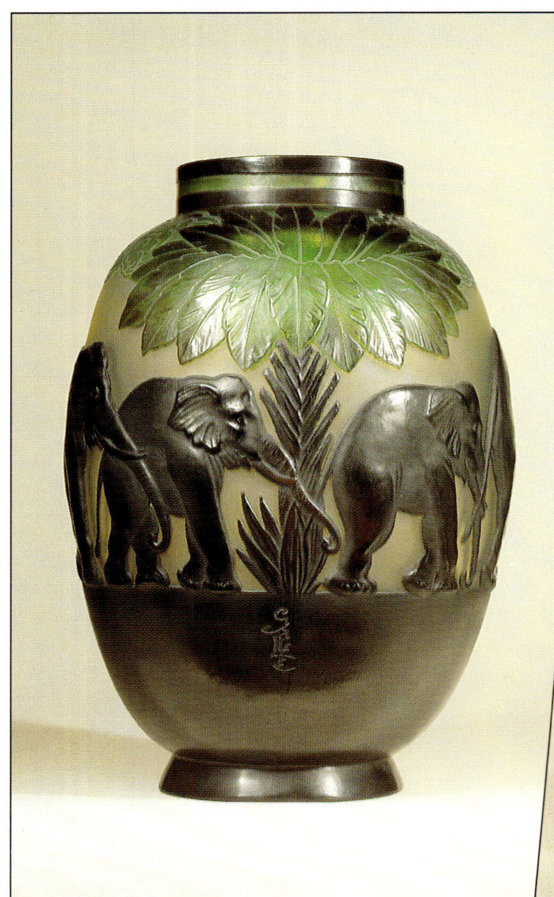

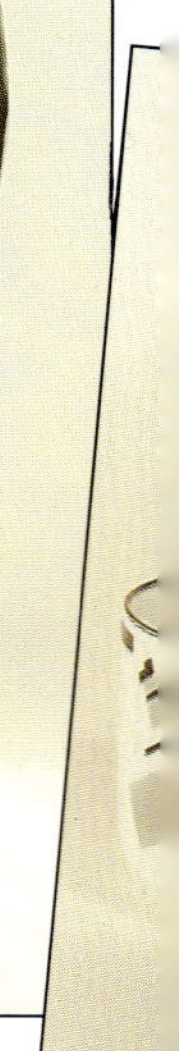

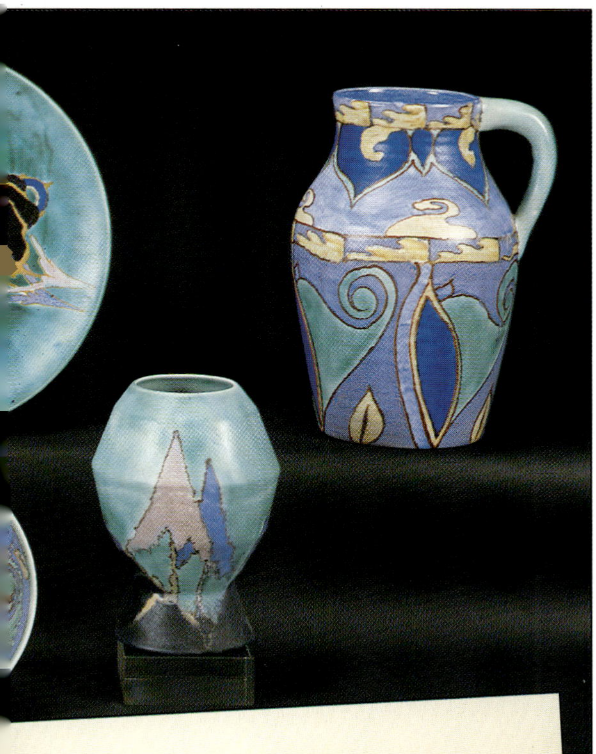

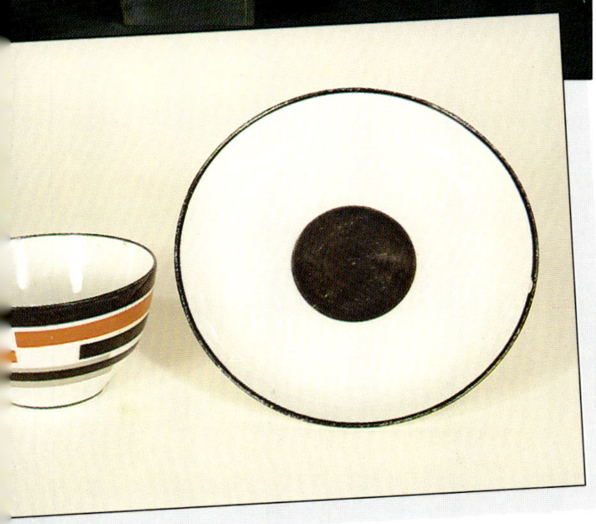

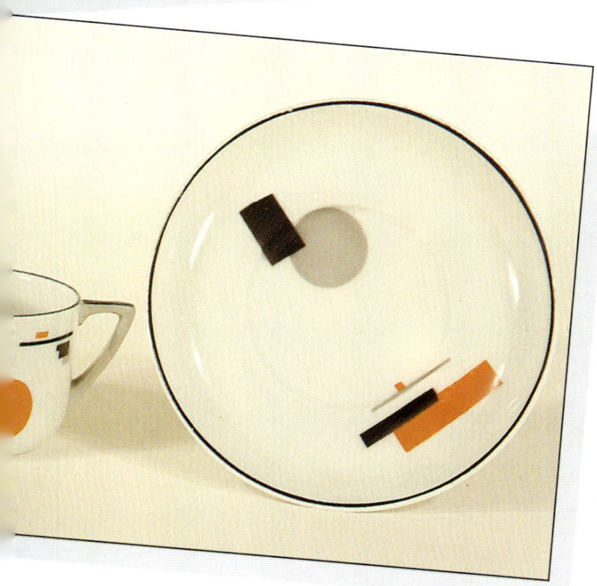

CENTRE LEFT Stark yet successful design for a porcelain cup and saucer by the Russian Ilya Chashnik.

BELOW LEFT Suprematist porcelain cup and saucer from Russia by the designer Nikolai Suetin.

for a fraction of the price of a one-off statuette in expensive materials like gold, bronze, ivory, or silver.

The more rectilinear tendency in Art Deco was also responsible for some novel, if not always successful, reinterpretations of established ideas about design of household objects. Teacups could be square, oval, conical – pretty well any shape that could contain liquid – teapots could be playfully disguised as motor cars, or have their spouts shaped like the prow of an ocean liner. A functional object could be ornamental as well. They were, and still are, delightful objects to have around.

In Holland, the Art Deco style also caught on, not so much in the area of the traditional Delft blue output from the Porceleyne Fles, but in other studios like the works in Gouda that produced Gouds Plateel. In Denmark, Royal Copenhagen also responded quickly to the developing taste. Most of the factories in Europe moved with the fashion but also continued to produce their old and tested traditional designs for the less adventurous.

The relationship of the factory to the designer, and in particular the studio potter, was often problematical. England provided a good case history that must have had equal relevance to the situation in other countries. When factories like Royal Doulton, Carlton, Wedgwood, and the Shelley Potteries in Staffordshire started to produce and popularize Art Deco design they began to endanger the survival and integrity of the individual craftsman potter. Potters of the calibre of Michael Cardew, William Staite Murray and, most notably, Bernard Leach found a lot wrong with the new direction ceramics were going in. The production of the straight-sided vases of the "Midwinter" range from Shelley Potteries, were considered by Leach, in particular, to be perverse and untenable. In 1934, Leach actually closed down his pottery and went to Japan where he felt tradition and expertise were still highly regarded and appreciated. There were, however, still some designers who could find inspiration from their individual work and not be overly snobbish about the idea of having copies made. Richard Joyce, the main designer for the Pilkington works throughout the 1920s, was a case in point. His favourite motifs were animals and in this he helped to bring the craft potter and Art Deco closer together.

The most individual of all the ceramic

RIGHT Plate in primitive style, featuring jungle animals and foliage.

BELOW RIGHT A collection of the highly decorative pottery by Clarice Cliff. Simple forms are jazzed up through daring though sometimes less-than-successful colour combinations.

designers, however, and now the most sought after and collected, is Clarice Cliff. She was born in 1900 and, after a long apprenticeship, rose to the post of art director of the Wilkinson and Newport Companies. Her most famous designs were the "Bizarre" range which were strongly-coloured and abstract. Often loosely based on flower motifs and landscapes, her work was highly innovative. The designs for her plates were sometimes hexagonal and sometimes even square. Cliff also managed to tempt artists to work on designs that she then manufactured. The artist Graham Sutherland designed a limited edition table set for Cliff, and others that she worked with included Ben Nicholson, Barbara Hepworth, Paul Nash and the Bloomsbury artists Duncan Grant and Vanessa Bell, whose earlier experiments at the Omega Workshops made them particularly suited to the job. It was odd how artists who worked with ceramics seemed to flourish in that medium, while craft potters themselves did not.

Ceramics throughout the '20s and '30s enjoyed a great period of success; even the arrival of materials such as plastics, bakelite and phenolic resin made few inroads on the market. Art Deco ceramics provided the style with a huge boost, because they were attractive and readily available, and even now the best designs do not look particularly dated.

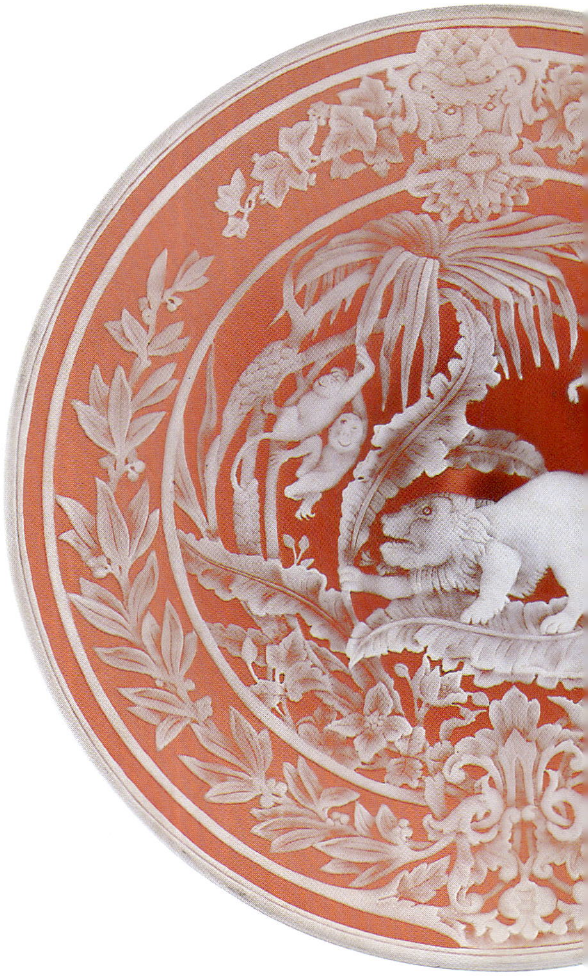

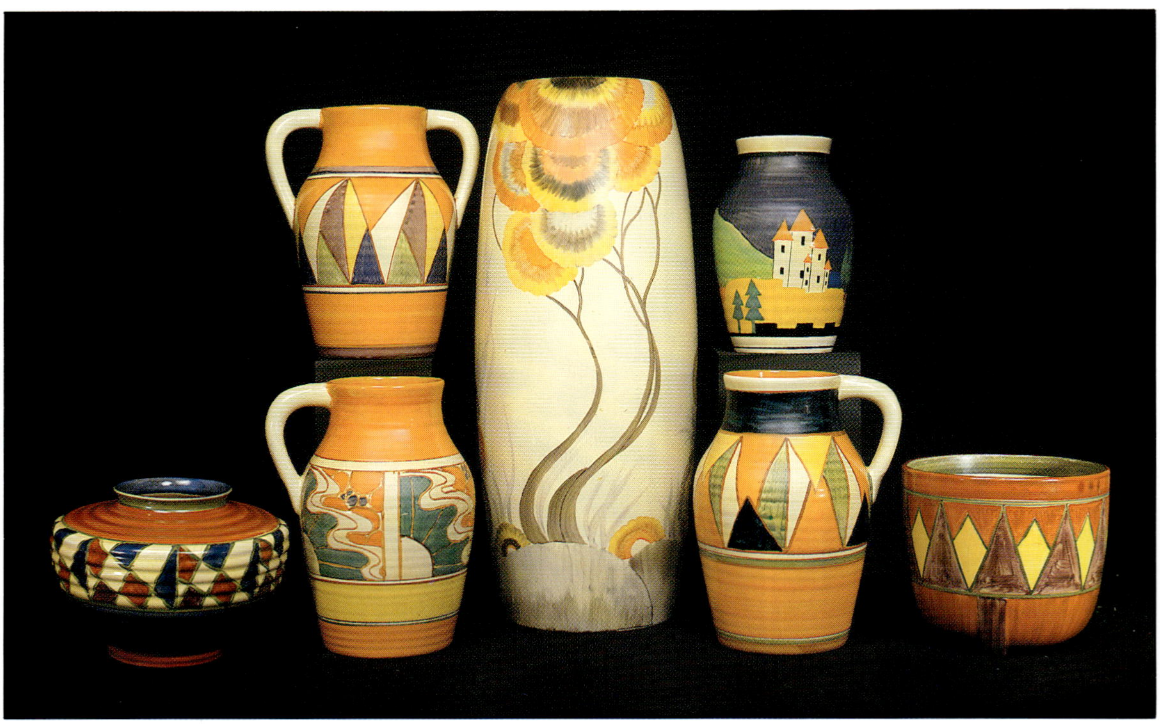

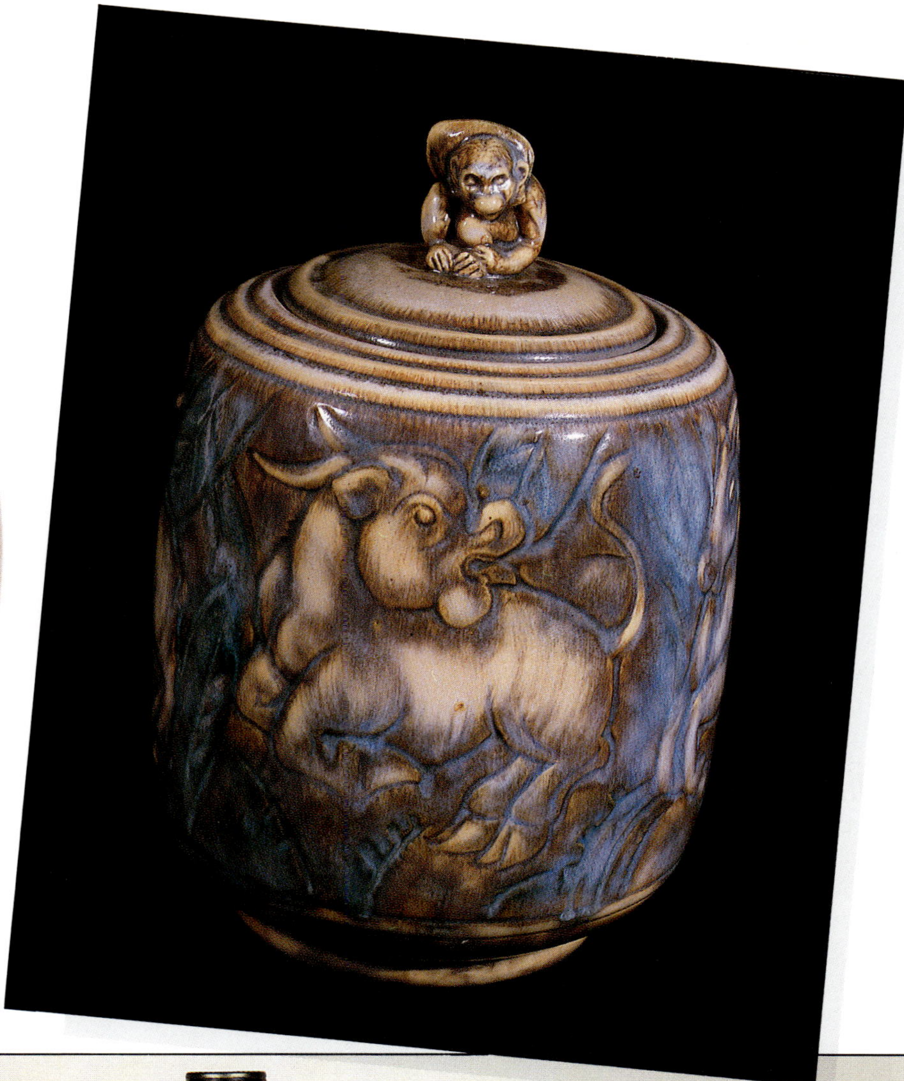

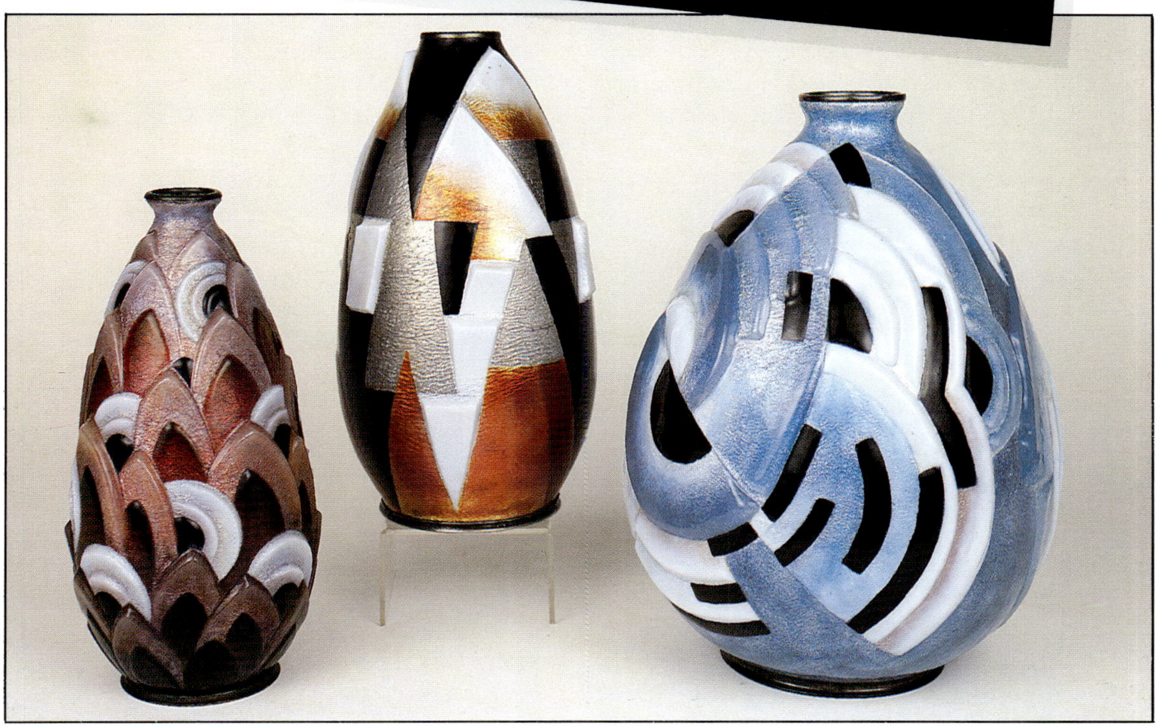

LEFT Eccentric oriental interpretation of an animal vase from the Sèvres porcelain factory.

BELOW LEFT Three silver and thickly enamelled vases by Camille Faure, that owe much to abstract painting, and arguably manage to cross the slim dividing line between vulgarity and beauty.

RIGHT Pâte-de-verre vase of 1925 by Gabriel Argy-Rousseau on the theme of fishes playing in the sea diving in and out of the waves.

FAR RIGHT Deeply-etched example of a glass bowl by Daum, Nancy, with an almost mediaeval feeling.

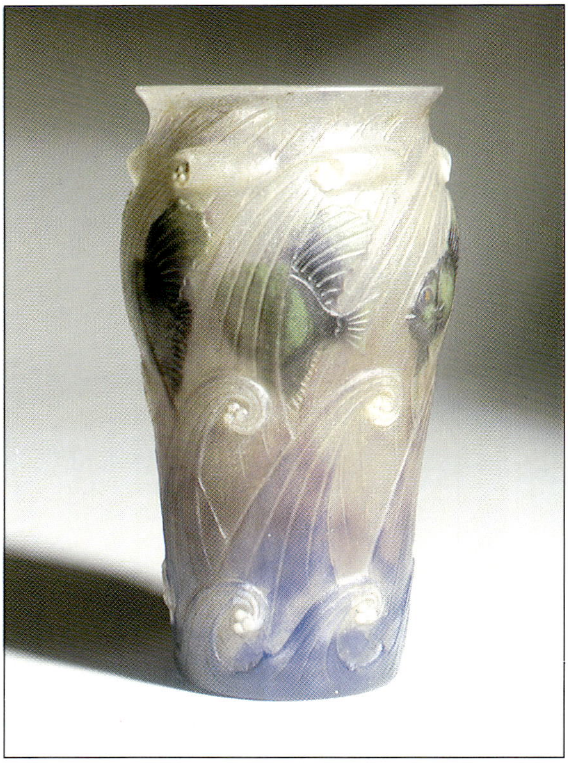

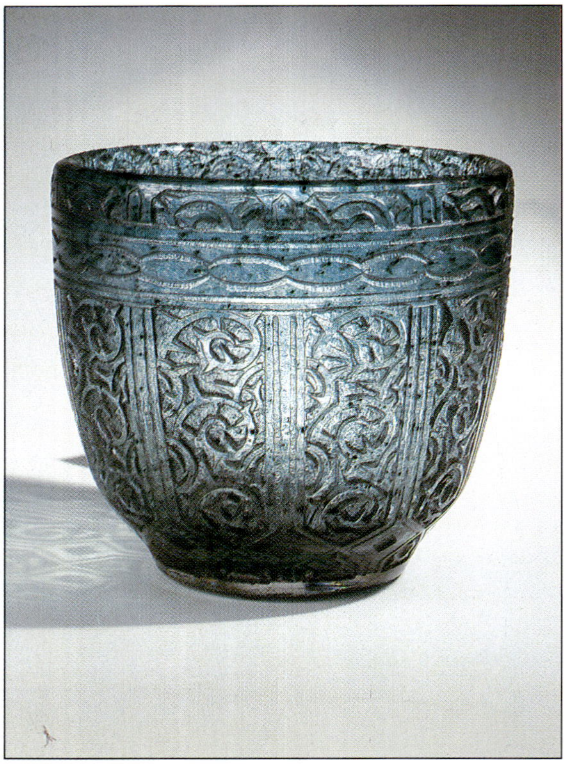

GLASS

The importance of glass to the development of taste in the 1920s and '30s is often overlooked. The Art Deco glass that is collected by connoisseurs is often limited to the vases, glasses and lamps designed by René Lalique and Daum. Those pieces are of course particularly rare and beautiful, but they only represent a small percentage of the glass produced, and do not give a full picture of all the uses to which glass could be put. Glass was not only used for table ornaments or vases, or even jewellery, but was also an important part of a whole architectural project on the grandest scale. At its plainest, a glass sheet is transparent – almost invisible. It was that particular quality of glass that many of the modernist architects exploited. Le Corbusier's Pavillon de L'Esprit Nouveau at the Exposition des Arts Décoratifs et Industriels stood as a statement against superfluous decoration. It also showed how to use the window as the only ornament and break in the structure of the building. Many architects, including Robert Mallet Stevens, Mies van der Rohe, Walter Gropius and Le Corbusier himself used glass for its properties of transparency. The modern buildings of the 1930s started off the boom in what we now call curtain walling, that is floor to ceiling glass walls in which the division between the interior and exterior space is minimised as far as possible.

Newly-invented types of glass compound allowed for a greater range of applications. Vitroflex could be bent round pillars and curved walls in ways that would be difficult to imitate with plain standard glass. The fragility of glass could also be overcome. Not only was glass used for mirrors and larger furniture ensembles, but some new types of glass would stand up to high heat. In the late '30s, the designers Raymond McGrath and Elizabeth Craig worked on various oven to tableware prototypes for the British Heat Resisting Glass Company. The designs themselves were hardly novel, but showed that the traditional limitations of glass need no longer be so restricting. Even within the traditional areas of glass usage such as for vases and lamps the Art Deco period saw a revival of many old techniques and the invention of some new ones. René Lalique, the master of glass manufacture, began to use moulds and casts in order to be able to manufacture large numbers of glass sculptures. Maurice Marinot discovered methods of catching bubbles between skins of glass in his vases, other makers used the etching and engraving techniques, while yet others exploited the *pâte de verre* technique.

Two of the largest projects during the period to use glass extensively, apart from the Exposition des Arts Décoratifs et Industriels, were the Grand Hotel at Dax in France, and the bathroom designed for Tilly Losch by Paul Nash. The entrance hall to the hotel was a dynamic extravaganza, its hundreds of plates of glass giving the visitor the impression of walking into the heart of a diamond as big as the Ritz. The Tilly Losch bathroom, which James Clark, Eaton and Son, constructed for Nash, was up to the minute in its use of mirrored walls, chrome and glass. It looks as modern today as it must have looked precociously ahead of its time. In America the designers Joseph Urban and Donald Deskey also used glass panels extensively in their interior designs. The precedent for abstract patterned or stained glass in America had already been set by Frank Lloyd Wright in the Avery Coonley Playhouse, and later in his mammoth project for the Midway Gardens in Chicago. If many of the modernist practitioners favoured the clear aspect of sheets of plain glass, there was still great support and understanding of the decorative potential of worked glass.

France had kept alive the skill of working glass throughout the 19th century with the most exciting contributions to the medium coming from Baccarat and Emile Gallé. Gallé was the master of the Art Nouveau style, and René Lalique was his direct heir. Born in Ay-sur-Marne in 1860 Lalique was one of the oldest practitioners of the Art Deco style. Turning to glass manufacture in 1902 he quickly recognized its expressive potential. Lalique was particularly important because not only did he achieve total mastery of the small ornament, vase and statuette, but in the 1920s he started to design glass furniture. Following the example of Baccarat's etched glass furniture in the mid 19th century Lalique reinvented the form in a totally modern way. He was followed in this by other designers, most notably Robert Block and Serge Roche.

The highpoints of Lalique's career were his designs for the Exposition des Arts Décoratifs et Industriels

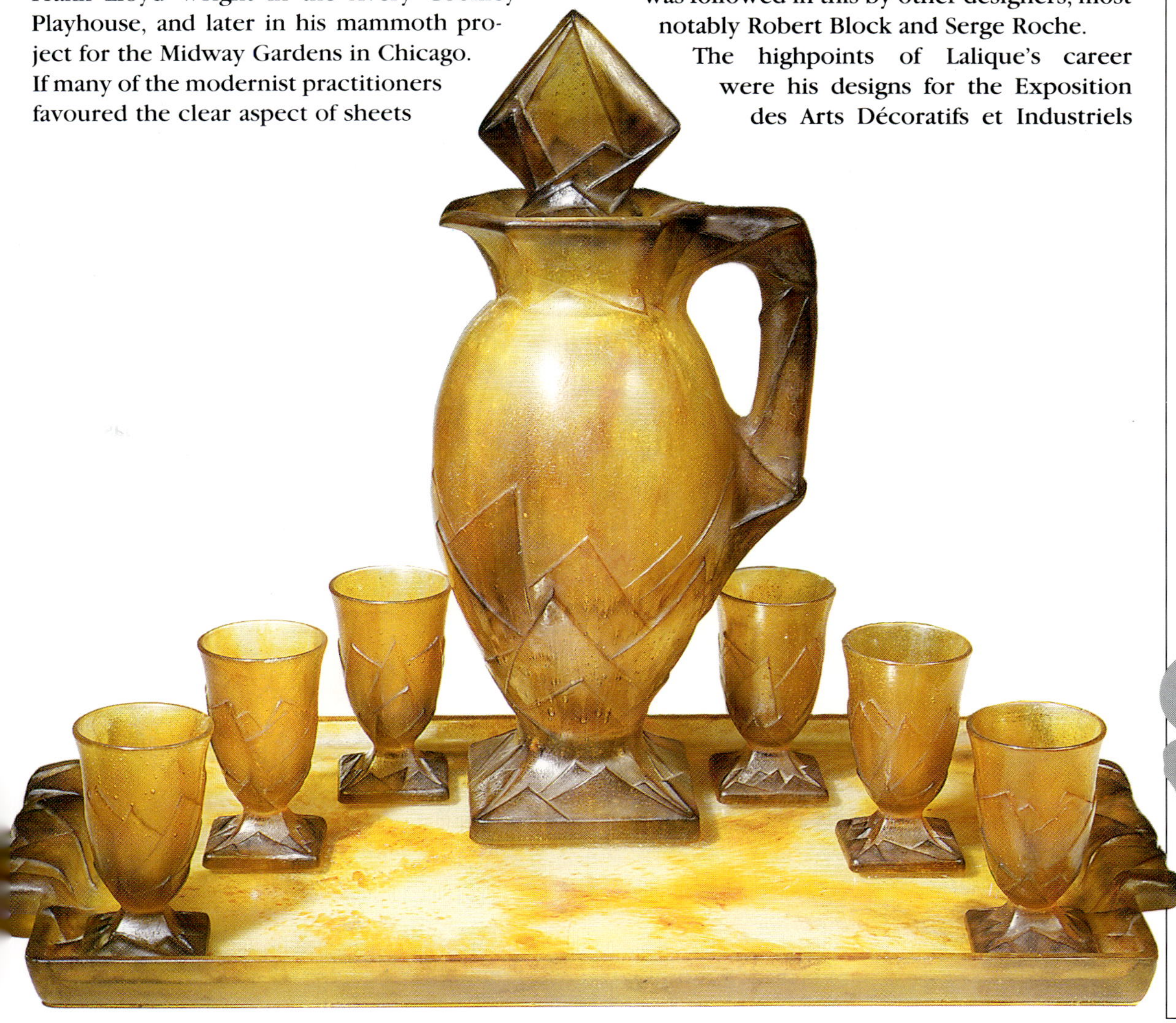

LEFT Vaguely cubist-inspired eight piece liqueur or water service, employing the pâte-de-verre technique, by Gabriel Argy-Rousseau.

RIGHT Delicately-shaped rectangular vase by E. Rousseau, with an image on the side of a grotesque figure.

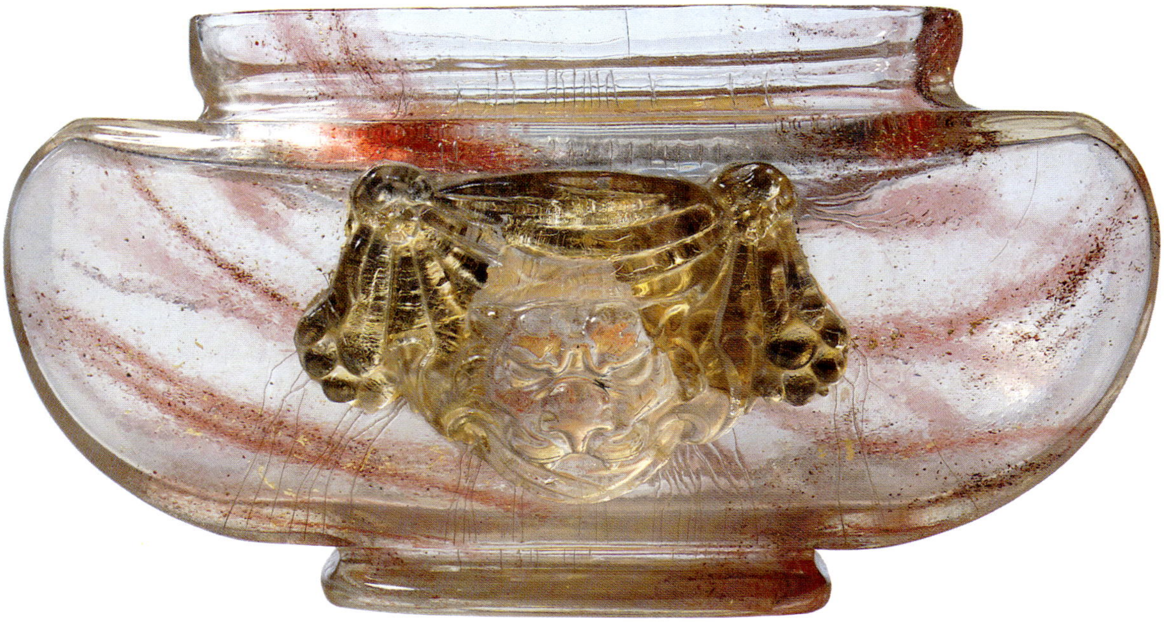

and the large *Normandie* commission. As well as having his own stand Lalique also participated in others. At his own, which was designed by the architect Marc Ducluzand, Lalique displayed examples of his work covering the complete range of his output. He was also asked to provide a glass fountain for the Exposition. Like a transparent Cleopatra's needle it rose with geometric ease through fifteen layers to an astonishing height for a glass construction. For the Primavera pavilion designed by Sauvage and Vybo, Lalique supplied the glass "cobblestones" that diffused the light into the central space through the ceiling canopy. Lalique also provided a dining-room setting for the Sèvres pavilion in which he displayed his glassware on a glass table, lit from above through squares of glass set into the ceiling.

In Lalique's work other designers could see the unification of the disparate strains of Art Deco design. He was at once luxurious, elegant, practical, interested in abstract design, showy, intimate and, above all, the supreme craftsman. Among his smaller pieces, he created delicately-coloured scent bottles, small glass plaques of nude bathers, statuettes of sleeping muses, and glass mascots for cars. The eagle mascot he produced later adorned the cars of Hitler's favoured staff members, a use that Lalique and other Frenchmen must have abhorred.

The method of working that Lalique favoured for his ornamental pieces soon found wider favour. He would first shape the object in another material and then take a plaster cast and pour molten glass into the mould. Apart from the advantage of being able to cast shapes that could not be blown, moulds could be employed for mass production. The results could be varied slightly by using variously coloured glass, or in the finishing process. Another designer who used this method was Marius Ernest Sabino, who favoured the nymph and animal motifs popular in Art Deco. The quality of pieces by Lalique, Sabino, Marcel Goupy and Alméric Walter is almost always a clarity that resulted from the use of few and discreet colours, but there were other designers who experimented with a far greater range, giving their work a heavier, opaque feel.

The revival of the *pâte de verre* and *pâte de cristal* techniques brought back the art of sculpting in glass. The method produced a cold glass compound that could be modelled like clay and coloured easily. Foremost proponents of this technique were Gabriel Argy-Rousseau, Alméric Walter and François-Emile Décorchemont. In comparison to that of Lalique, their work has a heightened sense of luxury and colour. Rich reds, oranges, mauves and blues blend delicately into each other without the strict demarcation lines that appear in other types of glassware.

Daum and Maurice Marinot specialized in the etching and enamelling of glass. By starting off with a thick glass vase, for example, they would cut back layer after layer with the application of acids, until the pattern was left as a deep relief. The Daum Frères factory at Nancy was quick to pick up on the experiments of Marinot in this field, and they mass-produced variations on the theme.

Glass had many possible applications, but one of its most inspired was when used in conjunction with the metalwork of Edgar Brandt. The screens, vases and lamps that Brandt constructed were beautifully illuminated by the glasswork of Daum and sometimes Schneider. The famous "Cobra" lamp discussed earlier could not only be bought in three sizes, but had a variety of coloured glass lampshades by Daum, enabling it to fit into the overall decorative and colour scheme of the client's home. The contrast of translucence and opacity was further heightened by the tactile contrast of solid metal supporting fragile glass. When Edgar Brandt manufactured doors and gates for specific settings such as the Paris shop for Paul Poiret, clear glass filled the spaces, so that the metalwork looked like sculpture suspended in air. When Brandt designed overhead lighting and chandeliers he would also draw on the talents and expertise of René Lalique.

Other European countries, as well as the United States, produced Art Deco glass of merit. The Leerdam company in Holland carried out designs for the architects Henry van de Velde and Frank Lloyd Wright, while the Orrefors company in Scandinavia also produced simple, good design. In America, the Steuben company, in collaboration with the Corning Glass works, produced many pieces that are on view at the whaling port of New Bedford. The most important designer for Steuben was Walter Dorwin Teague.

In England, the design and manufacture of glassware was carried out in much the same way as ceramics. The companies of Stuart and Sons, and Thomas Webb and Sons of Stourbridge invited the artists Graham Sutherland and Paul Nash to create new forms in glass. Another highly talented designer was Keith Murray, whose work for the Stevens and Williams company at Brierley Hill created new standards in Art Deco design. English glassware was never as inventive as that of the French, but what it lost in complexity, or colour, it made up for in simplicity. Where the English might engrave a vase with clear-cut lines, with the occasional ornamental motif, the French would burn or scour deep into the glass. Both were equally viable, and good examples of the fluid diversity of the Art Deco style, and of the new techniques available to designers in glass.

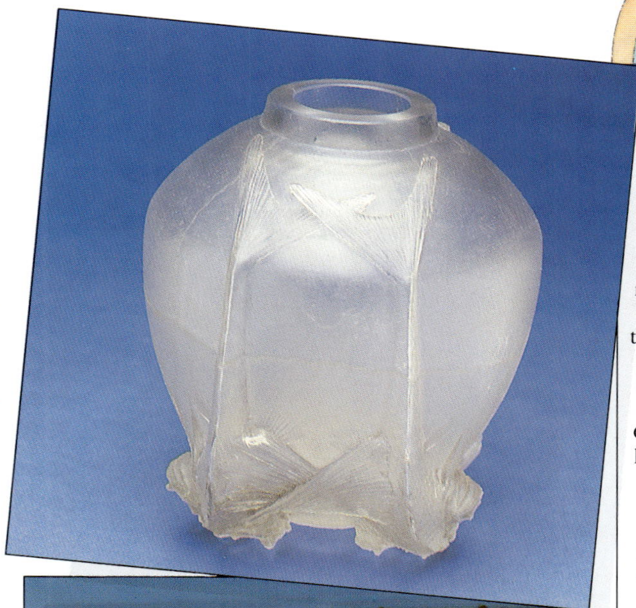

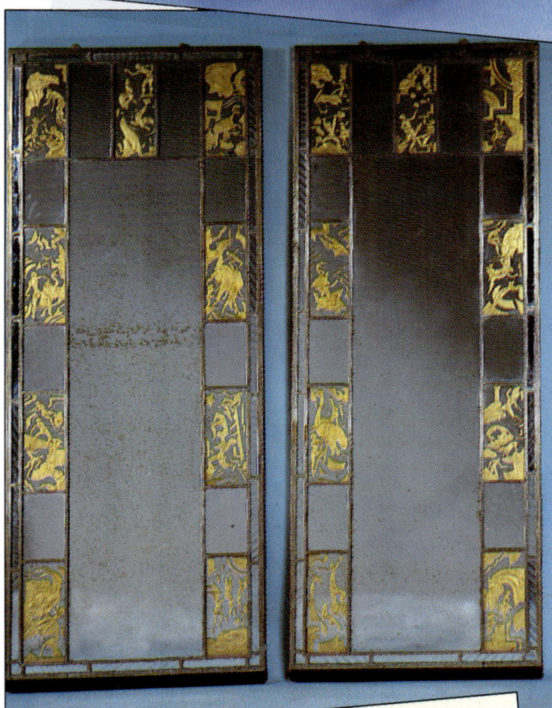

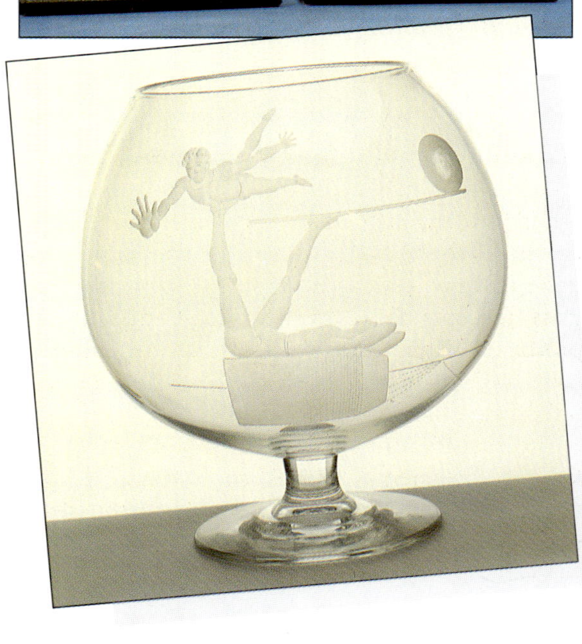

TOP LEFT A 1923 semi-translucent glass vase using the lost wax method by René Lalique. The common fish motif that is seen on the famous lacquered bed by Jean Dunand, and the playful pâte-de-verre vase by Gabriel Argy Rousseau, is here transformed into an extremely elegant, yet somehow disquieting image of disappearing fish. Frozen for that split second before they dive.

CENTRE LEFT Pair of 1936 Orrefors mirrored doors by Simon Gate, depicting eighteen scenes based on the circus theme, including knife throwing, juggling, trapeze artists, lion-taming, snake-charming, weightlifting, displays of strength by an elephant and a man, and the more unlikely pastimes of ostrich and tortoise racing.

BOTTOM LEFT Elegant, streamlined glass bowl by the Steuben Glass Works, United States, from 1939. The glass is engraved with a design of acrobats, which results in an astonishing play of perspective by Pavel Tchelitchev, sometime companion of the poet Edith Sitwell.

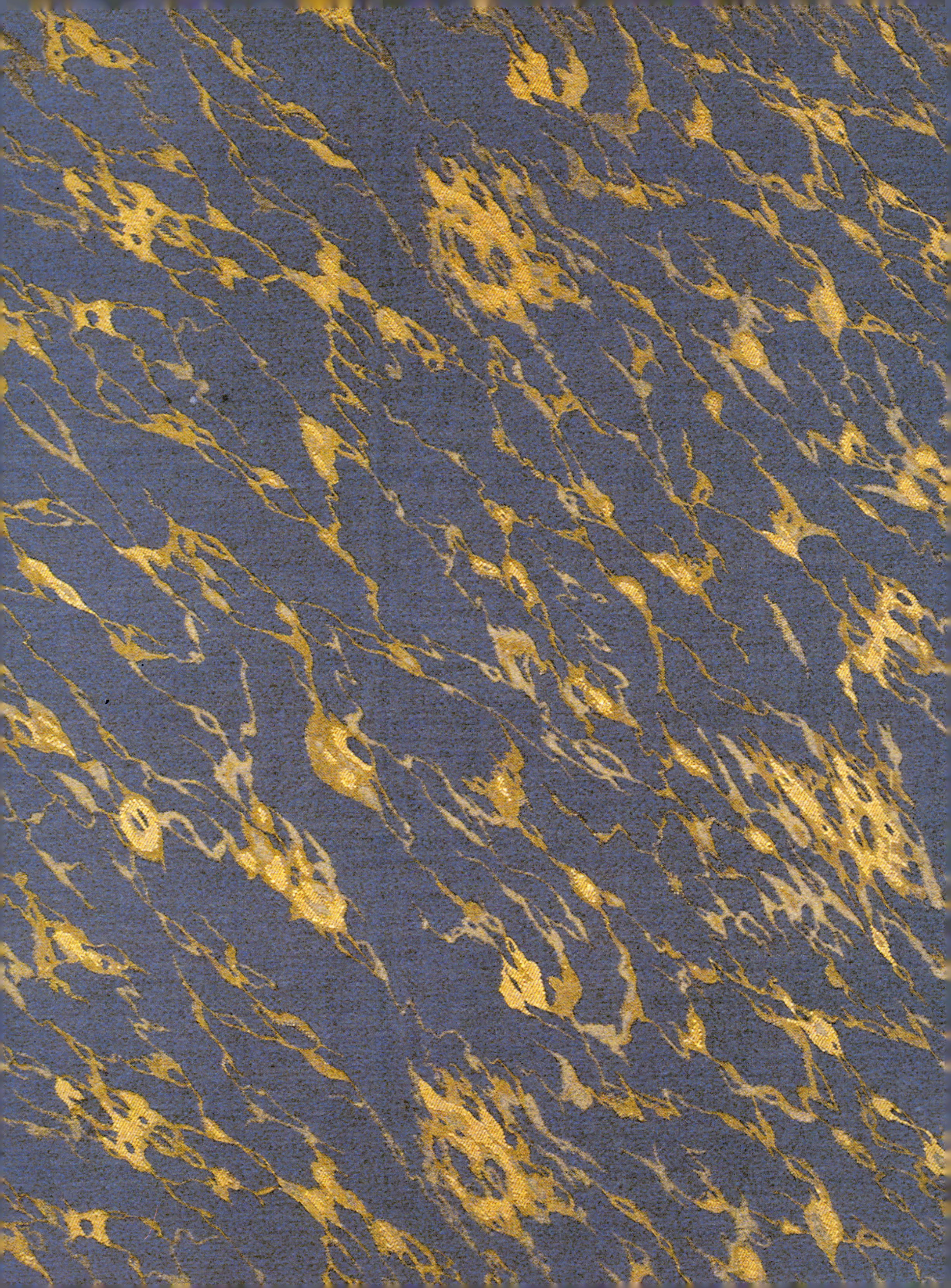

CHAPTER SEVEN

FASHION

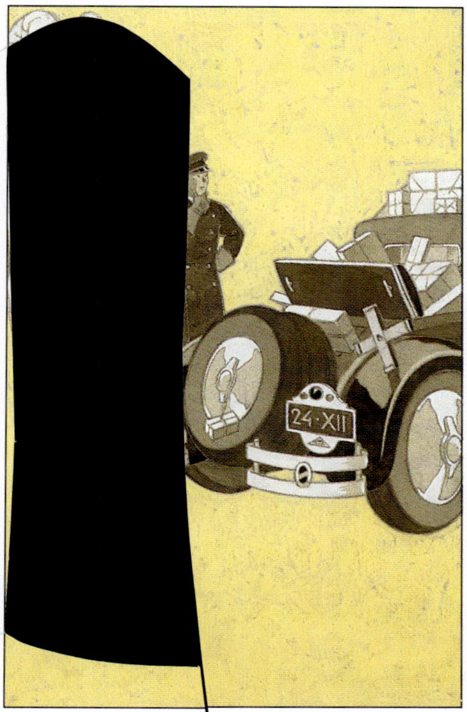

Witty sketch in pencil and gouache by Ernest Deutsch Dryden dated 1926. An angelic lady of fashion refreshes her appearance in her motor car laden with gifts as the bemused chauffeur and dog look on.

RIGHT A morocco crêpe day dress, and pâletot by Lucien Lelong, illustrated for Art-Gout-Beauté in 1922.

The world of fashion clothing and accessories is always quick to pick up on the latest changes in taste, even though it is fleeting and changeable as weather. The fashion that appeared in the 1920s and '30s is well known to anyone that has ever looked at films of the period. It has been repeated and diluted so many times since that it becomes difficult to place it historically, to see where it came from, or to notice how subtle modifications point to a dress being a '60s replica or the original. In itself, fashion may only be [redacted] important to people as the amount of [redacted] take in clothing themselves. For the [redacted] Parisian or New Yorker of the '20s [redacted] fashion was a vital part of life. The reason [redacted] rapid success of Art Deco was that [redacted] essentially a fashionable style. All [redacted] their day, but in the 20th century the [redacted] industry moved in response to [redacted] quicker than ever before. This has as [redacted] with built-in obsolescence as with a sense [redacted] and finesse; both feed off each other. [redacted] fluctuate quickly, so the industry has to [redacted] with something new, as clients try to [redacted] ahead of the rest of the pack. Fashion is [redacted] do with snobbishness and the desire to [redacted] the Joneses. With Art Deco, this was [redacted] important, since it was a total style. [redacted] collector lived amongst Ruhlmann tables, [redacted] sculptures, African chairs by Pierre [redacted] by Brandt and Daum, a coffee service by Sèvres or Clarice Cliff, place settings by Jean Puiforcat; if he or she lit your cigarette with a lighter designed by George Sandoz to the strains of Paul Robeson or a jazz number on the gramophone, as you examined the bizarre portrait by Tamara de Lempicka, or waited to hear from the travel agent as to whether he had managed to beat the waiting list for his or her forthcoming trip on the *Ile de France* across to New York, to spend a weekend with Scott Fitzgerald and crazy Zelda at one of their notoriously wild Long Island parties, before nipping over to Hollywood to set up a film contract – then you can guarantee that the cut of the husband's suit, the length and sharpness of his lapels, the width of tie, and the wife's dress by Schiaparelli worn for dinner at the Algonquin, or the Pierre, would be precisely in keeping. If so much effort in intellect, taste and money had been expended on creating the home environment, then the only things that could travel out of the door, clothes and jewellery, had to be as important; it had to complement the overall effect. In terms of design, the effect of fashion items on the other applications of Art Deco was fairly minimal; as a mirror to hold up and see the speed of the change, however, fashion was unrivalled.

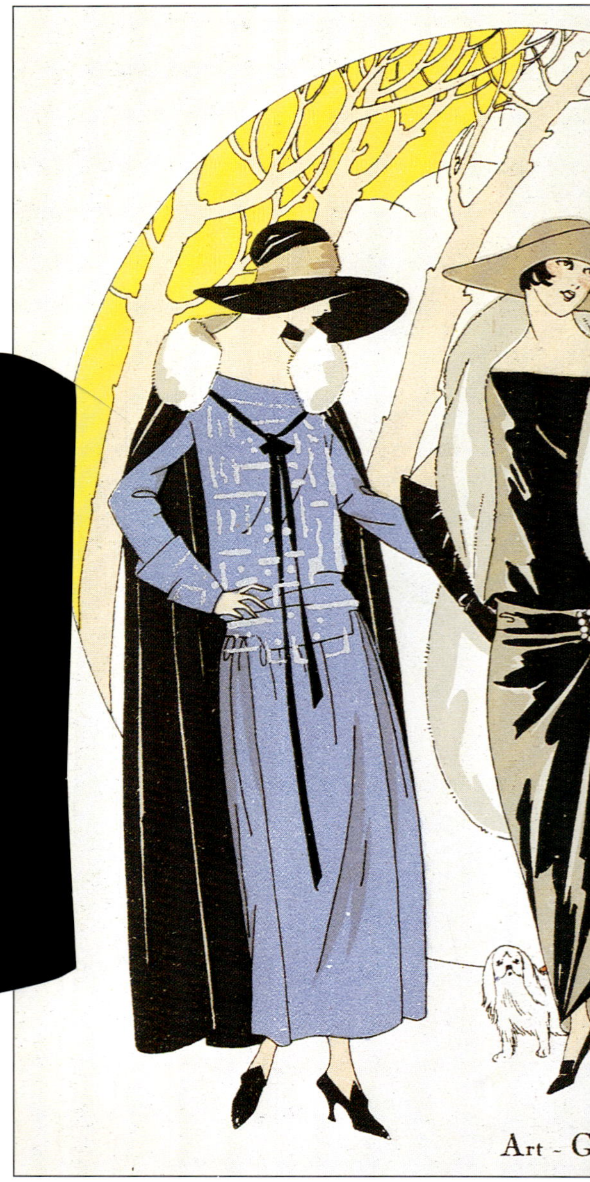

Sometimes, of course, the converse was true. The statuettes and Chryselephantine figures of Otto Poerzl and Ferdinand Preiss were direct reflections of the opera and ballet costumes, and the ballroom clothes, of the period. They were – if you like – knowing little nods; small elegant gestures of recognition that the owner appreciated the essence of what it was to be fashionable.

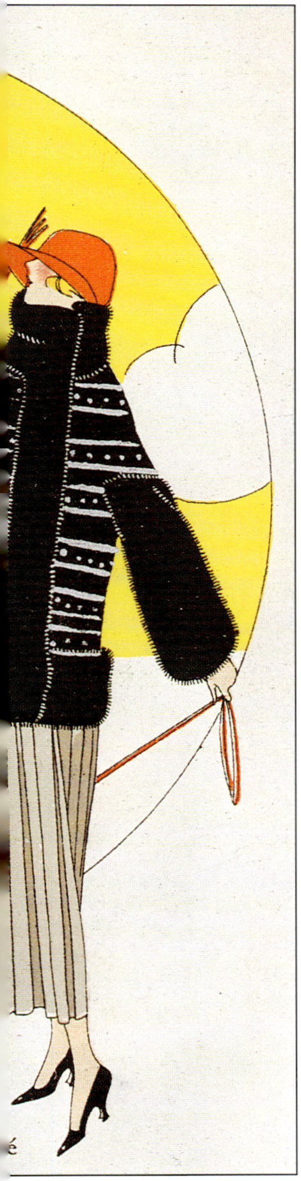

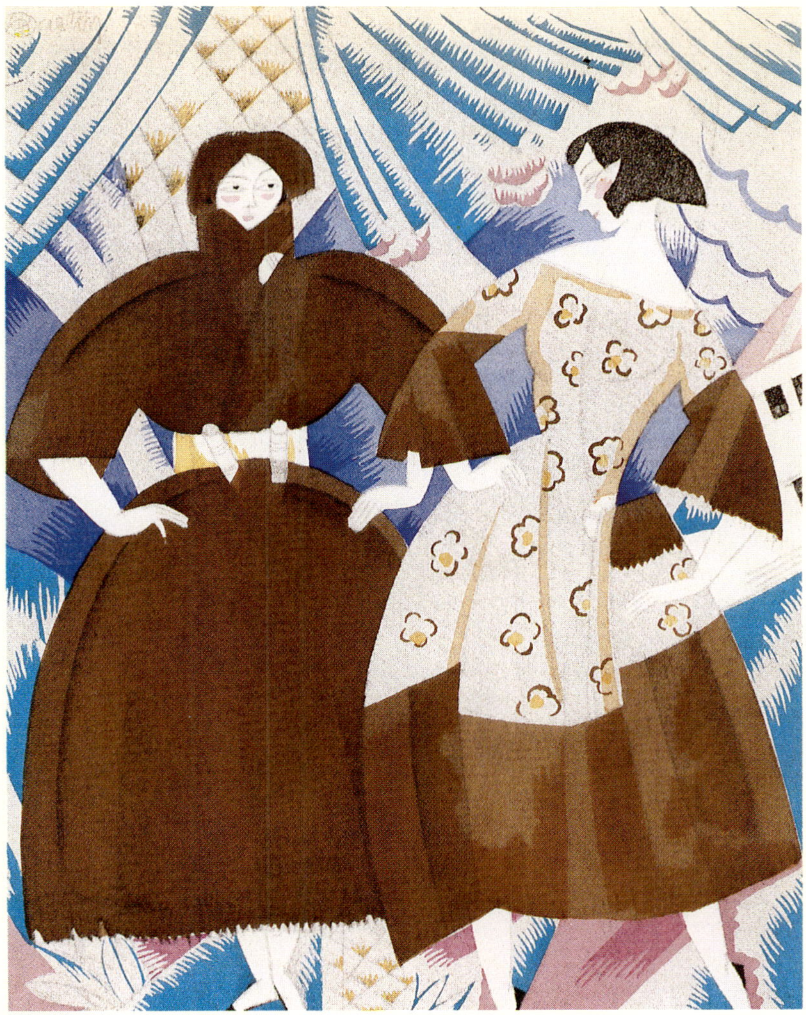

LEFT The Hindustan design by Paul Poiret of 1920 from the Gazette du Bon Ton.

It is not difficult to build up an accurate, if superficial, overview of fashion in the '20s and '30s from the statuettes by Preiss, the photo of Nancy Cunard in her African bangles, or photos of Picasso, Jean Cocteau and other *flâneurs* and poseurs in your mind.

There is a perverse rule in fashion that the poorer the economic climate is for the majority of people the more ostentatious the select, wealthy few become. The double standards of the "Roaring Twenties" in America particularly, where Prohibition cast a depressing cloud of double-dealing, suspicion and crime, reflected itself in the sexless, androgynous short skirts, bob cuts, and shapeless tops worn by the flappers. By the beginning of the '30s, when the reality was far more depressing and the comforting pedestal of wealth had been kicked away from under their feet of the erstwhile bootleggers, the fashion became fuller, the jewellery – even if it were paste – far more startling.

The top designers of the day included Schiaparelli, who at times courted the ludicrous inventions of the Surrealists, Coco Chanel, Jean Patou, Jeanne Lanvin, Worth, Nina Ricci, Paquin, Christian Berard and Mainbocher. Paul Poiret spread his influence and taste far wider than most of the other fashion designers. At the Exposition des Arts Décoratifs et Industriels, Poiret exhibited his designs on decorated barges just

RIGHT *L'heure du Thé* ("Teatime"), fashion plate from the *Gazette du Bon Ton, Paris.* The coat and veiled cloche hat are designed by Benito, 1920. Exaggerated high collars, already popular in Edwardian times, were still in vogue, but the plainness of the hat and figure-disguising shape of the coat are pointers to Art Deco fashion taste.

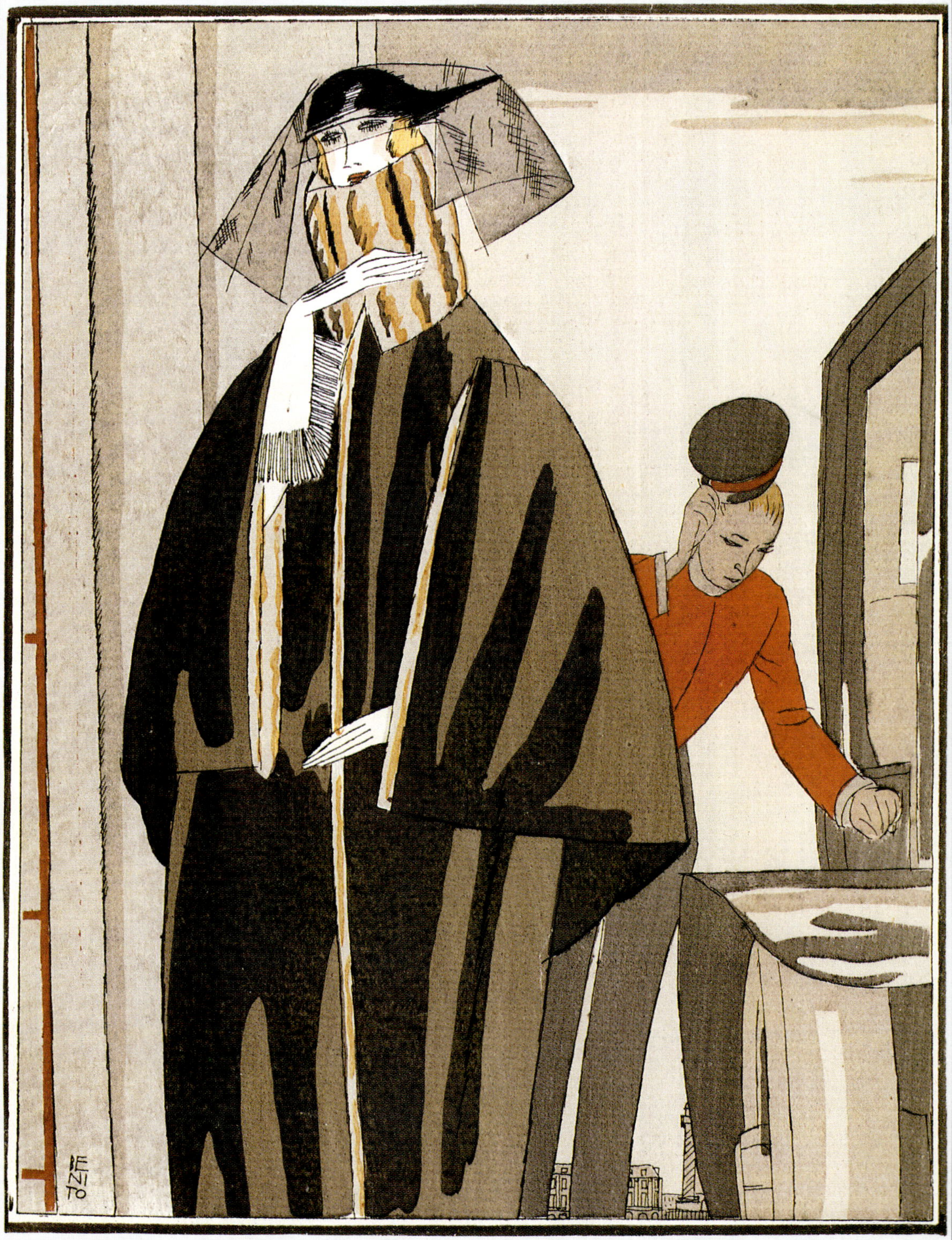

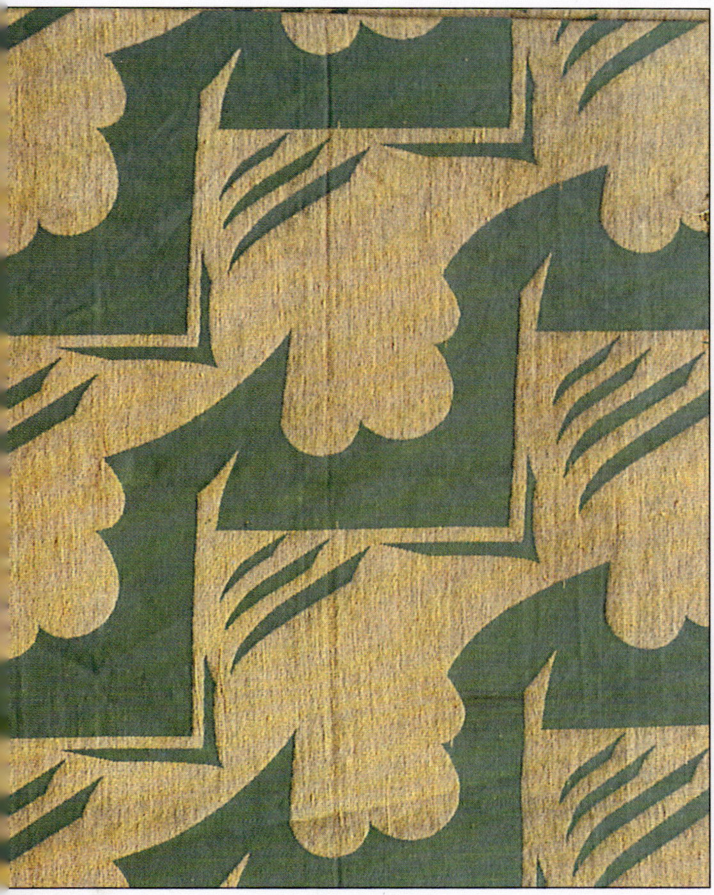

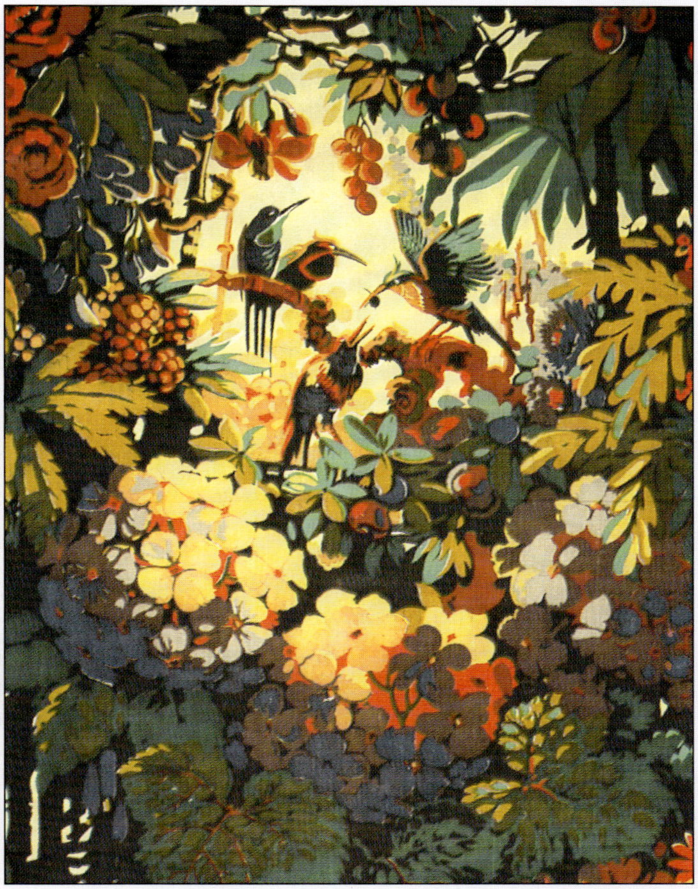

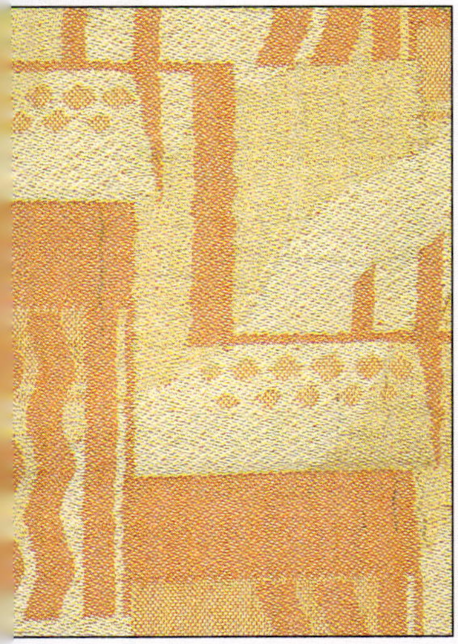

ABOVE **Braintree**, a cotton, cotton gimp and jute tissue designed by Alec Hunter in 1932.

Textile design was another area in which fine artists taught the established trade a great deal. In England, the ever-flexible Paul Nash and Duncan Grant produced dashing new pastel-coloured textiles. They were a direct attack on the heavy colours used in Art Nouveau Liberty designs and the work of William Morris and Co.

In France in the early 1920s the textile manufacturers and the tapestry weavers based in Aubusson found their industry in decline. Its revival in the 1930s was due in part to the large commissions for the liners *Ile de France* and *Normandie*, and the inspiration of a Madame Cuttoli. What she did was to invite France's greatest artists to produce painted designs that would then be faithfully copied by the tapestry weavers. The project clearly touched a chord with such artists as Pablo Picasso, Henri Matisse, Georges Rouault, Fernand Léger, Georges Braque, Jean Lurçat, André Derain and Raoul Dufy, all of whom contributed to the venture.

Dufy played an extremely important role in textile design. The fashion designer Paul Poiret had set up the Atelier Martine before the First World War, and it was Dufy who produced the most inspired designs for the workshop. The diluted character of his post-Fauvist style proved to be well-suited to textile work. Other designers like Emile-Jacques Ruhlmann also found it necessary to work in the medium in order to provide coverings for their furniture. In England, the American husband and wife team of Edward McKnight Kauffer and Marion Dorn produced work that typified the taste of the period. As in so many other things, the most outlandish and original designs were produced by Sonia Delaunay. The vivacity of her designs was matched only by the work of some of the best Russian textile designers.

RIGHT ("The Sweet Night"), fashion plate from the *Gazette du Bon Ton, Paris*. Clothes designed by Charles Worth, 1920. Note the skirt length which had already risen well above the ankles, even for formal evening wear, and the draping over bust and hips, obscuring the natural female shape.

FAR RIGHT 1922 drawing from Art-Gout-Beauté of a model wearing a white crêpe cocktail dress from the fashion house of Worth. Note also the furniture, which is a ragbag of Afro-Egyptian and neo-classical styles.

BELOW RIGHT Colourful 1925, Japanese-inspired textile design by the artist designer Raoul Dufy.

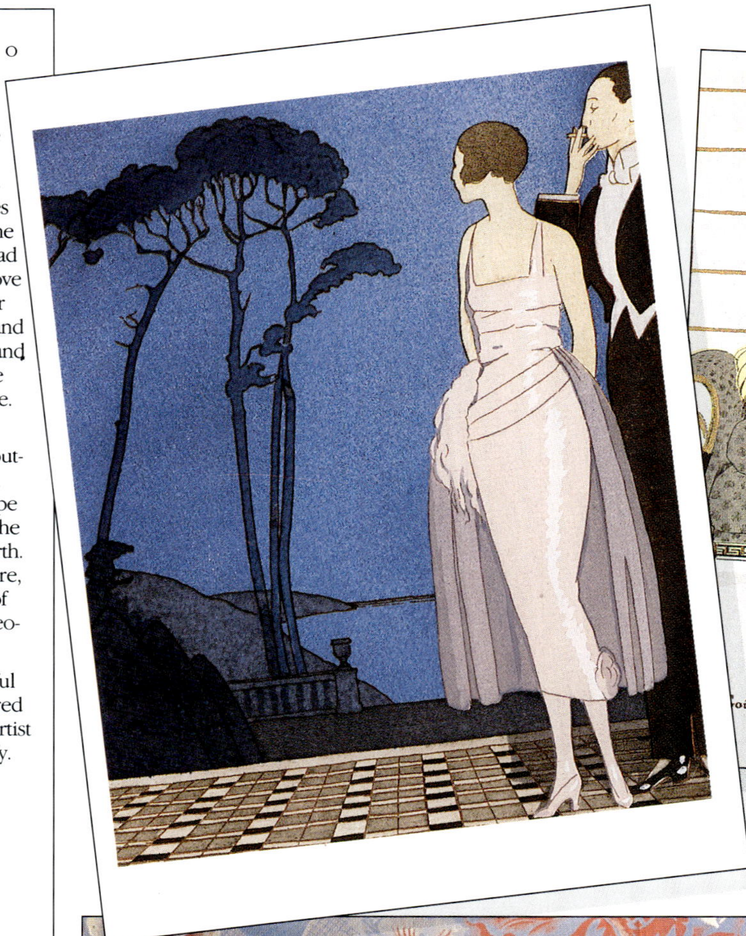

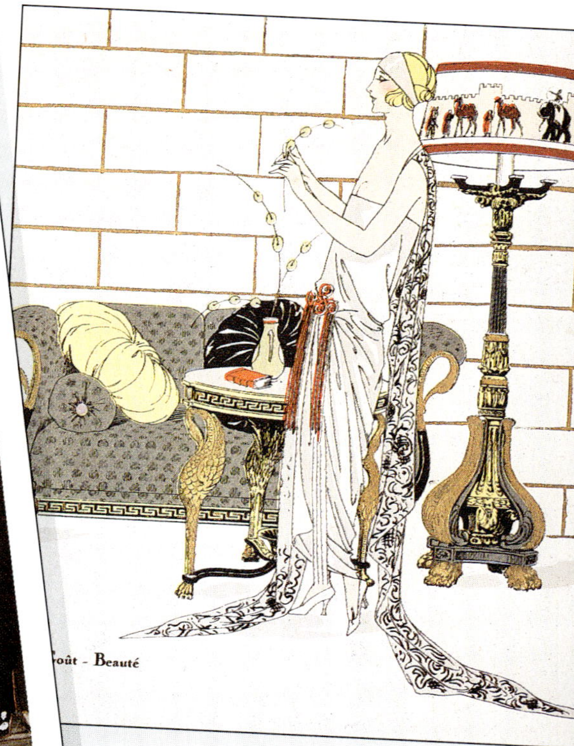

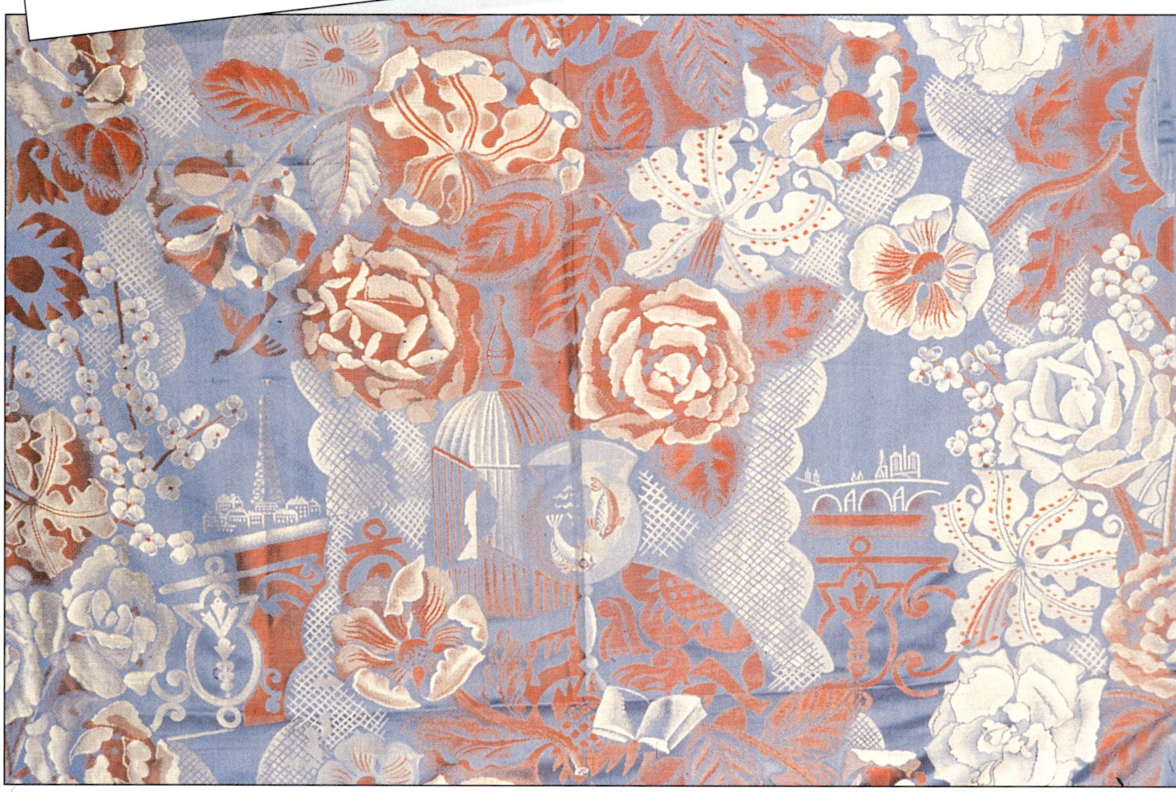

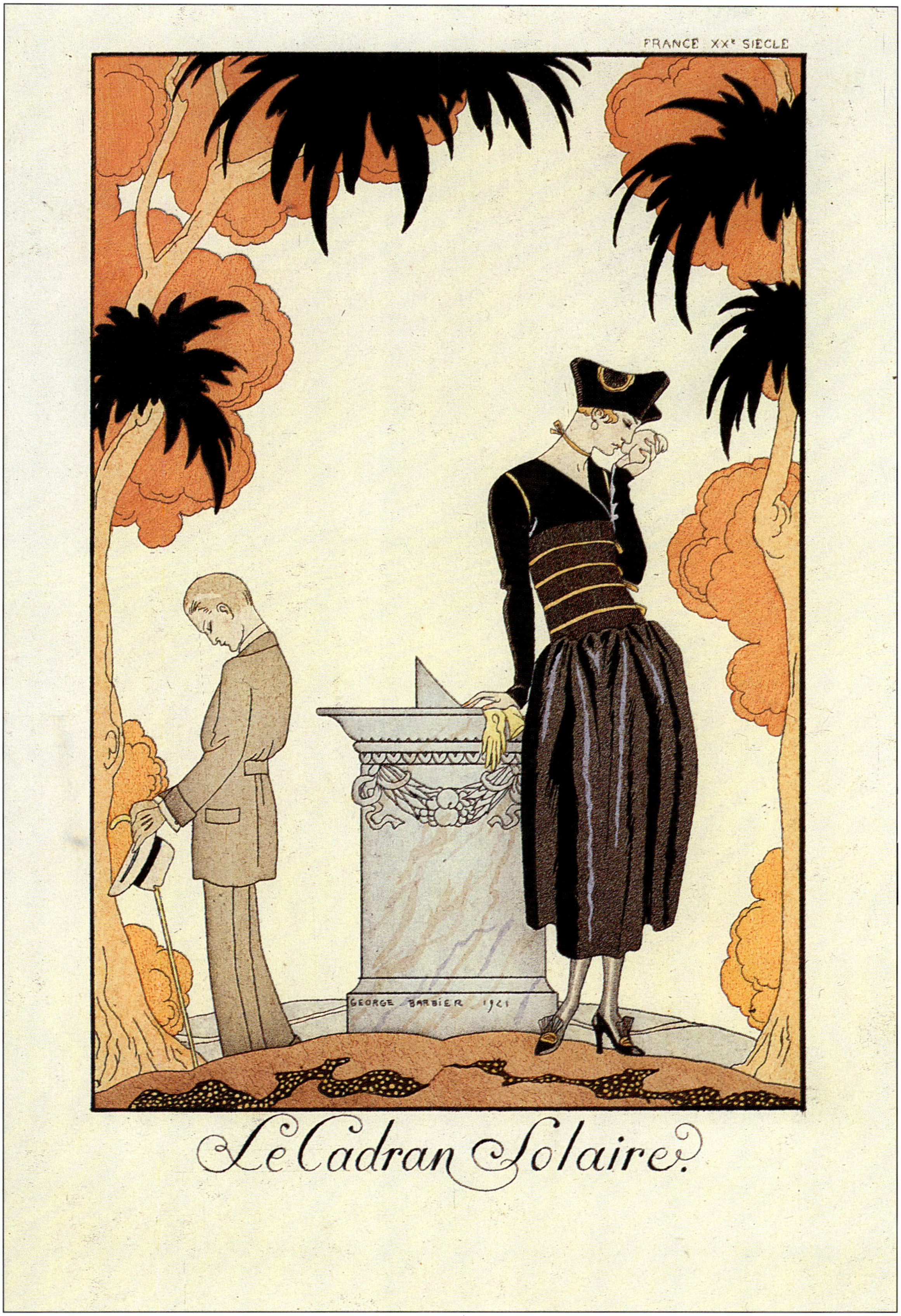

LEFT Fashion plate by Georges Barbier (1882–1932). Fashions for the 1921 'Le Cadran Solaire', stencil print from Falbalas et Fanfreluches, Almanach des Modes.

CHAPTER EIGHT

PAINTING AND DESIGN

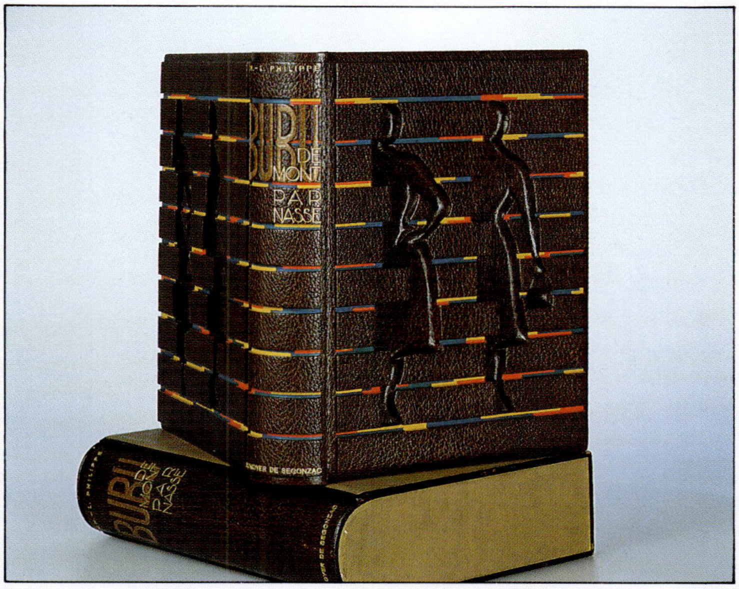

Highly rare and lavishly-bound copy of Charles L. Philippe's book 'Bubu de Montparnasse', with slip case. The design by Paul Bonet utilises the craft of leather tooling in relief to depict women silhouetted against multi-coloured stripes. The illustrations are by Dunoyer de Segonzac.

There is really no such thing as specifically Art Deco painting. It is possible to talk of Cubism, Surrealism, and Expressionism as coherent styles, but Art Deco painting never really existed in any convincing way. Strictly speaking, Art Deco derived its name from the Exposition des Arts Décoratifs et Industriels, which did not allow for a painting pavilion. Although the distance between the decorative arts and fine art is not as great as many people think, the best painting of the 1920s and 1930s certainly had little to do with the Art Deco style – if anything, the best painting and sculpture produced in Paris, Germany and Russia was itself an influence. What does still exist are examples of work by particular individuals that describe, or record in some way, the spirit of Art Deco.

Art historians looking back at the art between the wars find examples of the best art in the work of Picasso, Matisse and the Surrealists. There is really very little question that artists of the stature of Picasso, Mondrian, Kandinsky, and others pushed forward the limits of painting, enriching the visual language beyond a stale academicism. Although these artists are now seen as the giants of 20th century art, it would be wrong to disregard the contributions of less well-known artists who communicated their message more readily, and illustrated the taste of the age. Between the two extremes there is no contest on the grounds of quality, but minor art is often a more accurate indicator of public taste than works of geniuses ahead of their time.

The history books almost totally ignore the work of Tamara de Lempicka – surely the most representative of the period's portrait painters – the murals of Jean Dupas, the portraits of Kees van Dongen, or the later works of Raoul Dufy, reproducing instead the abstract innovations of Paul Klee, Pablo Picasso's classic nudes of immediately after the First World War, or the rigidly thought-out and constructed canvases of Piet Mondrian. This actually misrepresents the prevailing taste of the period. The artists commanding the highest prices at auction in Paris between the wars were Maurice Utrillo and Maurice Vlaminck. In retrospect, we can see that the host of canvases they produced then were just watered-down versions of their early work, but that was what the public wanted. There is no use either in being highbrow or snobbish about the decorative arts of the period – even artists as

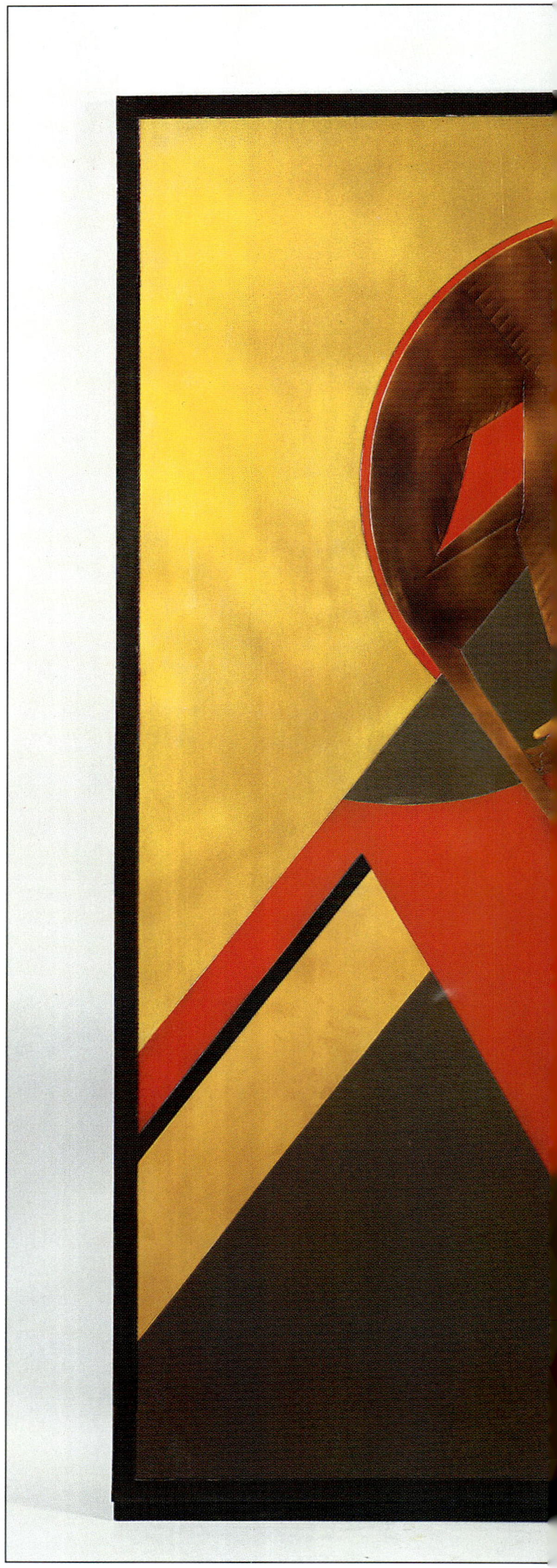

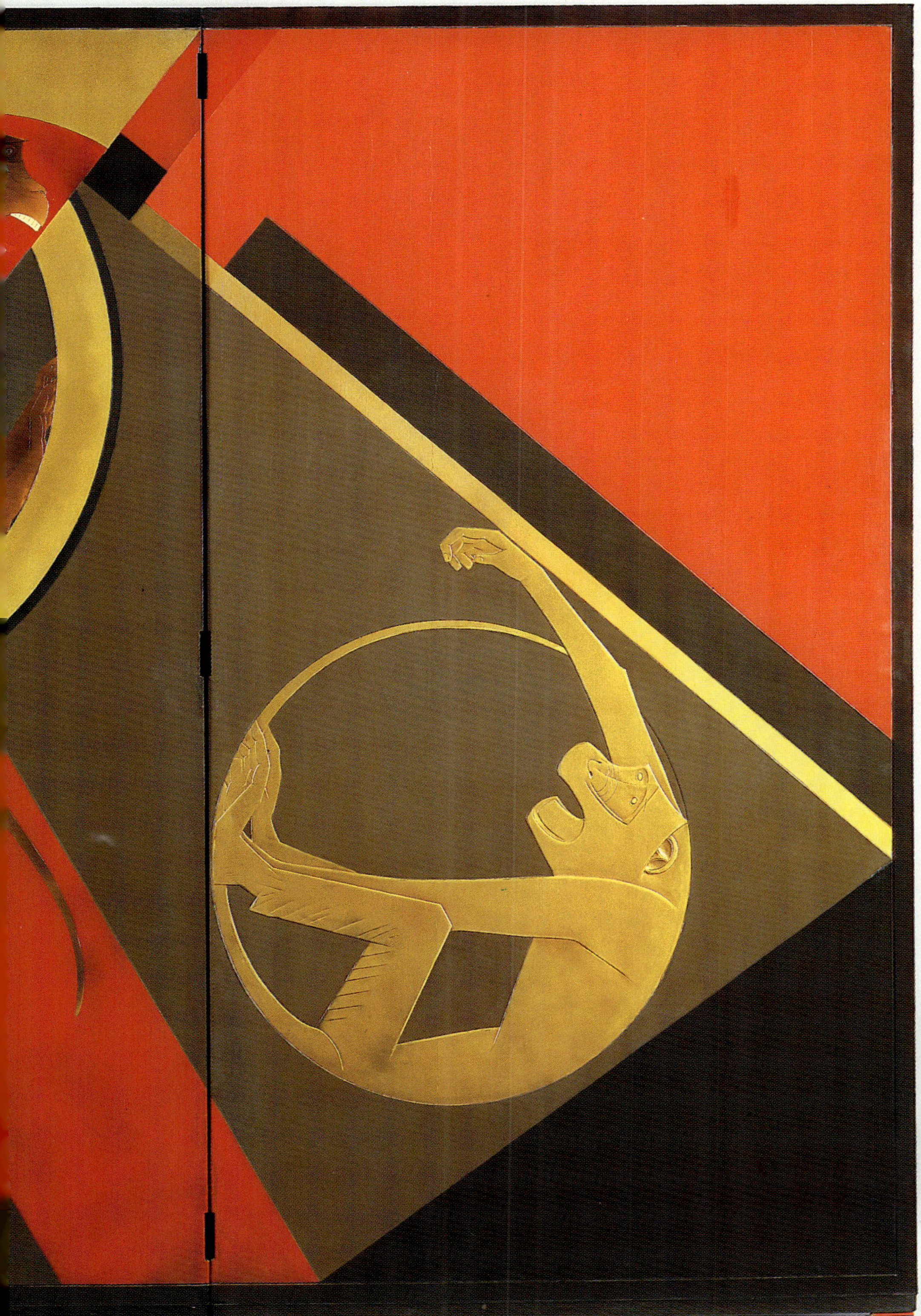

CHAPTER 8

LEFT One of the most exciting examples of Art Deco design. This two-part lacquered wood screen, dated 1928 by Leon Jannot, is an enormously successful solution to the problem of juxtaposing highly naturalistic subject matter with bold striking abstract design. The tails of each ape are dramatically employed to both contain and energise the complex design.

great as Picasso turned their hand to stage design, pottery and furniture.

What is perhaps curious about the painting that reflected the taste of the period most accurately was that it was almost always figurative, and in particular there are a great number of portraits that, even if dismissed as vulgar and modish, gave a clear insight into the character and taste of their sitters. The many portraits or figure studies in the Art Deco style were really just illustrations of the period. It is in poster design, where there is no question of high or low art, that a style could truly be said to exist. Graphic artists of the calibre of Rockwell Kent and Cassandre could employ all the devices of Deco design, without needing to feel guilty. Their success relied directly upon their ability to reach the largest audience, to produce a popular image. Abstract art, which had taught so many designers the advantage of using clear form, and strong bold design, was not itself strengthened by Art Deco. It was, rather, watered down and made acceptable in its application to consumer items. Although there was generally little place for abstraction in Art Deco-style painting, there were exceptions to the rule.

Robert Delaunay and his wife Sonia had been deeply involved with the most advanced art in Paris since before the First World War. Quickly adopting the lessons of Cubism from Picasso, Braque, Juan Gris and Fernand Léger, Robert Delaunay produced paintings of Paris, the Eiffel Tower, Saint-Severin church and other motifs of the modern world such as the aeroplane and the motor car. By the outbreak of the war he had distilled his art into pure abstraction, where fields of intense colour collided with one another. Developing a style that was called Orphism, Robert Delaunay's work provided inspiration for Art Deco design. The sweeping circular curves and fields of intense colour could be easily adapted to almost any other medium. It was his wife, however, who really developed and used the possibilities of the Simultanist style to the full. Photos of Sonia Delaunay-Terk at the 1925 Exposition show her in Simultanist dresses sitting on a motor car also painted in the house colours. Her designs were all the rage, becoming *the* look for the wealthy, sophisticated and avant-garde culture vulture. Bright and pleasing to the eye, her style brought a refreshing change after the heavy, exotic palette made popular by Bakst and Erté costume designs for the Ballets Russes.

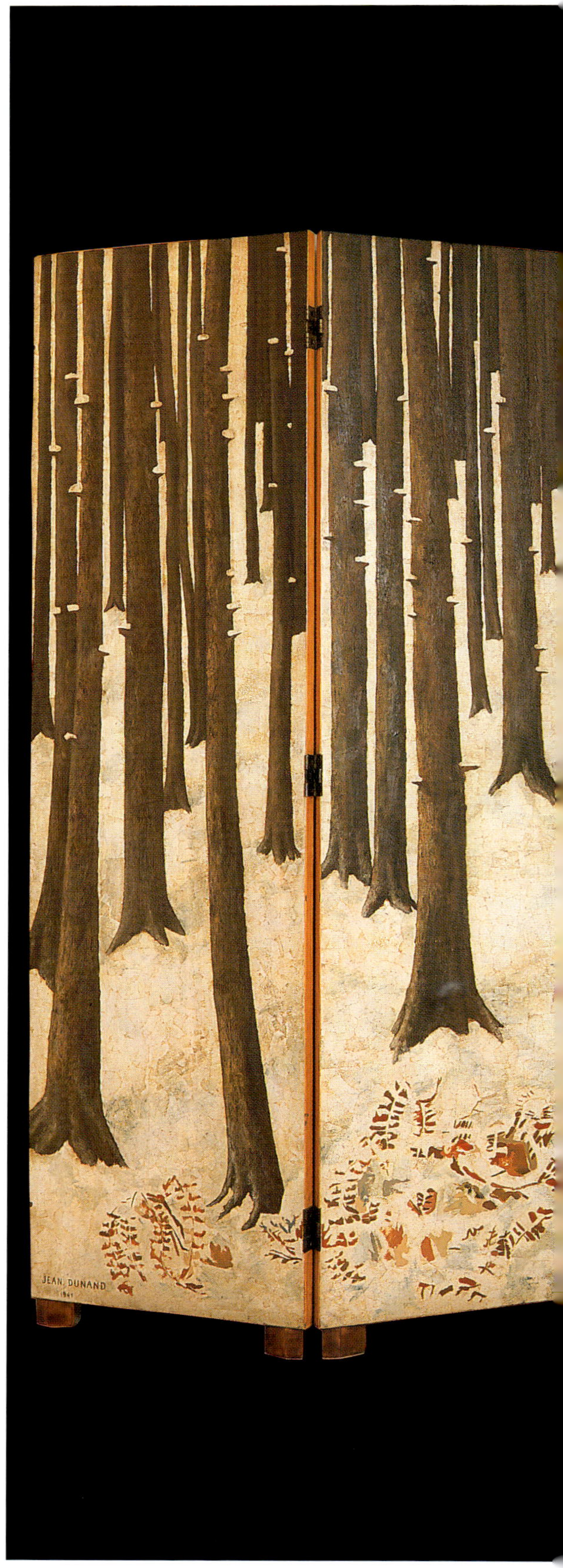

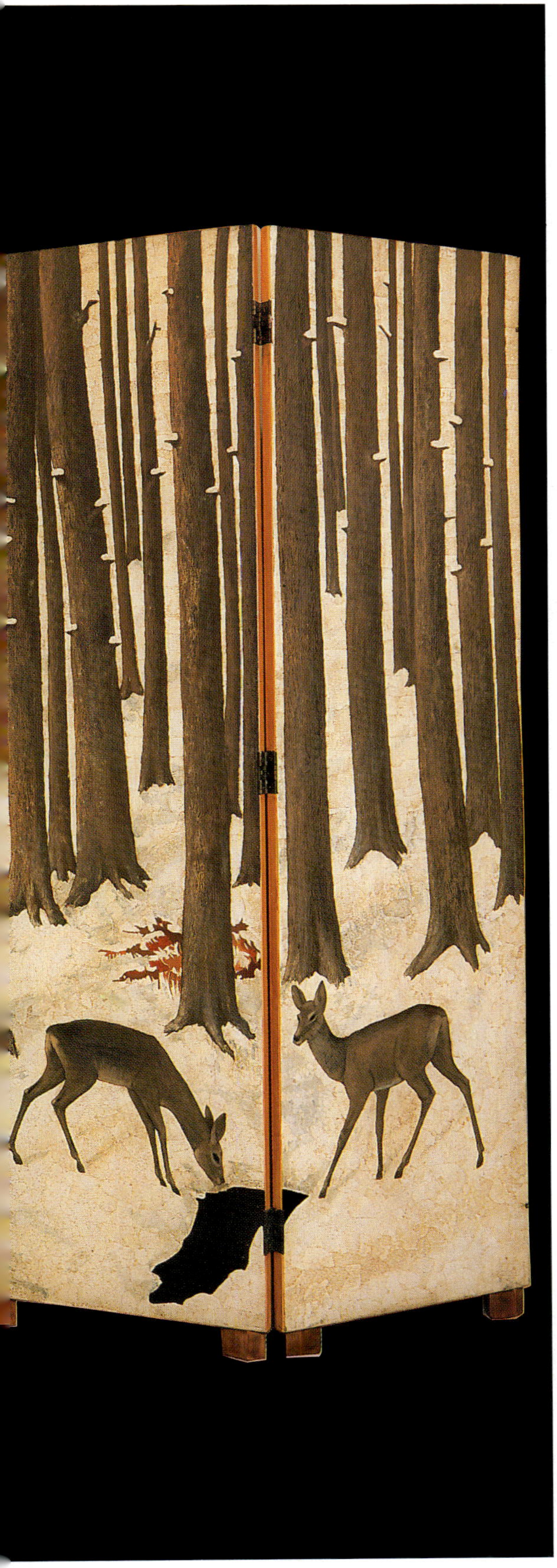

The cut was also far more practical, severe, and modern.

Another painter who is still regarded as important, and could be said to reflect Art Deco preoccupations was Fernand Léger. A friend and ally of Le Corbusier and Amédée Ozenfant, his pictures hung in the Pavillon de l'Esprit Nouveau at the 1925 Exposition. If Le Corbusier's architectural preferences were to provide a house that was a machine for living in, Léger painted large murals and canvases that reflected the age's obsession with machinery. His canvases are peopled with robot-like figures in the brightest of colour combinations. What he aimed to do was personalize the machine and employ it as subject matter, an attitude that ran throughout Art Deco in its more modernist vein.

The painters Henri Matisse and Raoul Dufy also contributed to Art Deco influence. Matisse's interest in exotic subject matter, inspired by his visits to Morocco, reflected the contemporary French obsession with the colonies. Oriental art had been in vogue since the mid-19th century, but Matisse's exquisite sense of decoration reinstilled it with a vigorous modern feel. Dufy, who had failed to win a commission for a large mural for the swimming pool of the *Normandie*, produced painting after painting of the Côte d'Azur and Marseilles and its sailors. The South of France became the playground of the rich.

The many-faceted nature of Jean Dupas' talent was also applied to painting. In Emile-Jacques Ruhlmann's "Hotel d'un Collectionneur" at the 1925 Exposition, Dupas displayed a large mural entitled *Les Perruches* (the parakeets), a theme that was equally dear to Matisse. His many murals and folding screens for the *Normandie* and other private commissions, although executed in lacquer among other media, were in essence large paintings. Exotic and rich in subject matter, they were fine examples of the decorative tendencies of painting in the Art Deco style.

Tamara de Lempicka, who had been a pupil of André Lhotte, was probably the most typically Art Deco of all the portrait painters. De Lempicka's portraits of women, in vogue again, are garishly hideous studies in eroticism. The Folies Bergères, Ziegfeld's follies, Josephine Baker dancing in the nude are all highly suggestive and informative portraits of the risqué fast set that Nancy Cunard was part of. Semi-clad nudes provoke with pointed breasts behind thin layers of diaphanous silk, or thin coverings of black

LEFT Late four-part painted screen by the French Master Jean Dunand, dated 1941 of two deer drinking at a watering hole in a snowy forestscape.

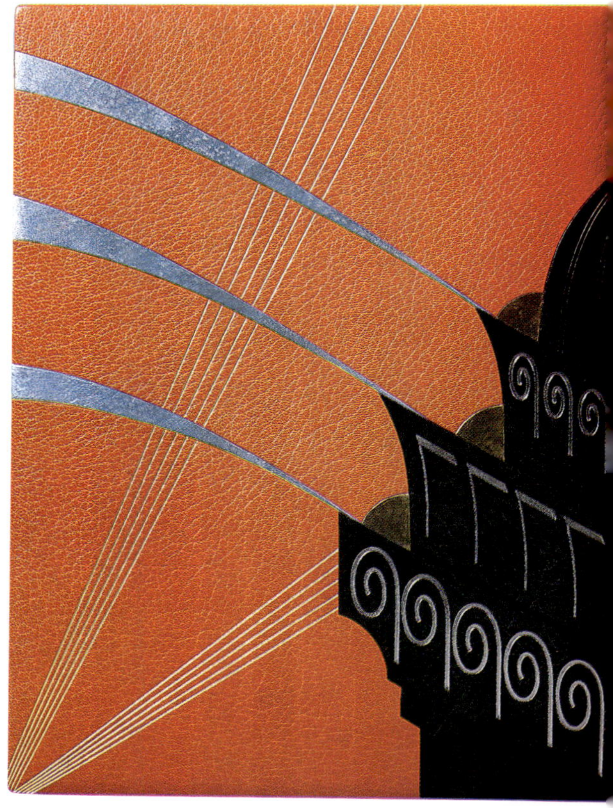

ABOVE RIGHT Exquisite Art Deco binding of 'La Mort de Venise' by Maurice Barres, Lyon 1936, with orange, black and palladium inlay. Bound by the craftsman J. K. van West, the artist is Henry de Waroquier.

Spanish lace. Like Foujita's sitters or the hermaphrodite little girls in Balthus paintings, de Lempicka's sitters look at the spectator with a coy, langorous look. Other painters of this sort of genre were Otto Dix and Christian Schad, who did for Berlin what de Lempicka had done for Paris, but better. Interesting and anecdotal, no Art Deco style painting is ever great art, it is more an example of entertaining camp.

POSTERS, GRAPHICS AND BOOK DESIGN

The history of poster design really started in the late 19th century. Before that, posters had been used to illustrate the ambitions and aspirations of political parties, or on a more intimate scale limited edition prints by Rowlandson, Gillray and Honoré Daumier had provided a forum for acid and biting criticism of the hypocrisies of the Establishment. By the end of the nineteenth century artists like Steinlen, Henri de Toulouse-Lautrec, Aubrey Beardsley and Edward Penfield produced works that truly understood the limitations and advantages of the poster medium. From them other graphic artists learnt the skills of successful poster design, and its role in 20th century society. A poster had to be inexpensive to mass-produce, striking in design, and arresting enough to catch the viewer's attention for long enough to tempt him to read the accompanying text. This latter attribute was not even essential, as the poster could work on the same level as a mediaeval stained glass window, educating and informing an illiterate audience and suggesting to them what they might like to acquire. Although the message was more mundane and down to earth than that of the mediaeval craftsman, the result in terms of beauty was not necessarily less. The best posters were equal to if not better than a lot of so-called fine art, and this was especially the case with Art Deco.

The Art Deco poster was the first full-blown example of a sophisticated understanding of the advantages and idiosyncracies of the world of advertising. This was hardly surprising as the growth of the advertising industry and the medium of poster design were inseparable. Art Deco, the style of the consumer age, was applied with great success to the promotion of all the

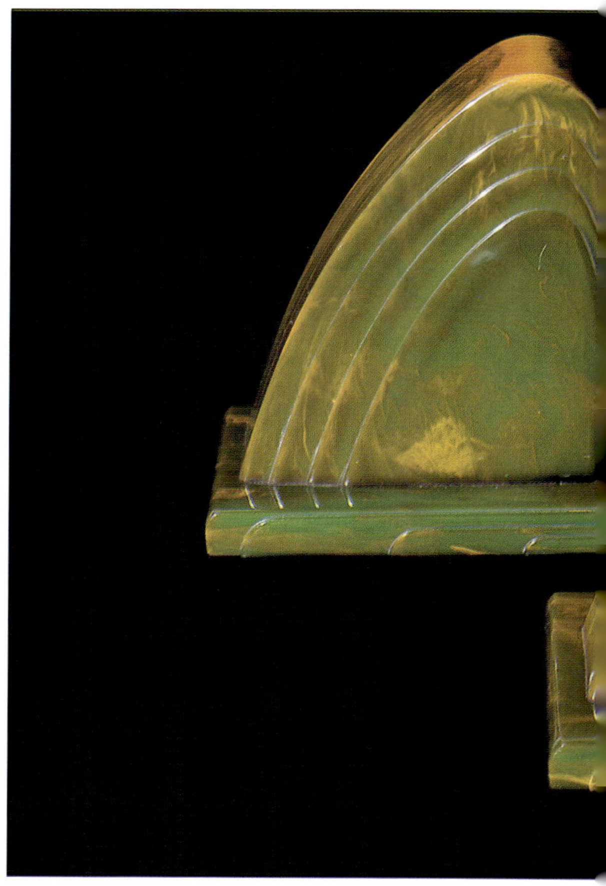

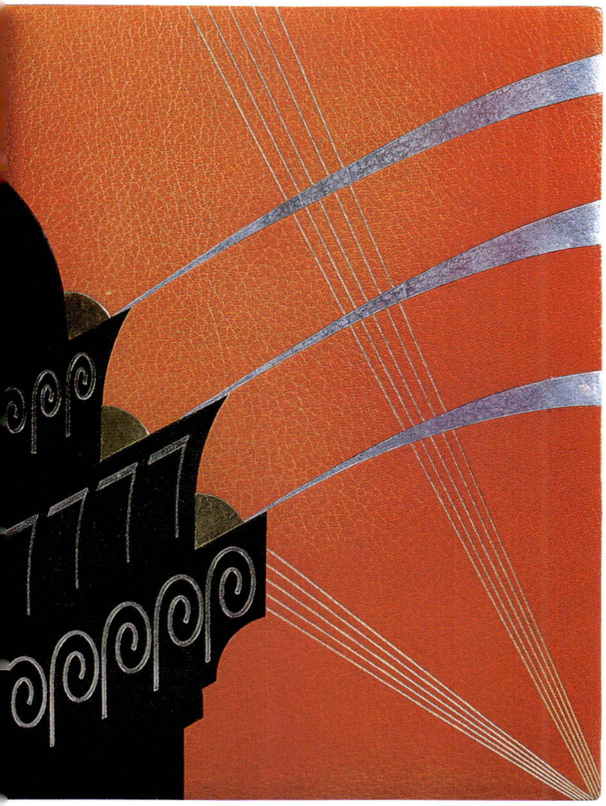

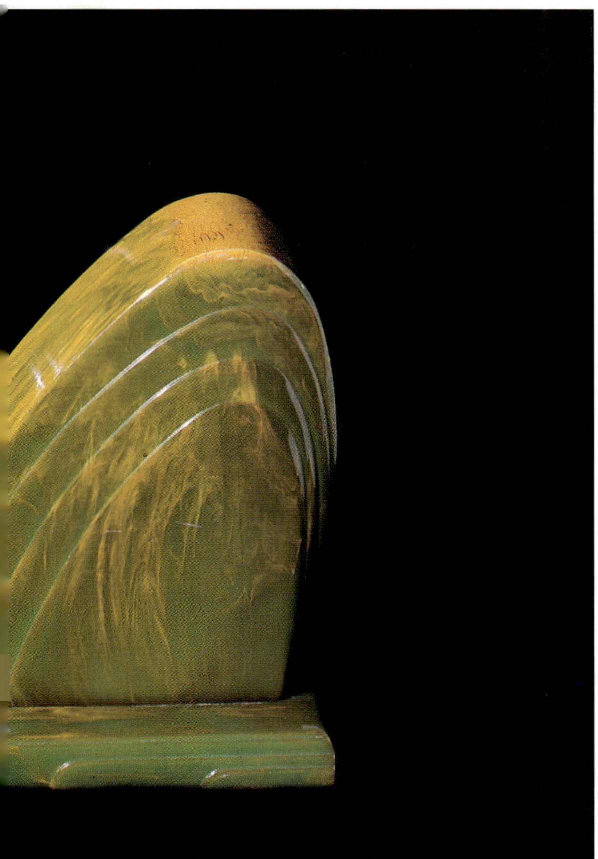

BELOW LEFT Pair of matching Carvacraft bookends, a Dickinson Product.

new consumer items; the gramophone (phonograph), radio set, the motor car (automobile), aeroplane, ocean-going liner, cosmetics, household appliances and, of course, the Hollywood movies. The one lasting theme and motif that ran throughout the Art Deco poster and illustration was that of the modish, chic, self-possessed and highly energetic woman. She would be the role model that any woman bent on self-improvement would have to emulate. Ever changing, she inspired people to part with their money in order to keep up with her. Unlike all the idealized nudes and nymphs that peopled Art Deco sculptures the women in posters were modern in every sense of the word. The sketches of Ernest Deutsch Dryden are a superb contemporary record. Women in the latest fashions stand with their companions around a Bugatti motor car ready to step in and set off to where? Deauville, Cannes, Long Island, or a weekend party at a country house?

The two greatest Art Deco poster designers were without a doubt Paul Colin and Cassandre. Both produced outstanding posters advertising rail travel and luxury liner voyages. Cassandre's most famous single work was the poster for the liner *Normandie*. The prow of the ship pushes forward out of the picture, as the majestic giant dwarfs the small tug beneath it. The stark outlines of the design and the stylized realism of the picture suggest to the viewer qualities that the *Normandie* certainly had, strength and elegance. Colin also produced posters to advertise the visiting Jazz giants at the Folies Bergères and other venues. It is with posters like these that the Art Deco style comes closest to gaining the name the Jazz Style. Deriving loosely from cubist painting with its disjointed sense of perspective, the colours are jazzed up, as unlikely combinations of electric blue are juxtaposed with reds and livid greens. The overall effect was initially jarring but then resolved itself into an energetic and fully comprehensible pictorial logic.

One of the most exciting areas of graphic Art Deco was the book jacket. Pierre Legrain, the furniture designer, had started his career designing book covers for Jacques Doucet. Other well-known designers were Paul Bonet, Louis Creuzevelt, Robert Bonfils and René Kieffer. Paris in the 1920s was the period of the small presses, but as well as this there was still a strong tradition of wealthy people, like Huysmans' hero des Esseintes in *Against Nature*, who had their

ABOVE RIGHT Poster design by Paul Colin of 1930 for the Pitoeff company's production of 'Les Criminels' by Ferdinand Bruckner at the Theatre des Arts.

FAR RIGHT Early example of cigarette advertising for the Celtique brand by the famous Cassandre.

BELOW RIGHT Poster advertising the production 'Gold Diggers 1935' starring Dick Powell, a Busby Berkeley extravaganza.

favourite books specially bound. Although book design may seem in some ways superfluous to the actual purpose of a book, no one who has held a fine-tooled morocco leather binding in the hand, and turned the pages of handmade paper can deny the sensual delights of sight, touch and smell, and the pleasure of good design and craftsmanship, that such a book can give. A particularly fine example was the collaboration on the book *Bubu du Montparnasse* in 1929 by Charles L Phillipe. The binding designed by Paul Bonet was accompanied by illustrations by the artist Dunoyer de Segonzac.

In America, the best designers of posters, books and illustrations were Rockwell Kent and Edward McKnight Kauffer. McKnight Kauffer also worked for Hollywood; his poster for Fritz Lang's masterpiece *Metropolis* is one of his best-known works. The common ground that all the best designers shared was simplicity, the use of a bold image, and a clear legible typeface that got the message across at a single glance.

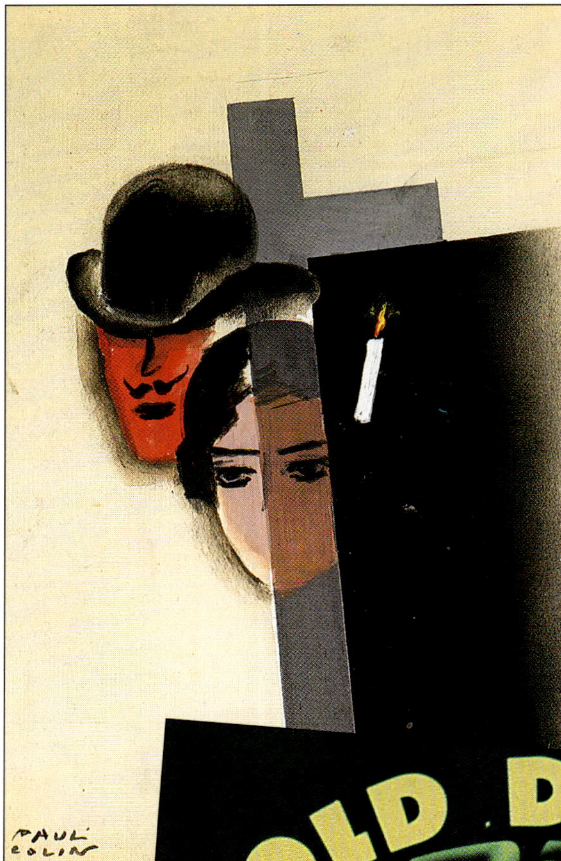

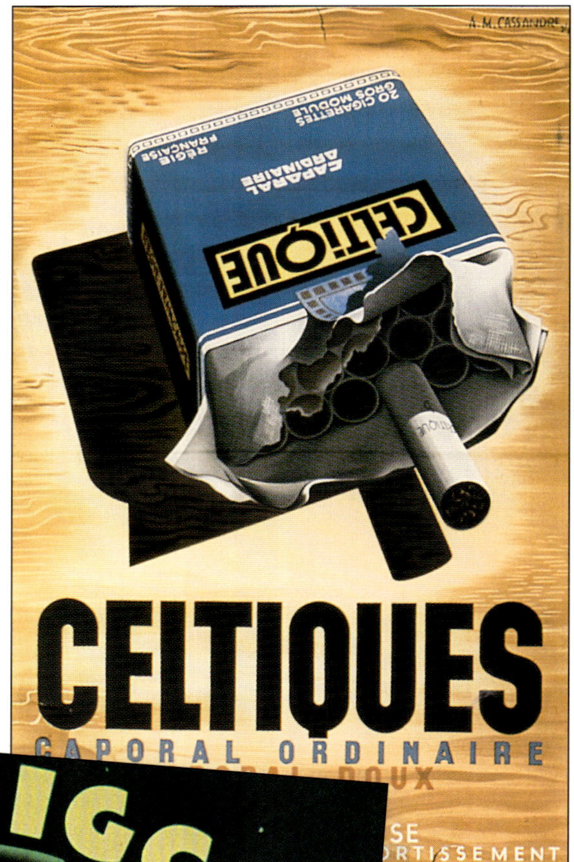

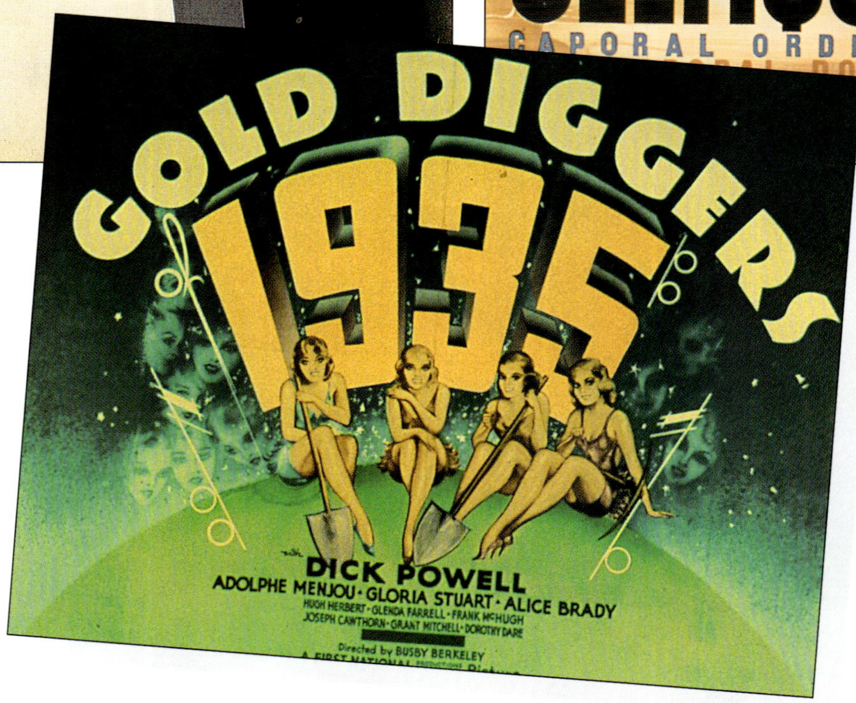

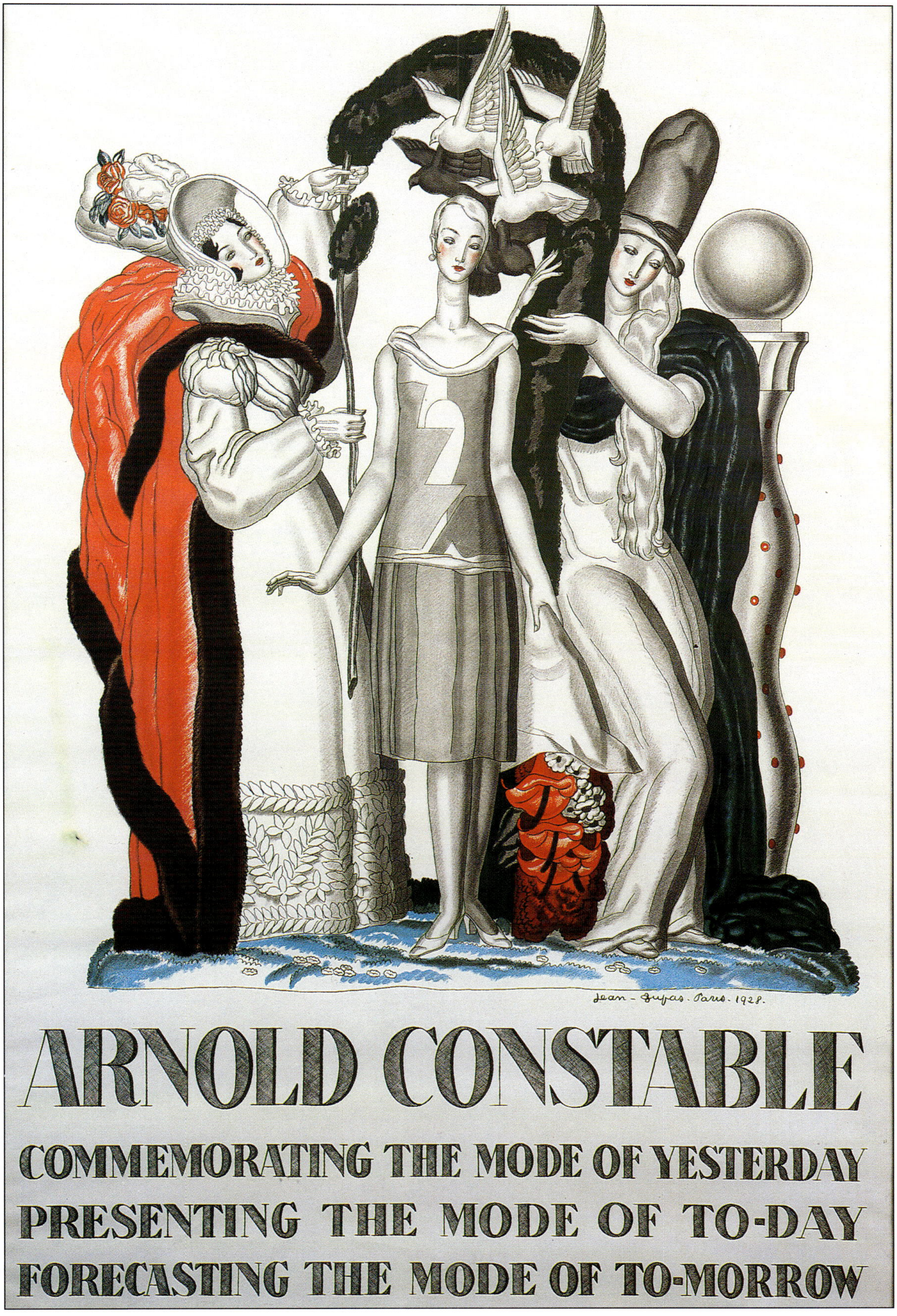

LEFT Limited edition lithograph and poster by Jean Dupas of 1928.

RIGHT Poster by Cassandre advertising the French Line service from New York to Europe.

FAR RIGHT Poster by Paul Colin advertising the Black Review that was then all the rage.

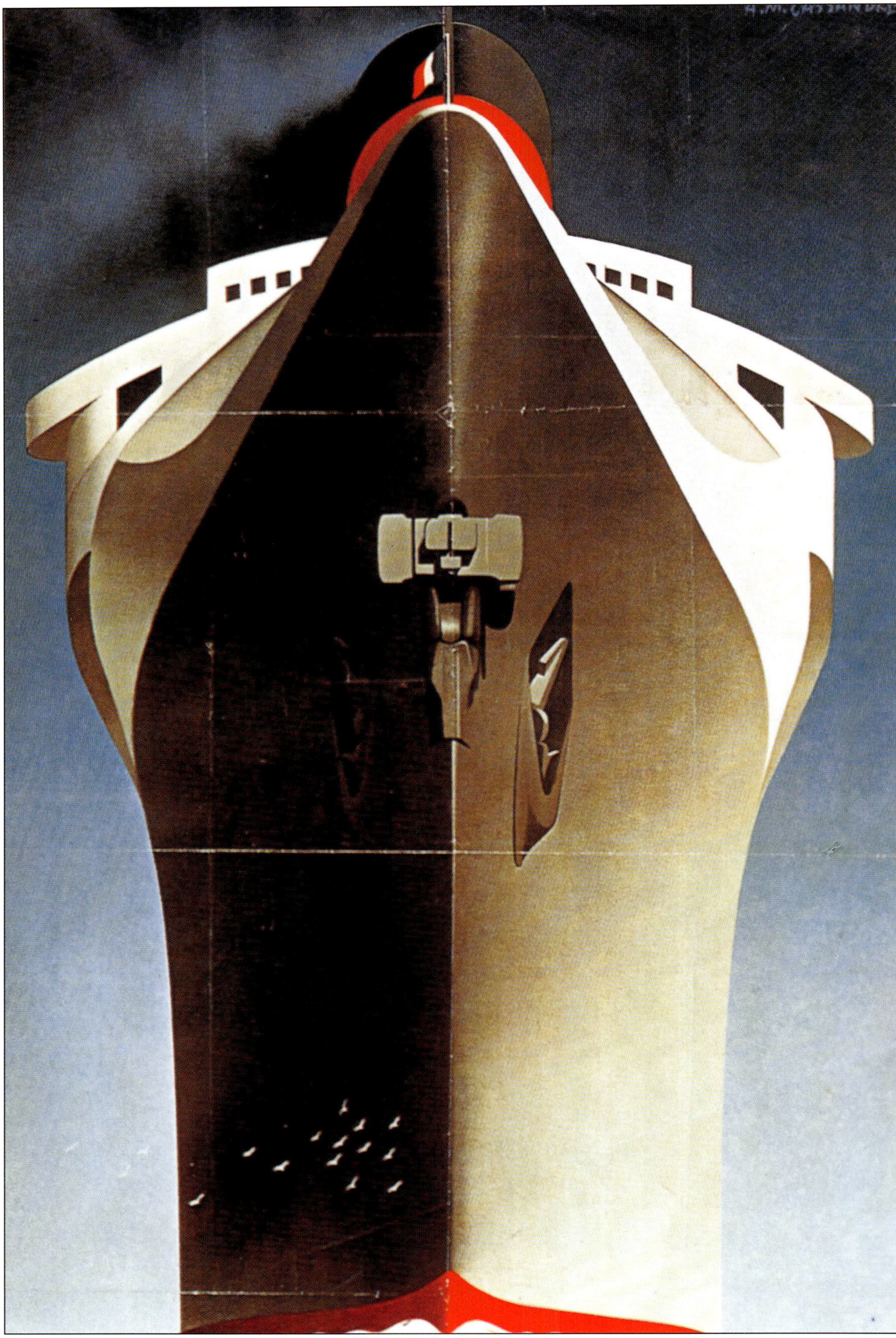

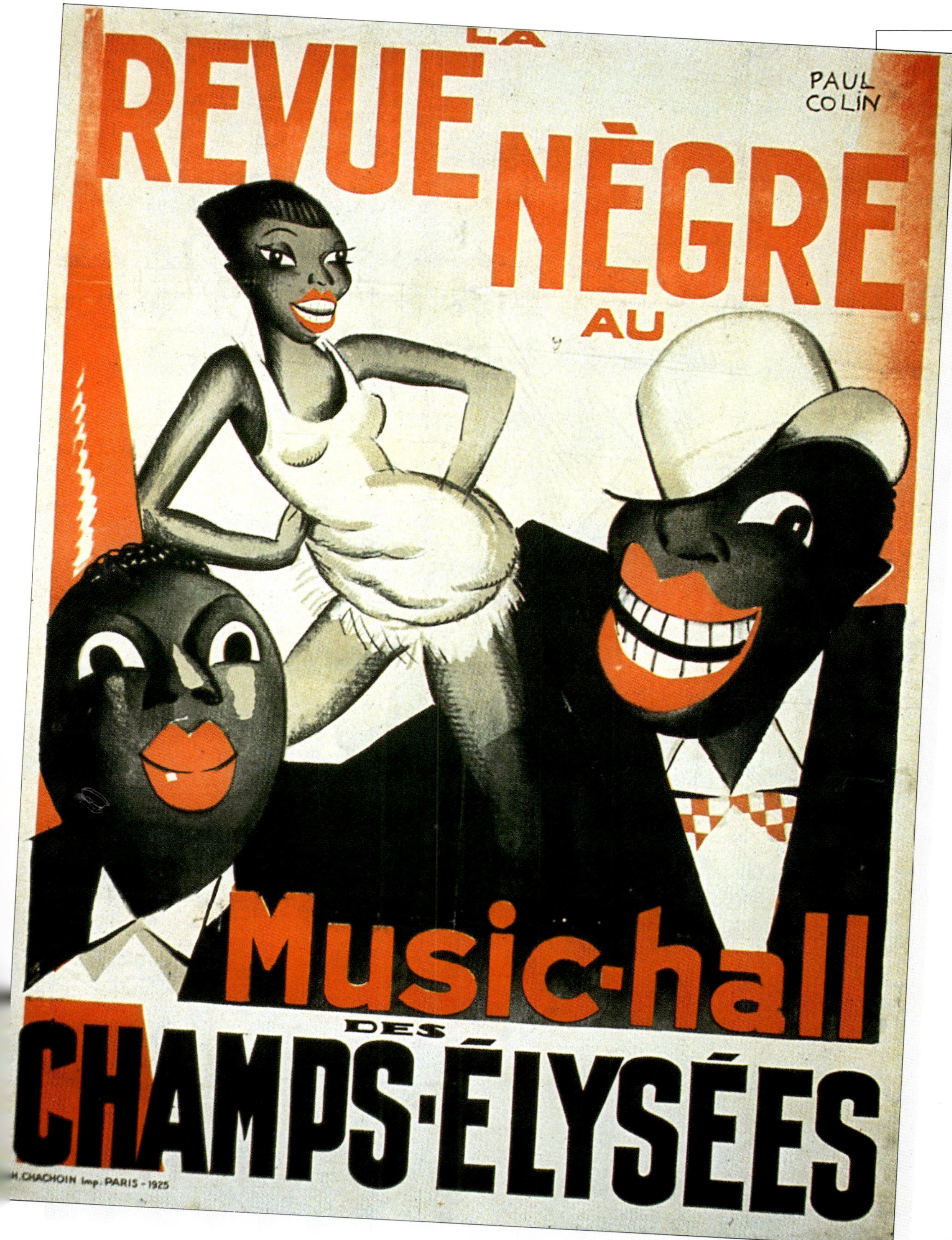
LA
REVUE NÈGRE
AU
PAUL COLIN
Music-hall
DES
CHAMPS-ÉLYSÉES
H. CHACHOIN Imp. PARIS - 1925

COLLECTORS AND COLLECTING

There are very few people nowadays who can afford to put together a comprehensive collection of top-quality Art Deco pieces. The best examples of work are still in the museums, notably the Metropolitan Museum in New York and the Musée des Arts Décoratifs in Paris. The three greatest private collections at the moment are those of Mr and Mrs Peter M Brant, and, in Paris, the collections of Alain Lesieutre and Felix Marcilhac. The depth and range of the last two collections is so astonishing, and the quality so consistently high, that any full-blown show of Art Deco could hardly take place without borrowing examples from these Deco connoisseurs.

Fortunately, the state of contemporary collecting in the Art Deco period was healthy. The major collectors and patrons then were the fashion designers Jeanne Lanvin and Jacques Doucet. Both of these promoted Art Deco by ordering the designs for complete interiors. Doucet, like most converts to the style, was passionate about his new interest. His patronage was particularly important for the furniture designer Pierre Legrain who, early in his career, was commissioned by Doucet to design book covers for him. The relationship between Lanvin and her favourite designer, Armand-Albert

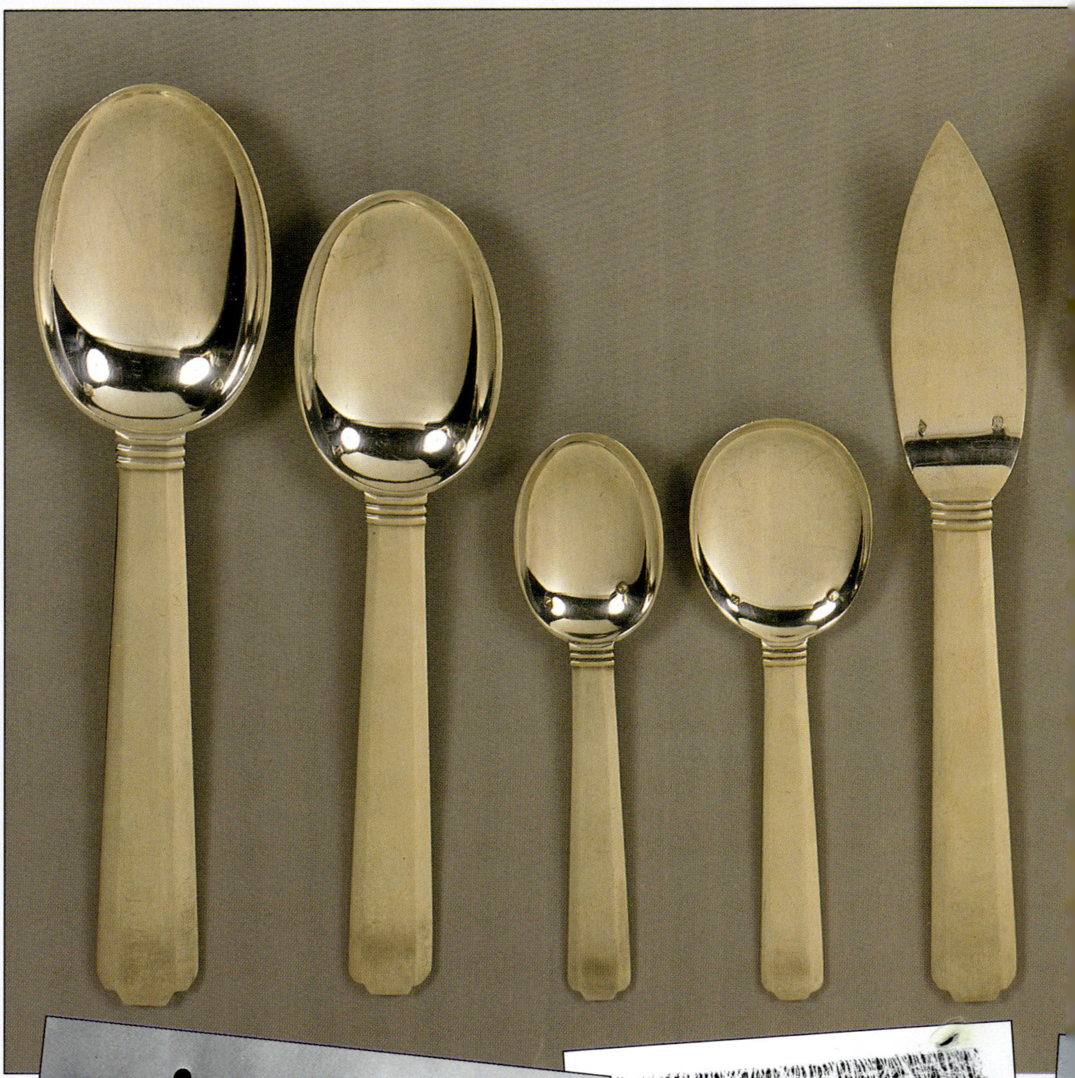

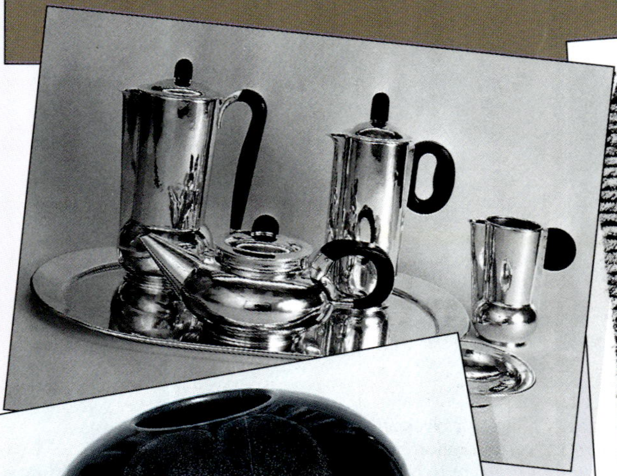

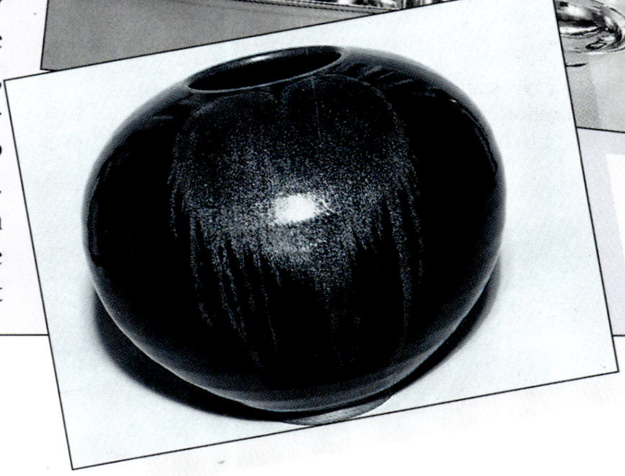

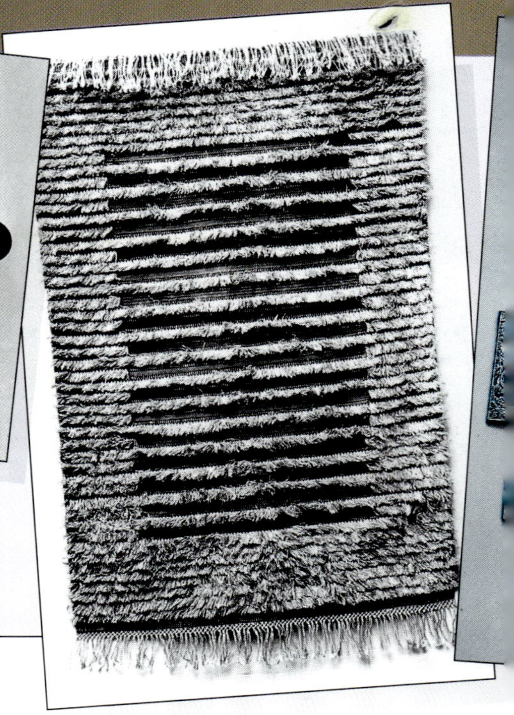

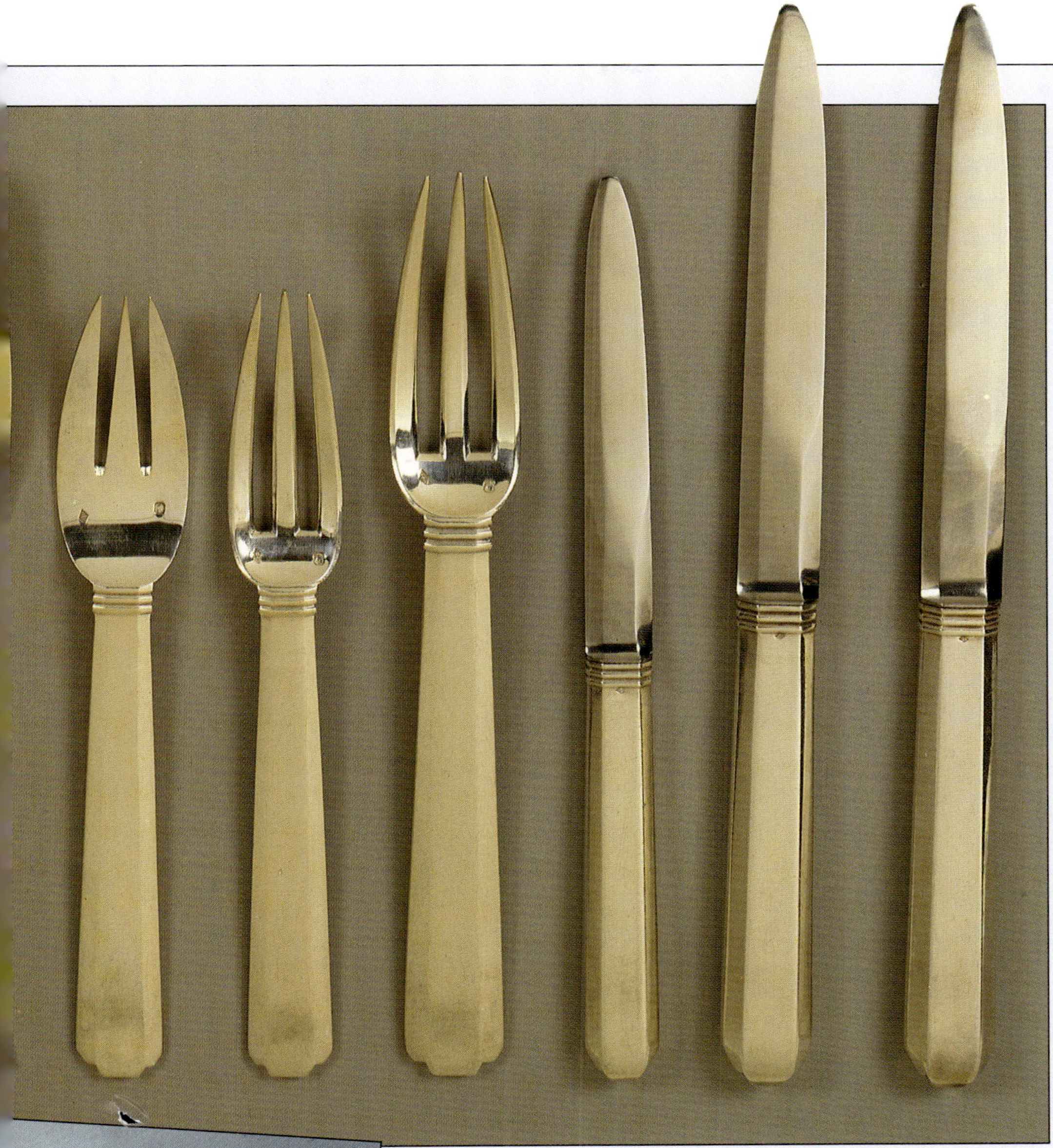

Rateau, was equally stimulating for both parties. In 1922, after decorating Lanvin's Paris apartment, Rateau joined her decorating firm as a director. America also produced two collectors of note, the Blumenthals and Templeton Crocker.

Although the major collections are now firmly established, and almost certainly destined to enter national museums eventually, Art Deco collecting is not out of reach of the average pocket. To build up a collection that is specialized in a single area is satisfying in itself. A collection of the mass-produced items, posters or Bakelite vanity sets is still possible to put together. What it needs is the same application and attuned eye that Marcilhac and Lesieutre have, and the bravery to buy on instinct and if necessary the willingness to spend just a little bit more for a special piece than the collector feels he can afford. Collecting can always be a gamble, but if the prime motivating force is the pursuit of objects that are beautiful, then the collector will never feel that his hobby has been worthless. The developing passion for the artefacts of the period teach the collector a great deal about a time that is not very far distant. It is also exciting to see at first hand the recurrence of aspects of Art Deco design in today's architecture, as well as every other aspect of the visual arts. Collecting can be a serious business, but it should never cease to be fun.

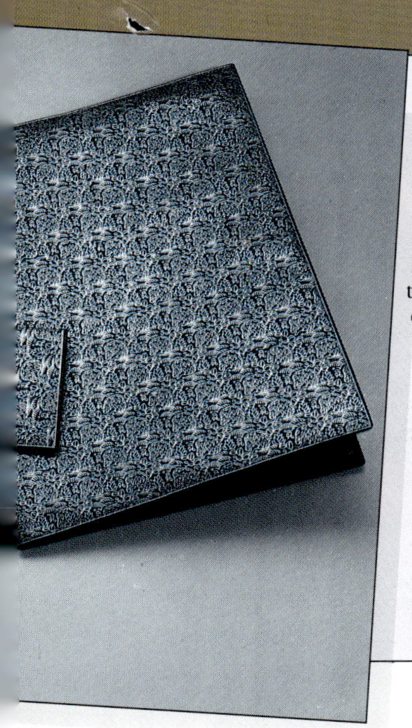

ABOVE Cutlery service designed by Jean Puiforcat.

FAR LEFT Tea service in silver with wooden knobs and handles designed by the Christian and Dell metal workshop of the Bauhaus. Although more traditional in style than much of the work of the Bauhaus metalworking department, note the originality of the totally unmatched handles on each piece.

BELOW, FAR LEFT Stoneware vase with mirror-black and rust-red iron glaze decoration by Charles Vyse, working in Chelsea, 1934. Note the Japanese influence.

SECOND FROM LEFT Swedish tufted carpet handwoven and designed by Marta Måås-Fjetterström, 1923. Båstad, Sweden.

LEFT Writing case, wallet and match-case, designed as a matching set in gold-blocked, tooled black leather by the Austrian architect, Josef Hoffmann (c. 1925). Hoffmann was a leading member of the avant-garde group of Viennese artists known as the *Wiener Werkstätte*.

CHAPTER NINE

JEWELLERY

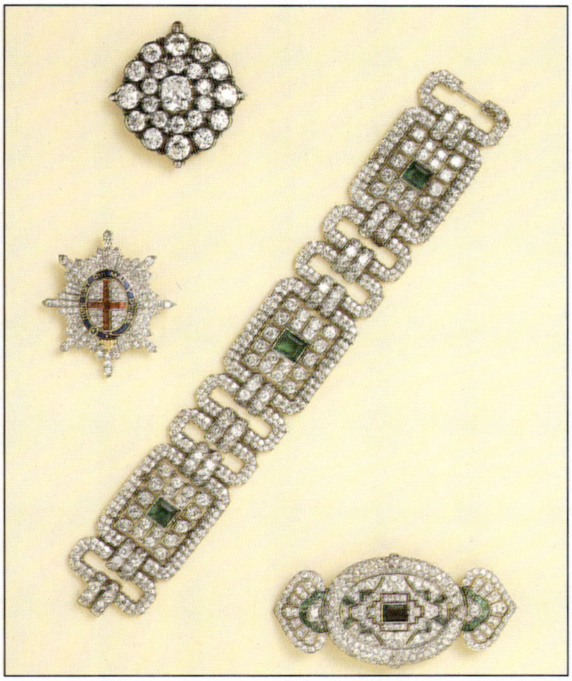

Diamond pendant brooch, a diamond calibre, ruby and enamel Coldstream badge brooch by Cartier, and a diamond and emerald bracelet and brooch by Lacloche.

RIGHT Stunning example of an Art Deco brooch by Georges Fouquet that is timeless in its elegance.

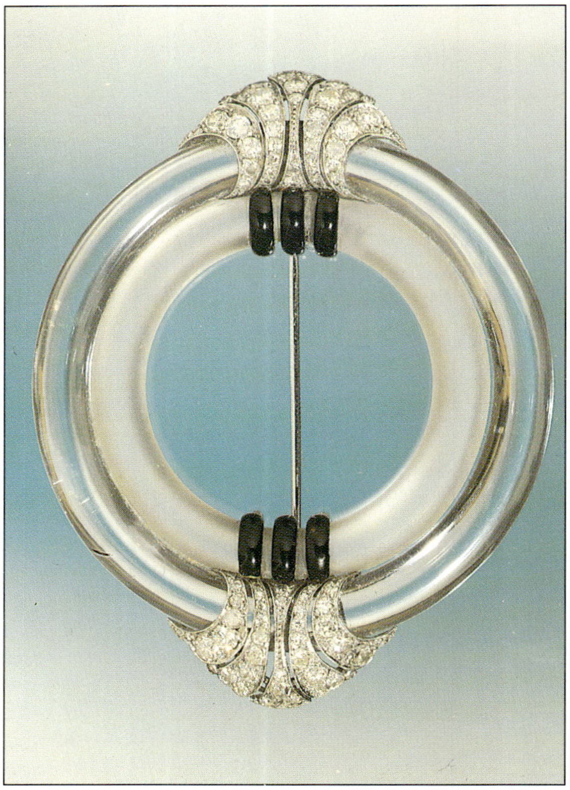

Jewellery is often regarded as a trivial luxury, a little extra touch that sets off an article of clothing. Apart from the wonderful creations by Jean Puiforcat in the area of tableware, it is in the field of jewellery that Art Deco reaches the very zenith of its stylishness. That is perhaps not so surprising when one considers the detailing on a Ruhlmann chest, or the fine finish of a Jean Dunand lacquerwork screen. Even though they were working in different materials, with a different sense of scale and purpose, they were really applying the care and craftsmanship to their work that is normally associated with the making of jewellery. If the designs for furniture or building interiors sometimes looked clumsy or not quite right, the intimate scale of jewellery could disguise those shortcomings.

The great names of Art Deco jewellery are now household words: Cartier, Boucheron, Lalique, Templier, Chaumet, Fouquet, Sandoz, van Cleef and Arpels, and Mauboussin. The established jewellers, Chaumet, Boucheron and Cartier, soon set the standard of the new jewellery.

The changes that took place in the field of jewellery in the 1920s and '30s occurred for several reasons. Firstly, the new style in women's clothing had changed the type of jewellery that was required to set it off. Sleeveless, low-cut dresses accentuated the two main areas where jewels could be worn, the neck and the wrists. A vogue that was to have little effect on the top-class jewellers was the wearing of heavy primitive bangles, although Jean Fouquet was one of the few to exploit the fashion with African-style bracelets. The short hair styles that became fashionable also did away with the demand for elaborate extras like combs and hat pins. If hats were worn they were usually small cloches that sat securely on the wearers' heads. The simple dresses, in contrast to turn-of-the-century styles, and the simple hats could be decorated with small brooches (pins) and clasps. The most important single innovation to take place was the invention of the double-sided clip or clasp. The clips could be used in pairs to hold together material, or separately as brooches and pins. The finest examples came from the major jewellery houses but they were quickly imitated in less expensive materials to cater for the larger market. At the cheaper end of the scale, hundreds of different designs were brought out for the buttons used on everyday wear.

As with furniture, the use of exotic new stones and metals was promoted. No longer limited to the traditional precious stones and metals, the jewellery designers made full use of new materials. The adoption of platinum as a setting meant that the other elements could be accentuated. Platinum is a far stronger metal than gold or silver and the settings for stones could therefore be reduced to just two or three retaining teeth. Other new materials were onyx, ebony, chrome, plastic, lapis lazuli, lacquered metals, agate, coral, Bakelite, rhinestones, jade, tortoiseshell, jet and moonstone. Used in conjunction, these materials offered up a riot of colour and contrasting textures. The types of jewellery produced were as various as the materials available: cigarette holders, rings, geometric necklaces, diamond and jet pins, glass pendants and wristwatches for day and evening wear.

The most beautiful objects of all were the small boxes, cigarette cases and notepads produced by Sandoz and Chaumet. Exactly the right size to support their simple abstract designs, the slim elegance of these containers makes much of the other Art Deco produced look tasteless in comparison.

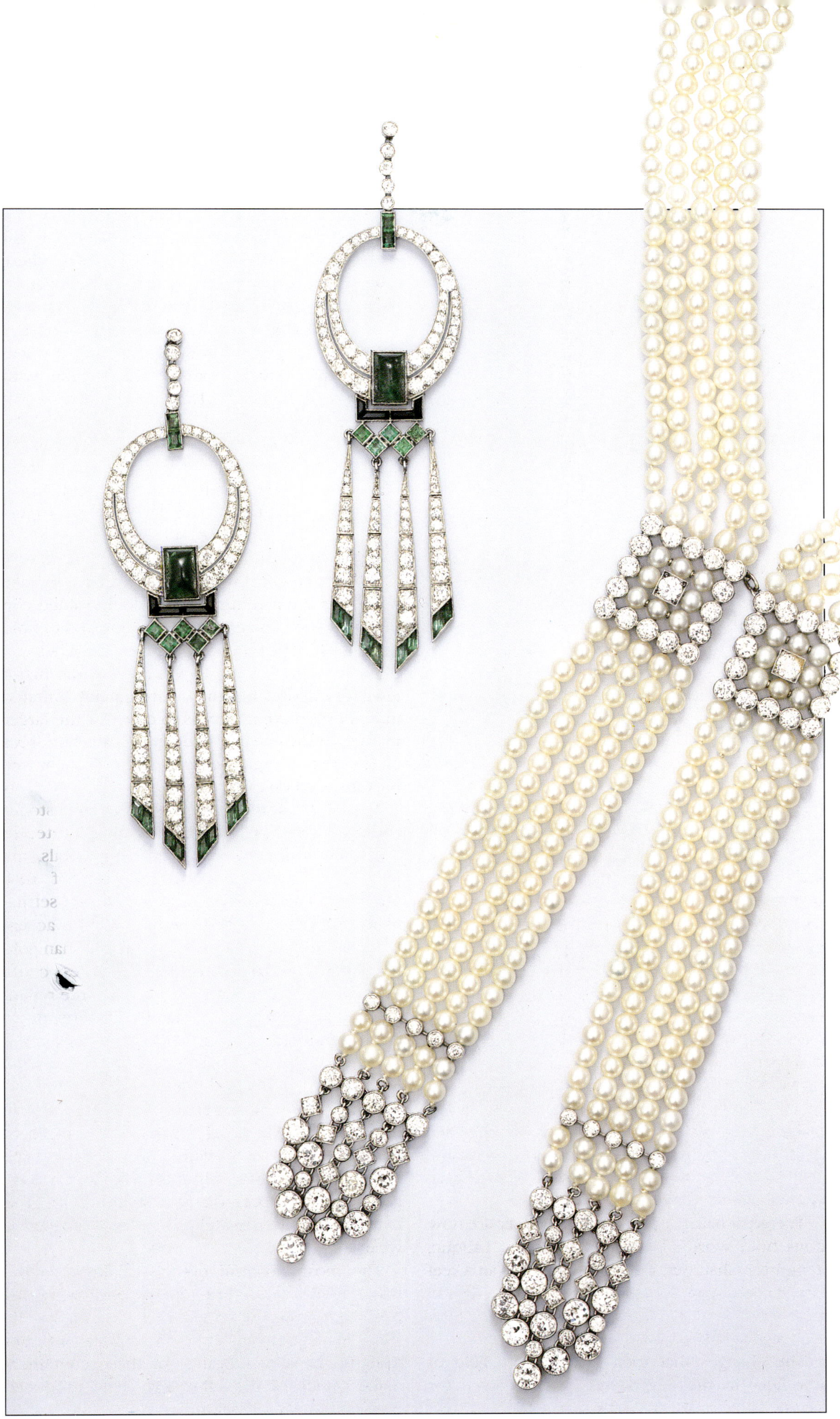

CHAPTER 9

LEFT Pearl and diamond necklace by Cartier, and a delicate pair of Art Deco emerald and diamond earrings by Van Cleef and Arpels.

RIGHT The fantastically popular Josephine Baker adopts one of the exaggerated and bizarre poses that sculptor craftsmen like Preiss, Gerdago and Poerzl would freeze and capture in their chryselephantine sculptures.

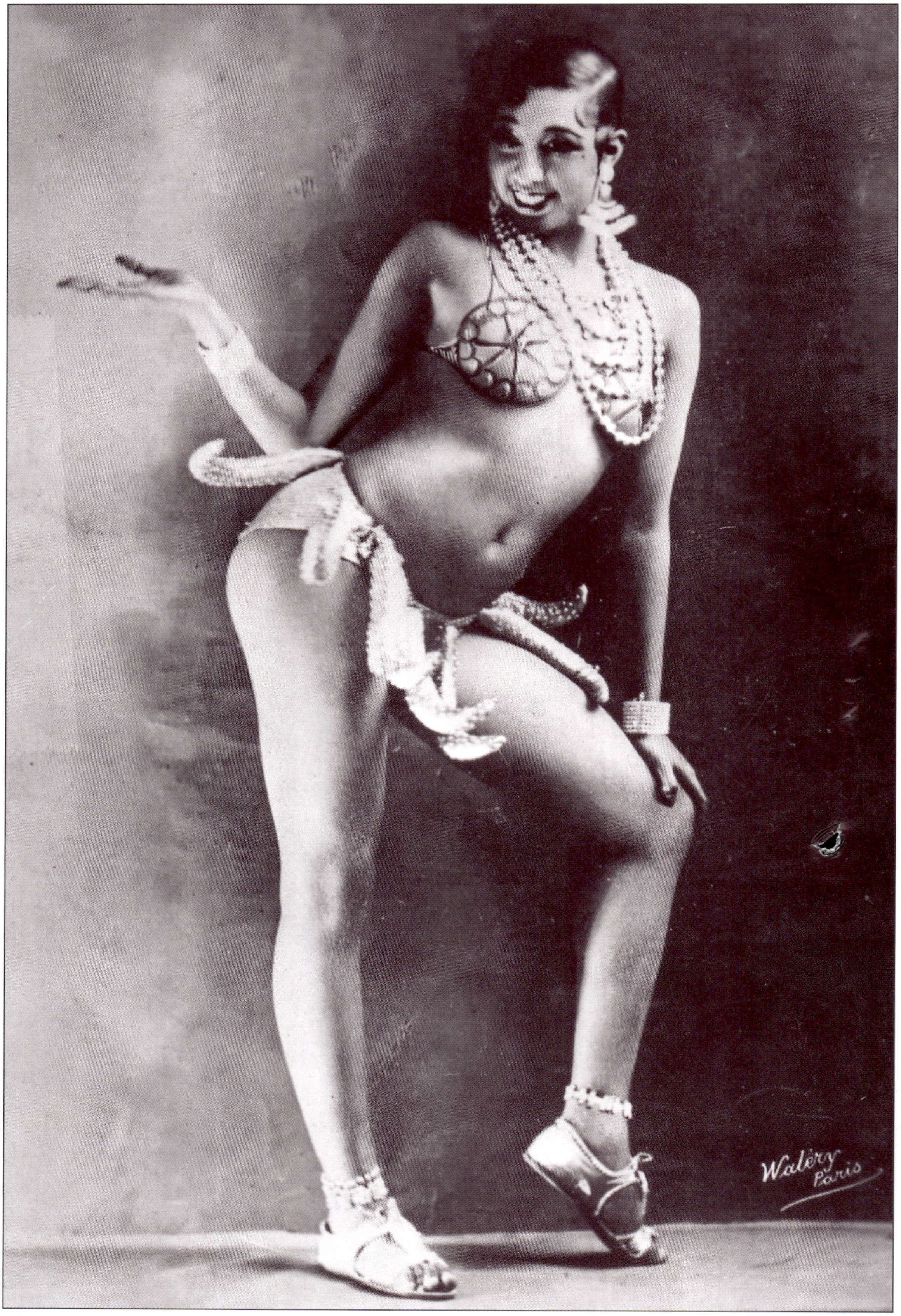

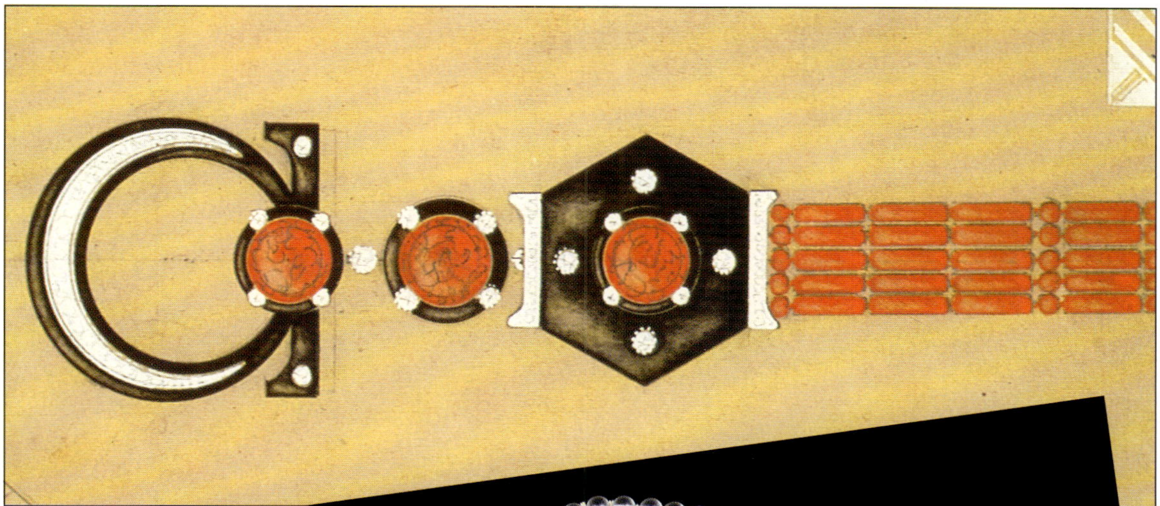

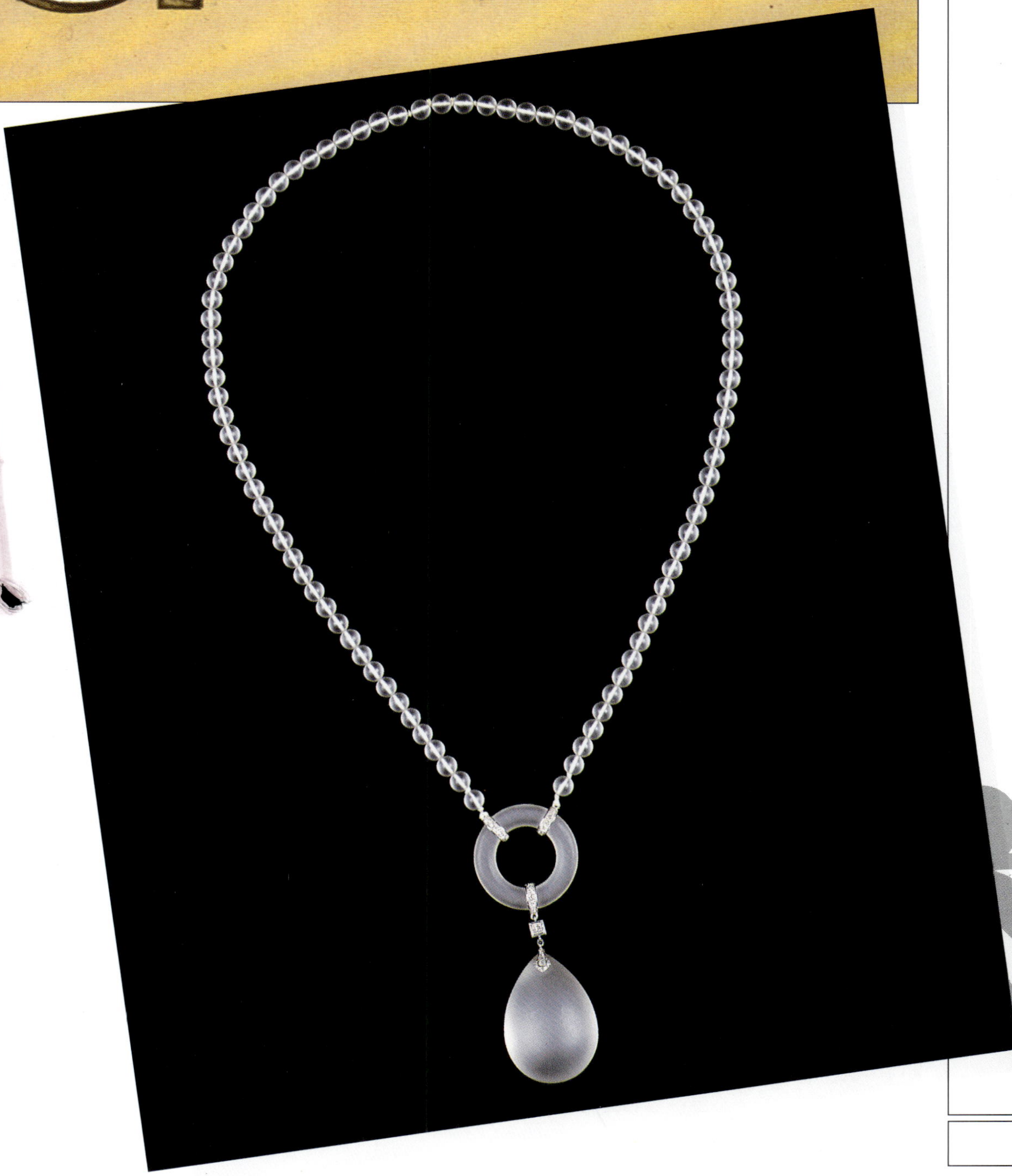

ABOVE LEFT Sketch for an elegant and simple article of jewellery by Georges Fouquet, 1924.

BELOW LEFT Simple rock crystal, platinum and diamond pendant necklace by Georges Fouquet, 1924.

ABOVE RIGHT Two powder compacts by Cartier c. 1925. On the left, an exquisite pierced gold piece, and on the right a black enamel compact set with diamonds.

BELOW RIGHT Millefiori-coloured cigarette case in cellulose nitrate, with a novelty clasp in the form of a hand. The flexibility of the material is perfectly suited to such objects, the hand slipping over the rounded edge securing the case shut. French, 1930s.

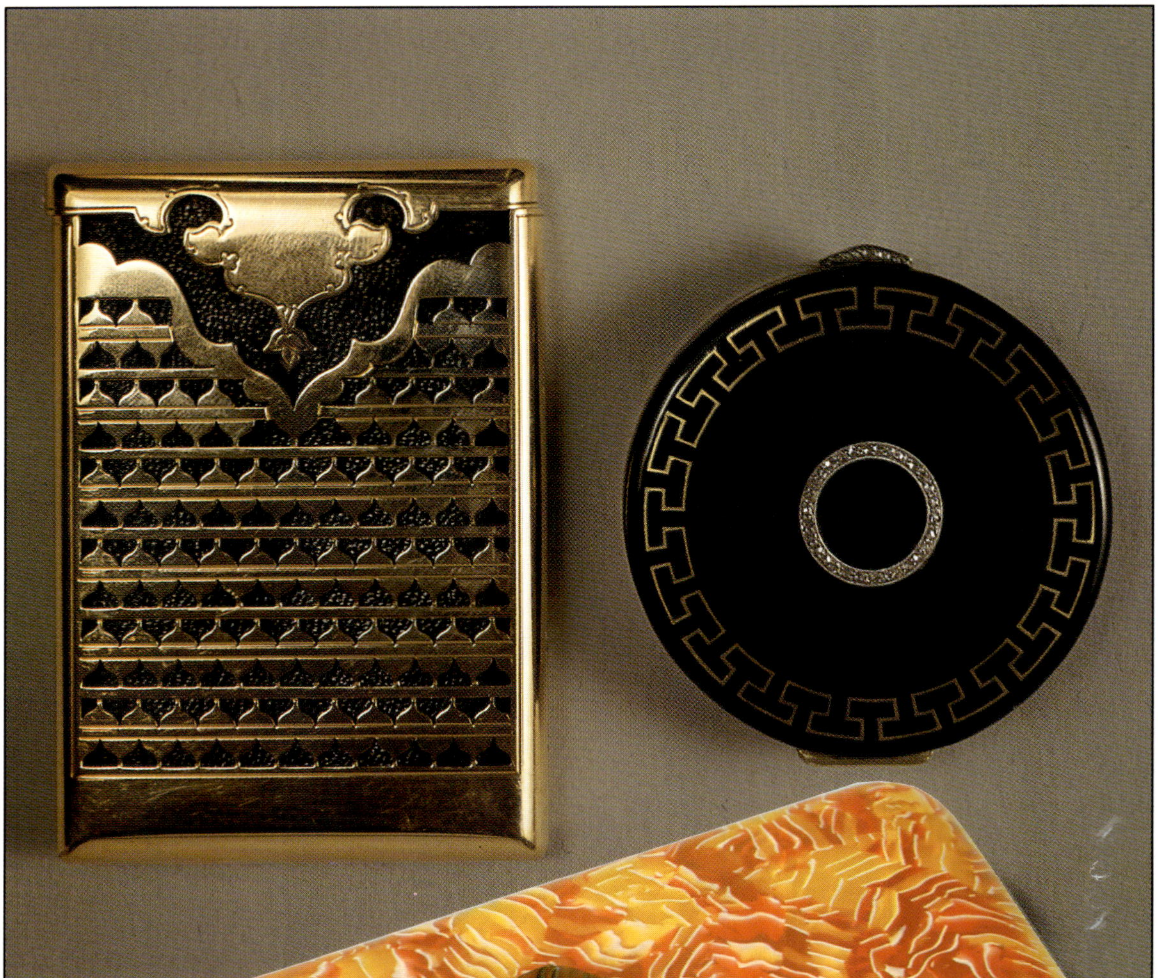

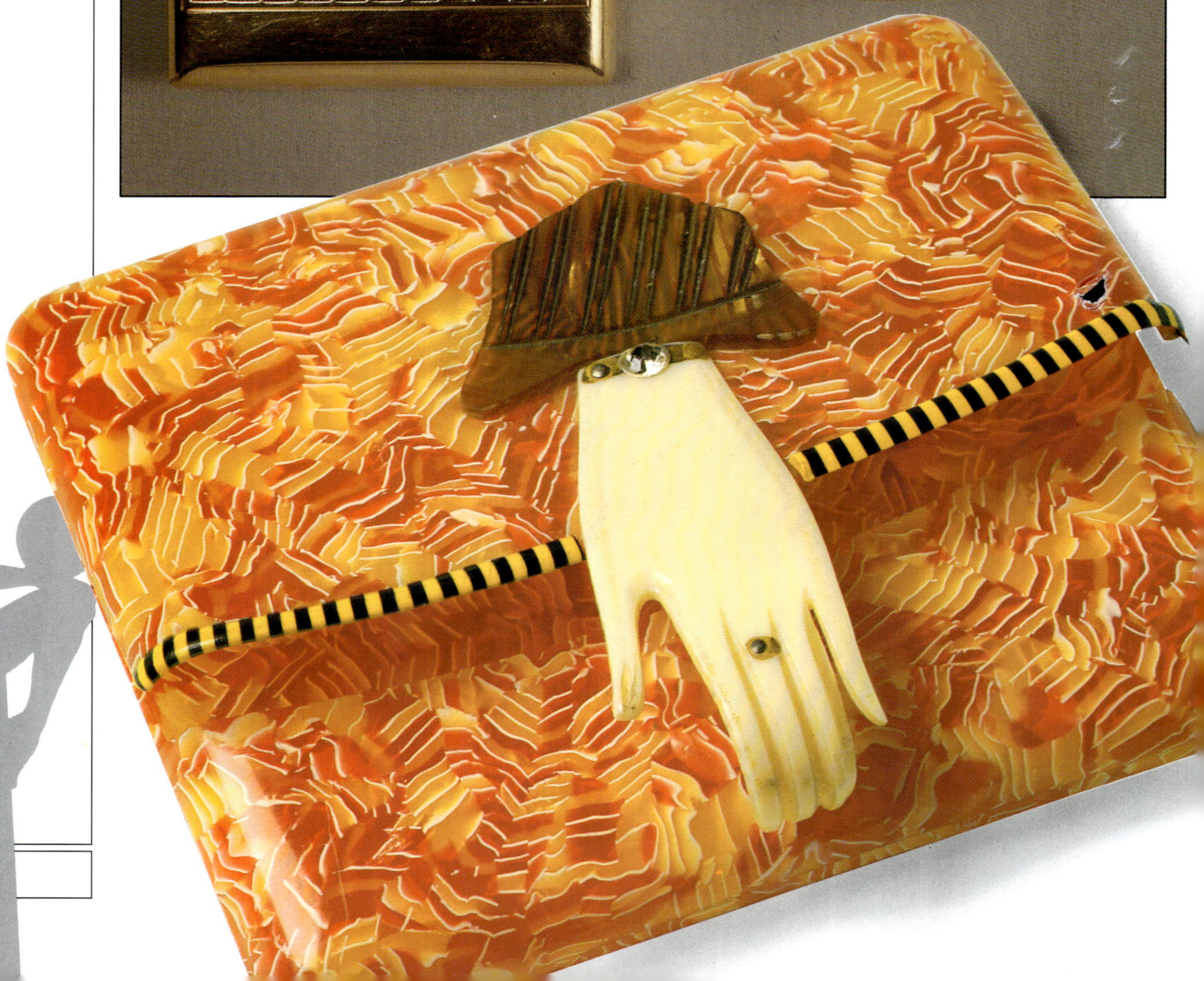

JAHRHUNDERTS. Staatliche Kunstsammlungen, Dresden, 1976

Le Corbusier: LE CORBUSIER ET PIERRE JEANNERET: OEUVRES COMPLÈTES DE 1910-29, Zurich, 1948 (5th edition)

Le Corbusier: TOWARDS A NEW ARCHITECTURE, London, 1927 (Paris 1923)

Lethaby, W.R.: FORM IN CIVILISATION, London, 1922

Mornand et Thome: VINGT ARTISTES DU LIVRE, Paris, 1950

Mornand, Pierre: ONZE ARTISTES DU LIVRE, Paris, 1938

Moussinac, Léon: ETOFFES D'AMEUBLEMENT TISSÉS ET BROCHÉS, Paris, 1925

Myers, Bernard S: EXPRESSIONISM, London, 1957

Natzler, Gertrude and Otto: CERAMICS, Catalogue of the Collection of Mrs. Leonard M. Sperry, Los Angeles Country Museum of Art, 1968

Neuwirth, Waltraud: WIENER KERAMIK, Braunschweg, 1974

L'OEUVRE DE RUPERT CARABIN 1862-1932, Exhibition Catalogue, Galerie du Luxembourg, Paris, 1974

Olmer, Pierre: LE MOBILIER FRANÇAIS D'AUJOUR, H'UI (1910-1925), Paris, 1926

Olmer, Pierre: LA RENAISSANCE DU MOBILIER FRANÇAIS, Paris, 1927 WENDINGEN, special issue devoted to Eileen Gray, 1924

Poiret, Paul: EN HABILLANT L'EPOQUE, Paris, 1930

Polak, Ada: MODERN GLASS

Polak, Ada: NORWEGIAN SILVER, Oslo, 1972

Pevsner, Nikolaus: AN ENQUIRY INTO INDUSTRIAL ART IN ENGLAND, Cambridge, 1937

Pevsner, Nikolaus: STUDIES IN ART, ARCHITECTURE AND DESIGN, London, 1968

Quénioux, Gaston: LES ARTS DÉCORATIFS MODERNES, Paris, 1925

PLASTICHE, Magazine of the Bakelite Society, 105 Blackheath Road, London SE10

Rademacher, Helmut: DAS DEUTSCHE PLAKAT VON DEN AUFGÄNGEN BIS ZUR GEGENWART, Dresden, 1965

Rapin, Henri: LA SCULPTURE DÉCORATIVE À L'EXPOSITION DES ARTS DÉCORATIFS DE 1925, Paris, 1925

Read, Herbert: ART AND INDUSTRY, London, 1934

Rochas, Marcel: VINGT-CINQ ANS D'ELÉGANCE À PARIS, Paris, 1951

Rochas, Marcel: LE JARDIN DU BIBLIOPHILE, Paris, 1930

Rochas, Marcel: LIVRE D'OR DU BIBLOPHILE, Paris, 1925

Rochowanski, Leopold Wolfgang: WEINER KERAMIK, Vienna, 1923

Rosenthal, Leon: LA VERRERIE FRANÇAIS DEPUIS CINQUANTE ANS, Paris, 1927

ROYAL COPENHAGEN PORCELAIN, 200 YEARS OF Catalogue of an exhibition circulated by the Smithsonian Institution, 1974-1976

EXPOSITION RETROSPECTIVE E.-J. Ruhlmann, Musée des Arts Décoratifs, Paris, 1934

Schaefer, Herwin: THE ROOTS OF MODERN DESIGN, London, 1970

Schiaparelli, Elsa: SHOCKING LIFE, London, 1954

Schmidt, Rudolf: DAS WIENER KUNSTLERHAUS, Vienna, 1964

Singer, Charles, Holmyard, E. J., Hall, A. R., Williams, Trevor (editors): A HISTORY OF TECHNOLOGY. VOLUME V. THE LATE 19TH CENTURY C.1850-C.1900, Oxford, 1958

'THE STUDIO' YEAR-BOOKS OF DECORATIVE ART, London 1906-30

Todd, Dorothy and Mortimer, Raymond: THE NEW INTERIOR DECORATION, London, 1929

Verne, H. and Chavance, R.: POUR COMPRENDRE L'ART DÉCORATIF MODERNE EN FRANCE, Paris, 1925

V Wingler, Hans M.: THE BAUHAUS, Boston, Mass., 1969

THE YEAR BOOK OF THE DESIGN IN INDUSTRIES ASSOCIATION, London, 1922, 1924-25, 1926-27, 1929-30

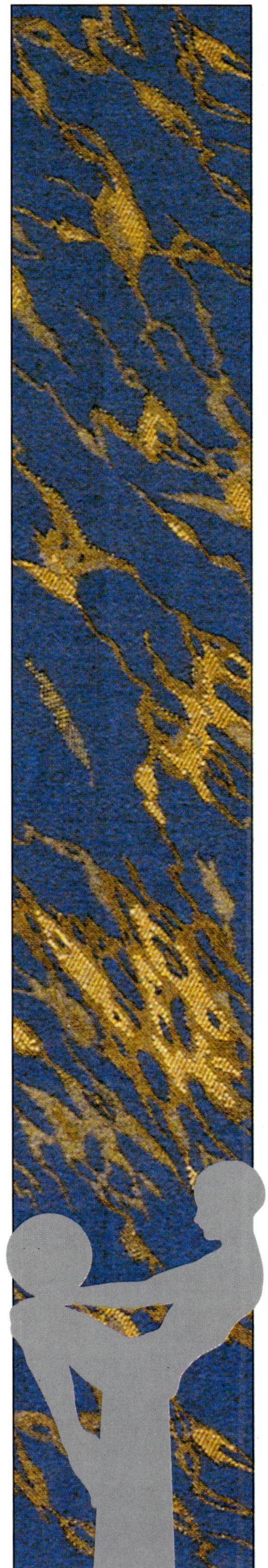

MUSEUMS WITH ART DECO COLLECTIONS

Most Art Deco items are in private or company collections. Furthermore, few art museums yet have special Art Deco collections, though many host travelling Art Deco exhibitions from time to time. Here are a few museums which have Art Deco items of particular interest.

AUSTRIA Historical Museum of the City of Vienna, Karlsplatz, 1040 Vienna 4
Museum of the 20th Century, Schweizergarten, 1030 Vienna 3

CZECHOSLOVAKIA Arts and Crafts Museum, Stare Mesto 17, Listopodu 2, Prague

CANADA Art Gallery of Ontario, 317 Dundas Street West, Toronto, Ontario

UNITED KINGDOM Brighton Museum, The Old Steyne, Brighton
Victoria and Albert Museum, Exhibition Road, London SW7
Gerald Wells Radio Collection, 23 Rosendale Road, Dulwich, London SE21
Jeffrye Museum, London E2
Southend Museum, Southend, Essex
York Castle Museum, York, Yorkshire
Lakeland Motor Museum, Export Centre, New Road, Blackpool, Lancs.

GERMAN FEDERAL REPUBLIC Ursula and Hans Kolsch, AM Ruhrstein 37B, D-43 Essen 1

FRANCE Musée des Arts Décoratifs, 107-109 rue de Rivoli, Paris 1
Musée de l'Ecole de Nancy, 38 rue du Sergent-Blandan, Nancy
Musée de la Publicité, rue du Paradis, Paris, 10e.

DENMARK Museum of Decorative Art, Copenhagen

SWEDEN Nordiska Museet, Stockholm
Rohsska Konstslo jdmuseet, Gothonburg

USA Drexel Museum, Drexel University, Drexel, Pennsylvania 19104
University of Washington Costume and Textile Study Center, Seattle, Washington 98105
Baker Furniture Museum, Holland, Michigan 49423
R.M.S. Queen Mary, Long Beach, California 90803
Norton Simon Museum of Art, Pasadena, California 91101
Barnsdall House Museum, Los Angeles, California 90029 (building designed by Frank Lloyd Wright)
Art Institute of Chicago, Michigan Avenue, Chicago, Illinois
Museum of Contemporary Art, Ontario Street, Chicago, Illinois 60611
National Museum of American Art, Smithsonian Institute, Washington D.C.
Metropolitan Museum of Art, 5th Avenue and 82nd Street, New York, NY 10028
Goodyear Rubber Exhibit, 1144 E. Market Street, Akron, Ohio 44316
Cooper-Hewitt Museum of Decorative Arts, 2 East 91st Street, New York, NY 10028
Solomon R. Guggenheim Museum, 1071 5th Avenue, New York, NY 10028 (building designed by Frank Lloyd Wright)

Index

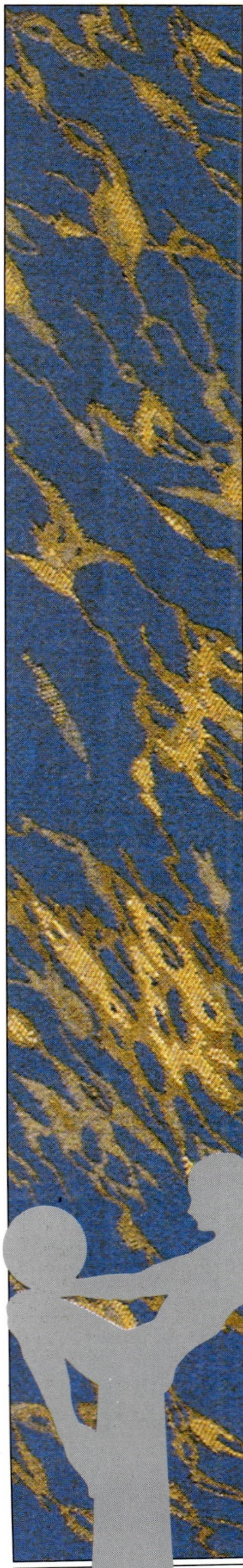

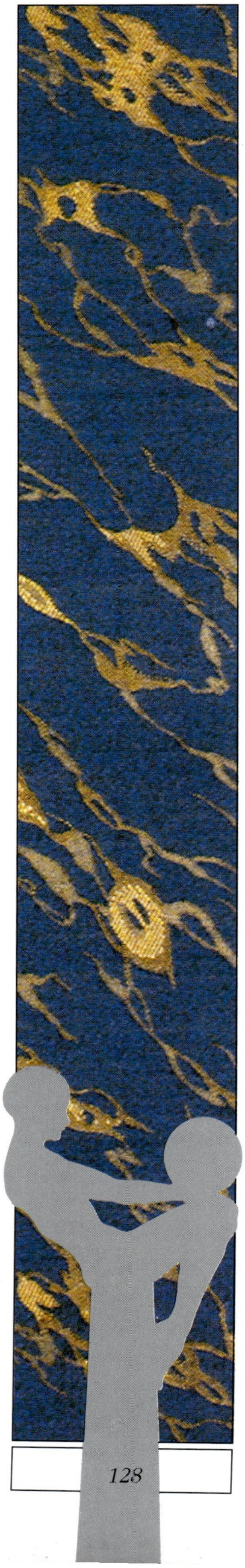